The Ecology of Att

To the Kolkata family,
those who left, those who remain

The Ecology of Attention
Yves Citton

Translated by Barnaby Norman

polity

First published in French as *Pour une écologie de l'attention*, © Éditions du Seuil, 2014

This English edition © Polity Press, 2017

P. viii, '2 + 2 = 5'. Words and music by Thomas Edward Yorke, Philip James Selway, Edward John O'Brien, Jonathan Richard Guy Greenwood and Colin Charles Greenwood © Warner/Chappell Music Ltd (PRS). All rights administered by WB Music Corp.

Polity Press
65 Bridge Street
Cambridge CB2 1UR, UK

Polity Press
350 Main Street
Malden, MA 02148, USA

ISBN-13: 978-1-5095-0372-8 (hardback)
ISBN-13: 978-1-5095-0373-5 (paperback)

A catalogue record for this book is available from the British Library.

Library of Congress Cataloging-in-Publication Data

Names: Citton, Yves, author.
Title: The ecology of attention / Yves Citton.
Other titles: Pour une ?ecologie de l'attention. English
Description: English edition. | Malden, MA : Polity Press, 2016. | Includes
  bibliographical references and index.
Identifiers: LCCN 2016020587| ISBN 9781509503728 (hardback : alk. paper) |
  ISBN 9781509503735 (pbk. : alk. paper)
Subjects: LCSH: Attention--Social aspects. | Perceptual learning.
Classification: LCC HM1176 .C5713 2016 | DDC 153.7/33--dc23 LC record available
at https://lccn.loc.gov/2016020587

Typeset in 10.5 on 12 pt Sabon by
Servis Filmsetting Ltd, Stockport, Cheshire
Printed and bound in the UK by CPI Group (UK) Ltd, by Croydon, CRO 4YY

For further information on Polity, visit our website:
politybooks.com

CONTENTS

ACKNOWLEDGEMENTS

Many thanks to Emmanuel Alloa, Alejandro Alvarez, Emily Apter, Maryvonne Arnaud, Bernard Aspe, Marc Bacchetta, Thierry Bardini, Christine Baron, Sarina Basta, Jacques Berchtold, Laurent Bigorgne, Aurélien Blanchard, Jean-Pierre Bobillot, Véronique Bolhuis, Robert Bonamy, Daniel Bougnoux, Dominique Boullier, Patrick Bourgne, Sylvain Bourmeau, Frédéric Brun, Graham Burnett, Rosemary and Gilbert Citton, Jonathan Crary, Isabelle Creusot, Jérôme David, Christophe Degoutin, Xavier de la Porte, Georges Didi-Huberman, Estelle Doudet, Marianne Dubacq, François-Ronan Dubois, Cédric Duroux, Rita Felski, Georg Franck, Igor Galligo, Aurélien Gamboni, Florent Gaudez, Mélanie Giraud, Francis Goyet, Michael Hagner, Christophe Hanna, Pierre Hazan, Denis Hollier, Michel Jeanneret, Dominiq Jenvrey, Nedjima Kacidem, Deborah Knopp, Charlotte Krauss, Isabelle Krzywkowski, Jean-Pierre Lachaux, Marina and all the Kundu family, Daniel Lançon, Catherine Langle, Raphaël et Catherine Larrère, Bruno Latour, Benoît Laureau, Maurizio Lazzarato, Pierre Le Quéau, Fabienne Martin-Juchat, Jean-François Massol, Éric Méchoulan, Varinia Michalun, Bernard Miège, Rajarshi et Ranjini Mitra, Valeria Morera, Philippe Mouillon, Yann Moulier Boutang, Romi Mukherjee, the editorial committee of the journal *Multitudes*, Carole Musset, Frédéric Neyrat, Laura von Niederhäusern, Christine Noille-Clauzade, Charlotte Nordmann, François Noudelmann, Françoise Notter-Truxa, *The Order of the Third Bird*, Isabelle Pailliart, the participants in the *Économie de l'attention et archéologie des media* seminars at the Université de Grenoble, Matteo Pasquinelli, Jean-François Perrin, Philippe Petit, Dominique Pety, Julien Piat, Julien Pierre, Claire Pignol, Martial Poirson, Catherine Quéloz, Anne Querrien, Dominique Quessada, Anne-Julie Raccoursier, Gene Ray,

ACKNOWLEDGEMENTS

Philippe Régnier, le *Revue des livres*, Julie Ridard, Claudia Roda, Stéphanie Roussel, Dario Rudy, Liliane Schneiter, Jean-Paul Sermain, Jean-Claude Serres, the Settembrini family, Adrien Staii, Bernard Stiegler, Henry Torgue, Isabelle Treff, Nicolas Truong, Urs Urban, Marco Venturini, Jérôme Vidal, the team of the Villa Gillet, Slaven Waelti, Guy Walter, Olivier Zerbib.

Very special thanks to Hugues Jallon and Bruno Auerbach for helping me to frame and realize this project.

Are you such a dreamer
To put the world to rights?
I'll stay home forever
Where two and two always makes up five
I'll lay down the tracks, sandbag and hide
January has April's showers
And two and two always makes up five
It's the devil's way now
There is no way out
You can scream and you can shout
It is too late now
Because
YOU HAVE NOT BEEN
PAYING ATTENTION

Radiohead, *The Lukewarm* (2 + 2 = 5)

FOREWORD

A book dealing with the exhaustion of our attentional resources is a living contradiction: it explains to you why you will not have had time to read it. Our house is on fire, from minor daily emergencies to climate imbalance – and often in conflicting ways, coupling one person's drought with the prediction of another's flood, threatening even entire cities like Kolkata. And we look elsewhere. We fail to read the writing getting ever bigger on the wall. *Burn before reading!*

It would have been better to write a tweet, or a blog post for viral distribution – not a *book*, composed of sequential chapters and complete sentences. This either proves that we do not believe what we say: our attention is not as threatened, scattered, shattered and maimed as people claim. Or it is a futile effort: this book demonstrates that it cannot be read.

We will have to hedge our bets. Go much too quickly and much too slowly at the same time. Write incomplete sentences that are already far too long. Go into the details and ignore essential points. Be simultaneously too inflexible, too pretentious, too learned, and too cavalier.

In order to suggest different reading rhythms, the route will be punctuated by a hundred or so KEY-EXPRESSIONS, written in capitals, and accompanied on each occasion by *a concise definition in italics*. Readers in a hurry can gain an initial idea of the concepts discussed in the chapter, and only linger over those which are of direct interest. Through this system, the book will put forward a battery of concepts, principles, maxims and hypotheses, for which it will seek to provide rigorous initial definitions – hoping in this way to furnish a more precise vocabulary with which to explore, decipher and cultivate the surprisingly underinvestigated field of what may become an 'attention ecology'.

Advertising, literature, artistic experimentation, television, on-line courses, credit agencies, search engines, live performance, militant gardening, political organizations: over the course of the following chapters, we will touch on all these areas. For each of them, we will try to understand better how our various environments condition our individual and collective attention, and how, from the moment we start to reconfigure these environments, we do retain a certain power over our own fate. In a certain way, our attention is the thing that is most particular to us. And yet, it is only available to us as something to be alienated – both in the capturing apparatuses in which we are immersed by consumer capitalism and in the aesthetic experiences into which we dive most passionately.

If our attention is a battlefield where the future of our daily submissions and coming rebellions is at stake, then we are at a crossroads. Each of us can learn to 'manage' our attentional resources better, so as to become more 'efficient' and more 'competitive' . . . Or, we can learn to make ourselves more attentive to one another, and to the relationships from which our communal lives are woven. Depending on the directions in which we turn to look and listen, depending on the beings and the problems that we notice, depending on the devices and programmes that we plug into our senses – we will continue towards a consumerist growth that draws each of us in like moths to a flame. Or we will manage to build together the shared conditions of a life that is more tenable and more desirable, which is more attentive to the quality of what surrounds it than to the quantity of its finances.

INTRODUCTION
From Attention Economy to Attention Ecology

Questions concerning the attention economy take on very concrete reality when you walk around the centre of Avignon during the July Theatre festival. Hundreds of posters, stuck to and hanging from anything imaginable, try desperately to attract your attention. At the corner of every street, dozens of young people, sometimes in costume, hand out flyers promoting their show. Some of them act out a scene from their play in the middle of the road. Others try to start up a conversation, in the hope that they will redirect you towards the curtain-draped garage that their theatre company has rented for a small fortune. The passer-by is forced to lie (*I'm leaving tonight*) or be rude (shamefully avoiding eye contact with the people addressing him so jovially). Between the beggars sleeping on cardboard boxes, who ask him for a coin, and the histrions pleading in their hyperactive solicitations for him to look at them, he experiences almost physically a parallel with the economy of material goods, traded on the basis of money and survival, and the economy of cultural goods, traded on the basis of attention and reputation.

Of course, these two economies intertwine all the time. If I am not attentive to the presence of the beggar, I will not give him a coin – this is the defence mechanism that most of us have developed to keep our guilt to a minimum. And likewise, artists do not live on attention alone: posters, flyers and street theatrics are not only designed to make us notice their show, but also to make us pay out a few euros for an entry ticket. Cultural goods are *also* material goods, and material objects are only 'goods' within a system of value-creation that is eminently cultural – this value-creation strongly depends on the way in which we distribute our attention.

1

1. Posters for the Avignon festival, 2013 (photograph
by Mélanie Giraud)

Although they cross over and feed off each other at multiple points, these two economies are nevertheless rooted in two fundamentally different logics. While the calculations of the classical economy of material goods are based on the scarcity of factors of *production*, the attention economy is based on the scarcity of the capacity for the *reception* of cultural goods. Even if, thanks to the generosity of a state or private sponsor, the production of shows at Avignon were to be taken care of, so that they were all free to me, my ability to take advantage of this offer would be restricted by the limits of my attention capacity. Where our economic analyses have focused, for the last three centuries, on the growth of our productive forces, we must learn how better to take into account this (still largely unnoticed) second level constituted by our reception capacity – where our attention is the main factor. This second level is the subject of this work.

A Situation of Overabundant Supply

At the beginning of a third millennium characterized by an explosion in digital communication, a (too) simple way of bringing out the contrast between the two levels of the economy is to oppose a ('material') economy of scarcity to an ('immaterial') economy of overabundance. Even if this framing needs to be critiqued,[1] it provides a useful initial approximation. With its 1,258 shows in less than a month, the Avignon fringe festival is a perfect illustration of this overabundance, coming about in what seems to be a recent and vertiginous explosion: in 1966, there was just one theatre company outside the main show; two decades later, in 1983, there were still only fifty or so; today, there are more than a thousand. Inside the stone walls of Avignon, as in the virtual space of the internet, spectators and web users alike find themselves inundated by an overabundant supply which, while it has certainly managed to get itself made, struggles, in its reception, to meet the expectations of its producers.

Commensurate with the explosion noted in the number of fringe festival shows over the last half-century, there has been an explosion in the number of art-works made available for human attention over the last five centuries. In the Middle Ages, quite apart from the fact that literacy was exceptional, a monk would only have a few hundred, or at most a few thousand, works available to him. To produce each of them required weeks or months of labour. The vast majority of the population was only exposed to a very limited number of discourses (the weekly sermon), images (religious frescos and paintings) and spectacles (passion plays, jugglers, wandering musicians). With the progressive development of communication media and technologies – the printing press, travelling shows, periodicals, cinema, radio, television, and now the internet – the number of discourses, images and spectacles offered to human attention has grown exponentially.

Not long ago, the economy of access to cultural goods was very tightly bound up with the production economy of material goods: before the arrival of the paperback, it was fairly expensive to have a collection of novels, philosophical or historical works at home; before radio broadcasting and vinyl disks, it was difficult and/or expensive to listen to a symphony or an opera; before the invention of the cinema, then television, it was rare to see fiction produced with well-known actors and magnificent scenography. Not satisfied with their large-scale distribution in Western populations over the course of the twentieth century, such experiences are, thanks to the free access provided by Google Books or YouTube, in the process of universalization. For the (increasingly modest) price of a computer, or even a simple mobile phone, and an internet connection, billions of humans will soon have millions of books, images, songs, films and television series at their disposal for a marginal cost of zero. Avignon in July raised to the power of a thousand, twenty-four hours a day, three hundred and sixty-five days a year anywhere on the planet – such is the horizon of the attention economy.

3

This situation of overabundant supply of cultural goods is an essential characteristic of the epoch opening today with the rapid development of digital communication. But it goes well beyond the narrow framework of technological determinism: joining the 1,258 shows of the Avignon fringe are the six hundred new novels of the literary season, the multiplication of terrestrial and cable television channels, and the proliferation of university conferences where our scholars are in such a hurry to make themselves heard that they cannot find the time to listen to others. Because of a penchant for autobiographical outpouring, narcissistic vanity or the need to publish (and not perish), we find ourselves in the surreal situation in which, as the satirists note, when 'everyone starts to write', 'it is easier to find an author than a reader'.

In our overdeveloped countries, even for the least privileged among us – and even if the most well-off still dream of a rare book, an exorbitantly priced show or a masterpiece beyond their budget – our cultural frustrations arise less and less frequently from a lack of resources, and increasingly from a lack of *available time* to read, listen or watch all the treasures hastily downloaded onto our hard drives or recklessly accumulated on our shelves. Of course, nothing is truly free or immaterial: the electricity consumed by the servers supplying the web, the huge increase in toxic waste caused by the built-in obsolescence of our personal computers and mobile phones, the increasing proportion of household budgets taken up by connection costs, the debt spirals engendered by the ease of online purchasing, the new forms of exploitation and insecurity brought about by digital competition – all this calls for the pricking of the utopian bubble of *free* culture (free in both senses), and the recognition of the (ecological) scarcities, the (socio-political) constraints and the impasses of unsustainability that are still imposed and will continue to be imposed by the limits of an inescapably material economy.[2]

None of this is sufficient, however, to invalidate this obvious fact: our classical tools of economic analysis and conceptualization, while they may help to explain the (re)production limits of our material goods, are largely inappropriate for the situation of overabundance which now characterizes the circulation of cultural goods. In its classical definition, the economy endeavours to optimize the utilization of resources characterized by their scarcity. Our situation of overabundant supply is bound to overturn the machinery of reasoning and calculation developed by orthodox economists. So an ever-increasing number of voices have made themselves heard over the last twenty years or so, calling for the advent of *another* economy, which is not only possible but necessary if we are to orientate ourselves in this new situation of overabundant supply: an *attention economy*.

The Emergence of a Discipline

The themes of overabundance do not date from the end of the twentieth century. Faced with the crises of overproduction that have haunted industrial capitalism since its beginning, the sociologist Gabriel Tarde set out in 1902 the tenets of an *Economic Psychology* which may be considered a foundational monument of the attention economy. Already in his work we find three axes of analysis that will play an essential role in later reflections. Firstly, problems of attention are intimately connected with the establishment of the 'machinofacture' peculiar to the industrial mode of production, imposing on the worker an 'exhaustion of attention [that] is a new subtler form of torture, unknown to the crude purgatories of earlier times': 'Excessive attentional stability necessarily produces, through an inevitable reaction, the attentional instability that is characteristic of nervous disorders.'[3]

Tarde understood immediately, moreover, the extent to which advertising, necessary for the absorption of excess goods coming from industrial overproduction, needed to be considered in terms of attention: 'Interrupting attention, fixing it on the thing being proffered, is the immediate and direct effect of advertising.' He sensed perfectly the contagious implications of this: 'it is not just the fourth page of newspapers that is made up of advertisements. The whole body of the paper is a one big continuous and general advertisement.'[4]

But, above all, Tarde understood the way in which attentional alignment structures a whole new economy of visibility whose currency is 'fame', defined as 'the simultaneity and convergence of attention and judgment on a man or event which then becomes well-known or famous'. Even if fame as such in no way dates from the industrial age, the production of 'audiences' by the new media of the day (daily press, telegraph, cinema) institutes an entirely new power regime rooted in a mercantile economy, from the moment that competition between these mass media is subjected to the logic of the market. This new mode of valorization demands new tools – capable of measuring the attentional flux – which simultaneously indicate and structure our daily interactions: 'The need for a *fameometer* becomes even more apparent when celebrities of every kind are more abundant, more sudden and more fleeting, and when, despite their habitual impermanence, they do not fail to be accompanied by a formidable power, since they are a *good* for the possessor, but a *light*, a faith, for society.'[5]

Coming nearly a century after Tarde, we generally consider Herbert Simon to be the father of the attention economy. In a conference in 1969, published in 1971, he asserted that 'the wealth of information means a dearth of something else – a scarcity of whatever it is that information consumes. What information consumes is rather obvious: it consumes the attention of its recipients.'[6] At the same time, the futurologist Alvin Toffler was popularizing the notion of *information overload*[7] and the psychologist Daniel Kahneman published his works remodelling the understanding of attention, emphasizing the limited nature of our attentional resources.[8]

It is in the middle of the 1990s, however, that the attention economy really takes off. The honours go to the philosopher and architect Georg Franck for having developed, in a series of articles begun in 1989 and then collected into a seminal work published in 1998, the first (and no doubt still the best) analytical framework for this new field.[9] While Herbert Simon and Daniel Kahneman received Nobel prizes for their work in economics in 1978 and 2002 respectively, Georg Franck's conceptual work remains largely unknown outside Germany, and the more superficial, virally disseminated, interventions of Michael Goldhaber have since 1996 been considered responsible for launching the public debate on a 'new economy' whose principal scarcity is attention rather than the traditional elements of production. In a few articles much discussed online, Michael Goldhaber asserts that '[l]ike any economy the new one is based on what is both most desirable and ultimately most scarce, and now this is the attention that comes from other people'.[10] Both through the way in which the texts are disseminated and the striking discovery of the promise of the internet, this 'new economy' of attention seems intrinsically connected to the 'new digital technologies'.

In 2001, the management experts Thomas Davenport and John Beck published *The Attention Economy: Understanding the New Currency of Business*, a work which has become canonical for helping markets and managers maximize their efficiency and profit. Next to diagrams formalizing our 'attentional landscape' (*attentionscape*), we read that '[i]n the past, attention was taken for granted, and goods and services were considered valuable. In the future, many goods and services will be given away for free in exchange for a few seconds or minutes of the user's attention.'[11] From the middle of the 2000s, countless publications, particularly in Germany and the

Anglo-Saxon world, emphasized that '[a]ttention is now the commodity in short supply'.[12] It is possible broadly to distinguish three main attitudes.

A number of university economists set out to understand this new attentional economy by submitting it to the formalization demanded by orthodox economics, modelling their approach on that of Josef Falkinger who published two important articles opening the way to a rigorous quantification of the capacity for attentional attraction observed in our market interactions. An attention economy is here 'modelled as a family of senders, which employ costly signals to attract the attention of audiences and have an impact on them'. Saying that attention is a scarce resource implies that '[t]he exposure of subjects to signals is so strong that having an impact by absorbing part of their attention capacity requires them to send strong signals and to target them on audiences with relatively unexhausted perception capacity'. As a consequence of these principles, which together show that 'managing attention and attracting attention are becoming universal maxims in business and economics', [13] a whole series of more practical manuals became available to help optimize the mobilization of ever more precious attentional resources in an increasingly intense competitive environment. As highlighted by Emmanuel Kessous, Kevin Mellet and Moustafa Zouinar, studies of the attention economy by orthodox economists tend to 'oppose two logics. The first aims to protect attention from the overloading of information and to optimize its allocation; the objective of the second is to capture it in a profit perspective.'[14] There will be opportunity in the second chapter to see how this tension sometimes produces strange reversals of economic orthodoxy.

Another series of work challenges these advertising and managerial practices as it denounces the alienating effects of the attentional manipulations that technologies of attraction entail. The publications of Pierre Lévy, Jonathan Crary, Bernard Stiegler, Jonathan Beller, Franco Berardi, Dominique Boullier or Matteo Pasquinelli seek to understand the attention economy as rooted in an anthropological mutation extending well beyond the framework of market exchanges. These authors often envisage a capturing apparatus here, which organizes our desires and subjectivities according to the dominant logic of capitalist profit – with harmful consequences for our capacity for collective decision making and our individual well-being. To the same extent that they seek to understand attentional mechanisms, these works make every effort to denounce perverted appropriations or enable us to glimpse unexpected possibilities.

Finally, a third group of works deals with attentional questions by trying to measure the impact of new technologies on the development of our mental capacities and subjectivities. Often, an alarmist tone prevails here, asserting that the 'internet makes us stupid' or announcing a 'new era of obscurantism' to which we are destined by online surfing and video games.[15] Condemned to the superficiality of multi-tasking (understood as the simultaneous carrying out of several parallel tasks), 'the young' become physiologically incapable of concentrating, which is confirmed by the worrying increase in diagnoses of attention deficit disorders.

The Hypothesis of a Reversal

Whatever the case may be with these questions, to which we will return in the following chapters, the attention economy seems, from the middle of the 1990s, to have established itself as a great reversal taking the form of a challenge: the new scarcity is no longer to be situated on the side of material goods to be produced, but on the attention necessary to consume them. With the following slightly disconcerting practical consequence, which rapidly takes shape as a prophecy: my editor has taken advantage of your naivety and inherited economic ideology to sell you the book that you are holding in your hands (or the digital file that is currently scrolling on your electronic reader), as if he were the one with the rare and precious resource (the book and its contents) at his disposal; in fact, it is you, the readers, who have the upper hand – though no one has dared tell you and you have not yet realized – since, faced with the plethora of works written and disseminated each month, it is your attention, which you are mobilizing right now as you follow this sentence, that is now the scarcest and most fervently desired resource. In all fairness and in all logic, it is me, the author of these lines, who not only should be thanking you, but paying you for the service you are doing me when you dedicate your precious time to reading this book instead of the millions of texts, songs and films available on the internet. Which brings us to the prophecy: in a few years or decades, we will be able to request payment for giving our attention to a cultural good instead of having to pay for the right to access it, as is still required of us in this backward epoch.

As counter-intuitive as it may seem, a prophecy of this kind is already partially realized in our daily reality. Through what miracle am I able to benefit at no cost from the almost magical services of a search engine like Google, as well as from the thousands of very expensive and electricity-hungry servers that this business puts at my disposal? What is free here is nothing but the price already paid for my attention, which explains the dictum of the 'new economy': *if a product is free, then the real product is you!* More precisely: your attention.

A firm like Google lives off this attention in two ways. On the one hand, our searches – our interests, our questions, our clicking choices, the links that we establish or activate – give substance to Google's marvellous intelligence, whose algorithm would be but an empty shell if we did not continually fill it up with our collective intelligence. Google lives off our active and reactive attention, which continually nourish and refine the effectiveness of the formal apparatus put at our disposal. On the other hand, Google tends increasingly to sell our attention, our needs to know and our search choices, to advertisers that the firm allows to short-circuit the effects of our common intelligence: if they appear at the top of the page, it is not (only) by virtue of their relevance, substantiated by our multiple clicks, but because they have paid millions of dollars for increased visibility *regardless* of our collective intelligence, which would place them much lower if it were allowed to organize itself freely.

The lesson to be drawn from the way in which Google operates (as well as YouTube, Facebook and all their like) is as clear as can be: *our attention has a price*, and it is pretty high. For the moment, however, it is not paid *to us*: others skim off most of the profit. We find echoes here of Patrick Le Lay's famous declaration when he was CEO of the television channel TF1, and characterized his job as 'selling to Coca-Cola the time of [viewers'] available brains'. TF1 offers the shows it broadcasts for free because the product is our attention – sold to advertisers according to alchemical equations based on ratings and their multiple translations in terms of market segments, visibility, impact, manipulating behaviours, occupation of spirits and access to the imagination.

If the reversal heralded by the prophets of the attention economy is not yet blindingly obvious, this is perhaps because we do not want to see what the evidence is showing us. Why do large pharmaceutical companies offer free weekends to our doctors (in the form of 'conferences') – if not to take advantage of their kindly attention towards the products they are putting on the market? Why do editors of books for young people develop services which enable bloggers to receive new releases at no charge in exchange for a review – if not because attention is contagious and getting people to talk about you is a condition for survival in this 'new economy'? Why do reality TV shows tend to abolish the distance between those who watch and those who are watched, pushing them onto an uncontrollable roundabout – if not because the mass-media apparatuses produce attention by producing attention?

In a particularly sober and enlightening article, Katherine Hayles, Professor of English Literature at Duke University in North Carolina, suggests that we are living through a major, rapid and massive shift in the attentional systems and cognitive modes that characterize the generations of teachers and students mixing together in the classroom. The teachers conceive their lessons for a system of *deep attention*, imagining that participants are committed to 'concentrating on a single object for long periods (say, a novel by Dickens), ignoring outside stimuli while so engaged, preferring a single information stream, and having a high tolerance for long focus times'. For their part, however, students have formed the characteristic habits of *hyper-attention*: 'switching focus rapidly among different tasks, preferring multiple information streams, seeking a high level of stimulation, and having a low tolerance for boredom'.[16]

For all that we could introduce a few nuances, a few clarifications and a few changes in framing, we would do well to take these prophecies of the attention economy seriously. No, the 'new' attention economy is not going to 'replace' the old economy of material goods – for the good reason that it would not exist without these goods. No, hyper-attention fed by digital acceleration is not inevitably going to undermine the foundations of our capacity for deep concentration. But yes, something major is being reconfigured, in which the distribution of attention already plays a hegemonic role. It is quite right to hypothesize a reversal: what was an epiphenomenon – collectively paying attention to this rather than that – is in the process of restructuring the way in which we materially (re)produce our existence. Attention is *the* crucial resource of our epoch. We cannot reorient ourselves here without trying to understand better what is at stake in its circulation, its capture and its capacities. What can we do collectively about our individual attention, and how can we contribute individually to a redistribution of our collective attention? This, then, is the challenge of the reversal that we are living through – and these are the questions that will orient the whole of this book.

A Temporal Reframing

For the most part, today's discourses on the attention economy point to an essential problem, but the way they tend to frame it is generally debatable. The main aim of this brief work will be to contribute to a resizing and re-centring of our discourses on attention so as to take the opposite viewpoint to three deceptive commonplaces.

The first commonplace relates to the novelty of the 'new attention economy'. From the apparently local and anecdotal phenomenon of the Avignon fringe festival, which has grown almost tenfold since 1990, to the spectacular development of the internet over the same period, everything seems to indicate that the problems of the attention economy only started to be felt on a massive scale over the last twenty years. The statistical data gathered on Google Books Ngram Viewer – the attention measuring software that counts up the occurrences of words and expressions in texts digitalized by Google Books[17] – confirm this initial impression (Figures 2 and 3). In both the Anglophone and the Francophone corpus they show a spectacular take-off in 1996, the moment that Michael Goldhaber set off a polemic by announcing the radical novelty of the attention economy, which was immediately denounced as vague and illusory in a series of critiques.[18]

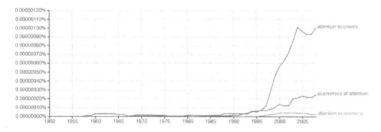

2. Occurrences of 'attention economy', 'economics of attention' and 'attention economics' in Google Books Ngram Viewer, Anglophone corpus 1950–2008 (consulted 23 April 2014)

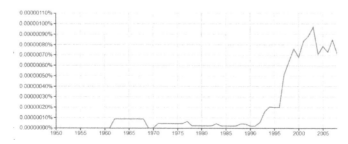

3. Occurrences of 'économie de l'attention' in Google Books Ngram Viewer, Francophone corpus 1950–2008 (consulted 23 April 2014)

11

Even if from the 1970s on there is much talk of 'information over-load', several technological and sociological convergences confirm intuitively the soundness of this periodization (the multiplication of television channels available on terrestrial or cable networks, the inauguration of unlimited subscriptions at cinemas, peer-to-peer file exchange on line, the establishment of free-access digitalized librar-ies, the development of alternative media and blogs, the emergence of YouTube and Google Books).

It is a good idea, however, to take a step back so that we can better measure the respective proportions of inertia and novelty in our situation of overabundant supply, and in the strategies it leads us to assume. As we have seen, the plethora of digital goods led Georg Franck and Michael Goldhaber to reinvent an attention economy that had been initially outlined by Gabriel Tarde following the crises of industrial overproduction at the end of the nineteenth century. The actors who endeavour to attract punters by acting out a scene from their show in the streets of Avignon are only reinventing the practice of *'parade'*, which had already been cultivated and refined by troupes promoting their shows at the fairs of the Ancien Régime. Ann Blair has recently shown that it was under pressure from informational overload that the Renaissance humanists and the philosophers of the seventeenth century developed measures relating to the book (tables of contents, indexes, references) and epistemology (Descartes's 'method') so that they could orientate themselves in the overabundance of texts, in which they already feared they may drown.[19] And it is not a third millennium sati-rist commenting on the six hundred books of the literary season, but the writer Charles Tiphaigne de La Roche in 1760, who wondered 'how to break through the crowd' and 'how to attract attention' when 'everyone has started writing and it is easier to find an author than a reader'.[20]

In his 2006 book titled *The Economics of Attention: Style and Substance in the Age of Information*, Richard Lanham is perfectly correct to highlight that the attention economy is more than two and a half thousand years old, given that rhetoricians have conceived of their work and their science since Antiquity as the skill of captur-ing, and then maintaining, the attention of an audience, whether in a judicial, political or artistic context. As he notes, a good part of the reflections and experiments relating to 'style', both formerly and today, should be (re)read in a context of competition for the conquest of attention, which is always painfully limited. So art historians and researchers in aesthetics and literature would be better placed than economists and specialists in marketing and management to under-stand what is at stake over the long term in the attention economy.

4. Occurrences of 'economy of attention' in Google Books Ngram Viewer, Anglophone corpus 1850–2008 (consulted 23 April 2014)

If we go back to Google Books Ngram Viewer and interrogate the machine on this broader basis, extended from a double temporal and disciplinary perspective, we see an entirely different periodization take shape. By taking the time span back to 1850 and introducing the English phrase 'economy of attention', used in disciplinary fields situated on the borders between psychology and aesthetics (more than cybernetic and economics), we overturn a number of preconceived notions about the attention economy (Figure 4).

Those who were concerned with the *economy of attention* between 1850 and 1950 often situated their reflections in an aesthetic order of questioning, which was more interested in the quality of the sensible and intellectual experience than in its quantification in productivist terms. It is this aesthetic dimension that this work will seek to reintroduce into our current discussions on the attention economy. Beyond being a choice of method and approach, this first reframing takes up a certain vision of the history of attention. This history largely remains to be written, despite the wish expressed by Charles Bonnet in 1783, which remains as pertinent than ever:

> We are missing a Book which would be more useful than any to have come from the human spirit; it would be a history of Attention. If this Book were to be well done and well thought out, it would topple all logics; because it would be a logic reduced to action.[21]

If we really are living through a great reversal in the relationship between the two tightly interrelated levels of our economic reality (the capacity for production of material goods and the capacity for reception of cultural goods), it is appropriate that this reversal should be situated in the expanded framework of the great transformation Western societies underwent, beginning in the middle of the nineteenth century, with the parallel developments of industrialization and marketing.

We should not be surprised that the most profound book on the history of attention comes from an art historian, Jonathan Crary, who analysed the way in which, at the meeting point of five convergent evolutions, attention becomes in about 1870 a socio-economic question of central importance. In *Suspensions of Perception: Attention, Spectacle and Modern Culture*, he reconstitutes in detail the series of transformations that we glimpsed just now in a few quotations from Gabriel Tarde's *Economic Psychology*. In the first place, the spread of assembly line work calls for the mobilization of a very particular kind of attention on the part of workers, who are required to remain alert for tasks that are repetitive and monotonous in the extreme. At the same time, and as a consequence of industrialization, the sale of goods produced in great numbers in this way, required capturing the attention of new masses of consumers through the emergence of the first forms of large-scale advertising and marketing. Starting in the same era, the development of experimental psychology of attention has closely accompanied – for a century and a half now – the incessant tensions and reconfigurations to which the evolutions of capitalism have submitted our capacity to be, to remain or to become attentive to certain phenomena rather than others. The second half of the nineteenth century saw the inventions of new media apparatuses multiply – from the intercontinental telegraph to the cinema, by way of the *Kaiserpanorama* and the first attempts at radio broadcasting – which all reconfigured our attention by serving as extensions to, and prostheses for, our senses (to take up the terms in which Marshall McLuhan characterized the media).[22] Finally, Jonathan Crary's book suggests convincingly that a whole section of the pictorial art of the era, from the Impressionists to Cezanne, staged either figures or ways of seeing that were characterized by unresolved discrepancies and tensions between attention and distraction.

> [S]ince the late nineteenth century, and increasingly during the last two decades, capitalist modernity has generated a constant re-creation of the conditions of sensory experience, in what could be called a revolutionizing of the means of perception. [. . .] the problem of *attention* becomes a central issue. It was a problem whose centrality was directly related to the emergence of a social, urban, psychic, and industrial field increasingly saturated with sensory input. Inattention, especially within the context of new forms of large-scale industrialized production, began to be treated as a danger and a serious problem, even though it was the very modernized arrangements of labour that produced inattention. It is possible to

14

see one crucial aspect of modernity as an ongoing crisis of attentiveness, in which the changing configurations of capitalism continually push attention to new limits and thresholds, with an endless sequence of new products, sources of stimulation, and streams of information, and then respond with new methods of managing and regulating perception.[23]

So, an initial temporal reframing with respect to the traditional association of the attention economy and the development of digital technologies is necessary. On the one hand, we will enrich our understanding of these phenomena over the very long term if they are re-situated within the aesthetic analyses and theorizations that have accompanied reflections on rhetoric and stylistics. On the other hand, the attention economy is inseparable from the evolutions produced and experienced by capitalism over the last one hundred and fifty years, from the beginning of the industrial modernization that continues to conquer the planet (today in China, Brazil and India) to the Taylorization of intellectual tasks affecting the reorganization of 'cognitive capitalism'.[24]

From the Individual to the Collective

The second reframing, which is implicit in the preceding point, entails getting away from an essentially individualist approach to attention. Under the influence of the methodological individualism that jointly characterizes orthodox economics, the experimental psychology inherited from the nineteenth century and recent developments in the neurosciences (with their appended cognitivism), most current analyses relate to the way in which a brain (in the position of subject) moves itself or experiences with respect to a thing or problem (in the position of object).

This individualist approach doubtless benefits from a certain intuitive obviousness. The experience that each of us has of our objects of perception comes to us in an individual mode. What is our attention at this precise instant? *I* look at the screen where the words I am typing on my keyboard show up; *you*, the reader, look at the screen or the page where my sentence has been recorded. When researchers set about analysing our attention in experimental conditions, they do indeed find themselves observing a confrontation between an *I*-subject on the one hand (identified with the brain, the mind, consciousness or formerly the 'soul'), which has attention to pay – with more or less compulsion, effort, desire or ease – and objects on the other (three-dimensional things, figures on a screen, smells, flavours, sounds, signs, voices, words, faces) which have a varying ability to attract or hold the attention we are able to pay to them. The infinite variations, experimentations and speculations on the multiple and nuanced relations that such subjects and objects may maintain have filled thousands of pages of scientific articles and scholarly works – from the experimental psychology of Gustav Fechner and Wilhelm Wundt, Théodule Ribot's treaty on the *psychology of attention*, Edmund Husserl's courses on the phenomenology of attention, and the management and marketing manuals that are proliferating today to help directors and advertisers better capture and captivate our attention, to the most recent discoveries in the neurosciences that have been so well summarized in a recent book by Jean-Philippe Lachaux.[25]

The practical consequences of this kind of methodological individualism pose a number of problems, however, as exemplified by the way in which society tends to diagnose and treat attention deficit hyperactivity disorder (ADHD). Even if the best textbooks on this disease go to the trouble in the foreword of situating it in the context of an 'acceleration in communications', of a 'technological revolution' or generalized 'channel hopping', they very quickly arrive at a diagnosis that is strictly limited to the interaction between a subject-child and the objects encountered in their environment. The screening tests focus on thirty or so criteria measuring the degree to which children 'fail to pay attention to detail or make mistakes in their homework or other activities because they are distracted', 'do not seem to hear when spoken to directly', 'get out of their chairs in class or in other situations when they have been asked to stay seated', 'respond before questions are asked', 'have difficulty waiting their turn', or 'interrupt or disrupt others'.[26] Other textbooks dispense with useless precaution. 'Why does he move so much? Why is he distracted?': the 'cause of the syndrome' is 'the inadequate secretion of certain neurotransmitters', provoking a 'slowdown in the transfer of information, which, in turn, changes the speed at which the part of the brain concerned functions'.[27]

ADHDs are rooted, therefore, in a 'disorder' (which is individualized, personalized, or more precisely neurologized) and a 'deficit' (the neurones do not work quickly enough). So it is not surprising that (starting in the USA) the main and most obvious way of 'managing' the disease is the broad distribution of Ritalin to a whole section of the young.[28] For a 'neurological disorder', a medicinal solution. This ignores the acceleration in communication, new media apparatuses and information overload; it ignores, in short, the whole evolution of 'the configurations of capitalism' highlighted by Jonathan Crary, which 'continually push attention to new limits and thresholds'. From the 'ongoing crisis of attentiveness' initiated in populations and lifestyles at least one hundred and fifty years ago, only subject-individuals remain who are pathologized for 'not paying attention to detail', 'being distracted by external stimuli', or 'having difficulty waiting their turn'.

As a consequence of this individualization of behaviours, we use chemistry to compel our children's attention (as well as our own), at all costs, to bend to the – unprecedented, completely artificial and terribly invasive – needs of a Janus-faced capitalism, which simultaneously advocates relentless productive discipline and limitless consumerist hedonism. So, it is in the broad framework of a vast *(in)attention economy* that ADHDs must be situated – rather than in the overly narrow framework of the subject–object relation or family dynamic. If we and our children are suffering from something, it is firstly from the very specific socio-economic illness that is 'mental capitalism'.[29] As Bernard Stiegler remarks:

> the great temptation is the desire to subject attention to a complete appropriation, to mobilize all of the 'time of available brains' – [. . .] an 'attention economy' has developed to capture attention by any means (given the competition between the media), which in fact leads to the destruction of all the systems that produce attention.[30]

Following the extension of the historical period necessary for an understanding of what is at stake in the attention economy, a second reframing necessitates the reversal of the current dominant approach, where questions of attention are focused on the relations that a perceptive subject maintains with certain perceived (or unperceived) objects. Which is why this book will suggest a triple path by which our traditional ways of conceiving attention will be reversed: instead of setting out from what is self-evident with respect to individual attention, so as to form the horizon of a collective attention, we will set out from the communal to open up the perspective of better forms of individuation.

So, a first section will begin by considering attention as an essentially *collective* phenomenon: 'I' am only attentive to what *we* pay attention to collectively. To understand the ways in which a subject becomes aware of an object, it is important to identify the collective 'attentional regimes' through which we are led to perceive our world – something the work of Dominique Boullier helps us to do. Probably counter-intuitively, but, it is hoped, enlighteningly, the first chapters will consider how attention is rooted in transindividual flows, distributed unequally over the surface of planet Earth and inside every social formation. Georg Franck's powerful analyses will help us to see attention as a new form of capital, whose circulation, distribution, monopolization and investment may certainly be considered in economic terms – with mechanisms for production, accumulation, financing, competition and exploitation. Media networks, of course, provide the infrastructure of this economy, so they will be placed at the centre of the analysis. Thanks to authors like Maurizio Lazzarato, Bernard Stiegler, Franco Berardi, Jonathan Beller, Kenneth McKenzie Wark and Matteo Pasquinelli, we will be able to understand better the nature, organizing principles and new classifications which reorganize contemporary capitalism around the new form of capital that is attention.

A second section will be dedicated to what psychologists refer to as *joint* attention. Starting at nine months, the baby moves from dyadic relationships (subject–object) to triadic relationships, where the attention of two subjects affects the way in which each considers the object. If adults divert their gaze, children learn to follow the direction in which they are looking: 'I' am attentive to what *you* pay attention to. Below the level of the great masses of collective attention as channelled by the media, and above the level of the couple formed by a mother and child or two partners in a loving relationship, the sphere of joint attention is the sphere of the 'small groups' studied by Roland Barthes in his course on communal life at the Collège de France. The pedagogic relation is one of the most important of these spheres: a classroom is a microcosm that can be understood neither as a sum of subject–object relationships nor as a crossing place for media flows. The tools of the macroeconomy of attentional capitalism must be swapped for the more refined tools of a microeconomy of joint attention, which we also encounter in the enclosed space of a live performance.

The co-construction of subjectivities and intellectual proficiency requires the co-presence of attentive bodies sharing the same space over the course of infinitesimal but decisive cognitive and emotional harmonizations. We find here the foundation of a particular quality of attention rooted in *care* – which is to say, the attentive consideration of the vulnerability of the other, of our solidarity and our responsibility towards them. But, so as to escape the constriction that threatens every dual relationship, we will also see the formation of the need for a certain detachment, something which is necessary in order for our attention to be 'joined' [*conjointes*] without being 'combined' [*confondues*]: the psychoanalytic notion of 'free-floating attention' will help us to formalize the detachment indispensable to all individuation.

So, in a third and final section we will be in a position to return to the relations of (in)attention that we maintain as subjects with the objects in our environment. The detour through collective and joint attention will, however, have led beyond questions of individual attention, refocusing them on the good use of an *individuating* attention. The fascinating lessons of the neurobiology of attention should be re-situated in the multi-layered systems that structure our sensibility and desensibilization. The intra-cerebral attention nano-economy, modelled in terms of zones, synapses, nerve impulses and neurotransmitters, only makes any sense if it is re-situated within the microeconomy of small groups in which we develop on a daily basis (family, office, business) and the macroeconomy of great media flows which take up and captivate our consciousness. Within the double framework provided by that to which *we* pay attention collectively, in the first place, and then by that to which *you* pay attention jointly with me, it is of critical importance to understand to what extent – and above all how – *I* can redirect the attention that gives direction to what I become.

This, then, is the object of individuating attention, for which our aesthetic experiences provide both a scale model and a full-size trial, an opportunity for practical exercise and for critical reflection. Knowing how to choose our alienations and our enthralments, knowing how to establish vacuoles of silence capable of protecting us from the incessant communication that overloads us with crushing information, knowing how to inhabit the switches between hyper-focusing and hypo-focusing – this is what aesthetic experiences (musical, cinematic, theatrical, literary or video-gaming) can help us do with our attention, since attention is always just as much something that we *do* (by ourselves) as something that we *pay* (to another).

Towards an Attention Ecosophy

This kind of approach imposes, however, a third discrepancy, which encourages a reframing of the vocabulary we have been using up to now to name the object of this reflection and this study. Attention economy, economics of attention, economy of attention: all these expressions, which help us to grasp the dynamic of a profound

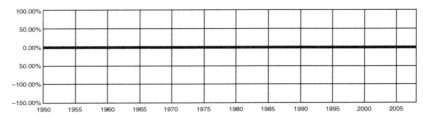

5. Occurrences of 'Attention ecology' or 'Ecology of attention' in
Google Ngram Viewer, English corpus 1950–2008 (consulted
23 April 2013)

formal reconfiguration of our lives, import an economic paradigm
into the heart of our future imaginings. Is the (collective, joint and
individuating) functioning of our attention really beholden to an
'economy'? We should doubt this as a matter of urgency.

This suspicion does not seem to be widely shared. Aurélien
Gamboni has produced an enlightening reframing, articulating his
discussion around a suggestion that we speak of an 'attention *ecology*'
instead of an 'attention *economy*'.[31] While it can be found sketched
out in the odd reflection on attention,[32] this phrase still only produces
a perfectly flat encephalogram in Google Ngram Viewer (Figure 5).

Making this until now lifeless line take off represents, however, an
urgent necessity, and is one of the ambitions of this brief work. Even
if, as we will see in the second chapter, it can be enlightening to consider attention as the 'capital' peculiar to a new level of the market
economy, you trap yourself in a narrow and distorting perspective
when you content yourself with an economic paradigm to account
for attention. Our linguistic habits no doubt push us in this direction: we 'pay' attention to this or that; these objects generally 'yield'
information in 'exchange' for this 'payment'; this kind of transaction
certainly 'produces' a kind of intellectual 'profit'. To keep to this
dominant economic paradigm – directed towards the maximization
of profits thanks to the reduction of costs in a context of market competition – is to suggest that everything can be understood in terms of
a 'better return', a 'more rational organization' or a 'more efficient
management' of our attentional resources, whether that be for advertising, managerial, production or activist purposes. These kinds of
metaphor, however, are as dangerous for the differences they conceal
as they are useful for the parallels they reveal.

We may address three main objections to this economization of
attention. Firstly, as we have seen already, the currently dominant

economic paradigm rests on a deceptive individualist methodology, which makes the collective the result of individual activities, when it is a matter of understanding how such individuals individualize themselves from the communal.

Secondly, our economic reasoning would seem to be a tool rooted in a purely instrumental reason: it only helps us to achieve more efficiently what we have supposedly already decided to do or desire. The economy (modestly) claims only to elucidate the optimal management of scarce resources, without allowing itself to go into the question of the ends to which we direct the use of these resources. The 'Great Society' dreamed up by Friedrich Hayek is admirably 'liberal' in that it endeavours to provide as many means of happiness as possible to the individuals that make it up, while leaving everyone free to provide their own definition of happiness (building churches to the glory of God, buying luxury cars to show off at the weekend, collecting stamps, studying Spinoza's philosophy). But attention cannot be reduced to a simple question of means. You cannot claim to be holding an axiologically neutral discourse (separated from any subjective value) on attention, for the good reason that attentional processes are inextricably linked to our processes of valorization. As we will see in the final section, attention is individuating because it is rooted in a circular dynamic – in a circle that may be vicious or virtuous: I valorize what I pay attention to and I pay attention to what I valorize. As soon as the means-resource conditions the end aimed at through it, it is no longer possible to claim – as does our economic ideology – that it is maximizing the means while leaving everyone free to choose their own ends. Making do with an economic vocabulary in the study of attentional dynamics therefore prevents us from posing the essential question: how – which is to say, inevitably, in which direction, to what ends – are we to direct the attention which gives direction to what we become?

Thirdly, and above all, the economic paradigm should be rejected because there is another which proves much more inspiring for conceiving the complexities of our attentional processes – the paradigm referred to as 'deep' ecology and theorized by Arne Naess, the Norwegian philosopher, as *ecosophy*:

> 'Ecosophy' is a compound of the prefix 'eco-' found in economy and ecology, and the suffix '-sophy' found in philosophy. [. . .] 'Sophia' need not have specific scientific pretentions as opposed to 'logos' compound words (biology, anthropology, geology, etc.), but all 'sophical' insight should be directly *relevant for action*. [. . .] 'Sophia' intimates acquaintance and understanding rather than impersonal and abstract results.[33]

21

In the same period in the 1980s when Naess published his best-known work, Félix Guattari took up the same term to designate the necessary concatenation of several essentially connected levels:

> An ecosophy, articulating together the ensemble of scientific, political, environmental, social and mental ecologies, is perhaps called to replace the old ideologies which abusively divided the social, the private and the civil, and which were fundamentally incapable of establishing transversal links between politics, ethics and aesthetics. [. . .] I call it *ecosophy*, not in order to include all these heterogeneous ecological approaches in one same totalizing or totalitarian ideology, but, on the contrary, to point to the perspective of an ethico-political choice for diversity, for creative dissensus, for responsibility with respect to difference and otherness.[34]

For both, the central affirmation of the ecosophical approach is that individuals do not pre-exist the relations that constitute them: 'Relationalism has ecosophical value, because it makes it easy to undermine the belief in organisms or persons as things which can be isolated from their milieux. Speaking of interaction between organisms and the milieux gives rise to the wrong associations, as an *organism is interaction*.'[35]

In the same way, we could say that *attention is an interaction*. It represents the essential mediator charged with assuring my relationship with the environment that nourishes my survival: a being can only persist in existence to the extent that it manages to 'pay attention' to that on which it depends for the reproduction of its life form. It must 'attend to' (*beachten*) that which enables it to live, it must be concerned for it in order to take care of it. *Paying attention is a genuine activity* – preceding any form of subsequent action: it implies weaving together observations and gestures while respecting the correct level of tension for maintaining tenable relations with our milieu.

Far from belonging to a purely technical expertise (as the prevailing economic discourse would have us believe), the activity of paying attention belongs to a genuine environmental *wisdom* – an *ecosophy* – in which the orientation of ends is inseparable from the calculations of efficiency. Analyses elucidating the mechanisms of an attention economy certainly warrant our interest as they reveal the new dynamics that are superimposed on the traditional economy, focused on the mercantile production of material goods. But these analyses must be reframed in the broader perspective of an attention ecosophy, which alone is capable of articulating the five levels of ecological reorganization necessary for the reproduction of the life forms that we value. The *biophysical* ecology of our environmental resources, the *geopolitical* ecology of our transnational relations, the *socio-political* ecology of our class relations and the *psychic* ecology of our mental resources all depend on the *media* ecology that conditions our modes of communication.[36]

This last level is at once the most superficial (superstructural), since it only seems to be the 'reflection' of the other four, and the most fundamental (infrastructural), since it is this that decides to what we pay our attention (or not). Whether the things that are most dear to us blossom or are crushed depends on this. This is why attention ecosophy is a question of vital importance to us. And this is why this work will begin with an analysis of the status of our attention in today's media systems.

Part I

Collective Attention

— 1 —

MEDIA ENTHRALMENTS
AND ATTENTION REGIMES

Let us imagine the surface of the Earth seen from Saturn through a high-powered telescope that would not only allow us to observe the movements of human bodies, even inside their houses, but also to record and speed up their developments over the centuries. We see them every day, going in their masses to the fields, factories or offices, taking public transport and getting into cars that coagulate in traffic jams. We think we understand that they move in this way because of functional necessity: producing food, clothing, tools, and the skills necessary for their continued existence.

From the eighteenth century, we notice that a certain proportion, negligible to start with but soon growing to a majority, remains almost motionless, their eyes fixed on sheets of paper or glowing screens. Some only give themselves over to this immobility in the evenings or at the weekend, when their productive movements have come to an end, but an increasing number give themselves over to it almost all the time, to the point that it becomes hard to tell when their immobility has a productive function and when it is relaxation unrelated to work. We see them make micro-movements which very subtly affect the sheets of paper or the screens they look at, and which suggest they are contributing to productive collaborations. But, starting in the twentieth century, we also see the proliferation of a variety of devices into which they seem to speak, and more recently make hand gestures, and which seem to allow them to communicate with each other with increasing speed and over ever greater distances.

Indeed, adjusting the telescope we see multiple networks, in the form of periodicals, telegraphic lines, radio waves or fibre-optic cables, being established between them with increasing density. For a few decades, this communication seemed to be organized from a few

27

central points, which sent out the same messages to all the surrounding places of reception; but, starting in the 1990s, highly interactive networks developed at a remarkable pace. At the beginning of the third millennium, the surface of the inhabited regions of the Earth seems to be completely covered by a thick, dense cloud of messages, sounds and images circulating in a great many directions – let's call this the 'mediasphere' – to the extent that, in the middle of this entanglement, it becomes very difficult to distinguish who is speaking and who is listening, who is producing and who is receiving, who is carefully working and who is having fun.

The Mediasphere Seen from Above

Despite their apparent physical immobility, all the Earthlings seem acutely mobilized by what circulates in this mediasphere. It is hard to fathom why, from the middle of the twentieth century, they are sometimes glued in their millions to little screens in order to watch trim young people push a leather ball around, climb mountain passes on bikes, or hit the top half of each other's body with large coloured gloves. During other less physical and essentially verbal contests, held every three or four years between people generally wearing ties, they seem to decide, through the insertion of paper into ballot boxes, who among them will take charge of the administration of their future interactions within vast associations called 'nations'.

However complex the effects produced by the entanglement of multidimensional communications mixing with each other in this mediasphere, we can clearly see from Saturn, if the unfolding of the decades is sped up, entire generations start to grow their hair, wear only black clothes, be outraged by the sexual escapades of a politician, cry over the death of a princess, buy up addictive gadgets or criminalize the wearing of certain clothes – all with striking synchrony. And so the general function of this entire mediasphere, of which we had difficulty deciding whether it related to the necessities of production or to the puzzling pleasures of entertainment, comes into view. The very fact of watching the same things together at the same time, even if in apparent isolation from each other, produces effects of communal valorization which are indispensable to the constant renewal of the system of production. As a local informant lucidly suggests,

> mass media, taken as a whole, is the deterritorialized factory, in which spectators do the work of making themselves over in order to meet

28

the libidinal, political, temporal, corporeal, and, of course, ideological protocols of an ever intensifying capitalism. [. . .] [T]he media, as a deterritorialized factory, has become a worksite for global production. The value of our look *also* accrues to the image; it sustains the fetish.[1]

Seen from Saturn, the mediasphere forms, therefore, the necessary counterpart to the industrial production line: in order for factories to offload the material goods that they produce on a mass scale, the media must produce subjects wanting to buy them. In other words: seen from above, human attention seems to be massively channelled by an entanglement of media apparatuses which enthral us [*nous 'envoûtent'*].[2] The media should be conceived more in terms of ecosystems (of diffusion) than as 'channels' (of transmission). As was so well analysed by Niklas Luhmann, they form a system that actively reconditions the reality that it is supposed faithfully to represent.[3] This ecosystem functions as an echo chamber, whose reverberations 'occupy' our minds (in the military sense of the term): most of the time, we think (in our 'heart of hearts') only what is made to resonate in us in the media vault by the echoes with which it surrounds us. In other words, media enthralments create an ECHOSYSTEM, understood as *an infrastructure of resonances conditioning our attention to what circulates around, through and within us.*

It would be terribly reductive – even if partially true – to characterize such enthralments in terms of an opposition between 'them' (the media, journalists, the powerful, rulers, elites, the *establishment*) and 'us' (the poor little ignorant people, shamefully manipulated by Machiavellian politicians, big bosses of multinational firms, spin doctors and storytellers). Media enthralments result from an echosystem in which we are all implicated (literally: 'folded') – with very different and harshly unequal (but nonetheless interconnected) levels of participation, responsibility, activity, exploitation and profit. Even if we are led to find its deplorable and degrading effects deeply repulsive, this echosystem can only be conjugated in the first-person plural: whether we like it or not it constitutes 'our' environment, 'our *milieu*' (another word etymologically related to the word 'medium') – we are what and who we are because we live in the 'middle' of it. We don't merely live *in* it: to a large extent, 'we' *are* it. And just like our atmosphere or climate, however unbreathable or overheated they may be, our media echosystem – with all its nuances, standardized sectors and no-go zones – is necessarily communal. Here as well, there is no plan(et) B.

Every time that – spontaneously or with reflection – 'I' give my attention to this rather than that, it is under the influence of a media enthralment to whose resonance, around (and inside) each of us, we all contribute. The morning radio, the evening TV news, the afternoon newspaper, Facebook pages, telephone conversations, constant texts and tweets – all of this continually in-forms the contents of 'our' (necessarily communal) thoughts.

The particular effect of media enthralments has less to do with efficient causation than it has with formal causation. Among the four causes distinguished by Aristotle,[4] besides the 'material' cause (the marble the statue is made of), the 'final' cause (the payment or glory the sculptor hopes to obtain through his work) and the 'efficient' cause (the gestures he makes with his hammer and chisel), the 'formal' cause designates the import of a pre-existing form on the development of a procedure. But, as Thierry Bardini, following Marshall McLuhan and Lance Strate,[5] rightly highlights, the formal cause relates to environmental permeability and recursive circularity: it is difficult to prove (and to admit) that I bought a Nespresso coffee machine because I fell into the crude trap of identifying myself with George Clooney, who does their commercials; on the other hand, it is reasonable enough to think that it is because we are *all* submerged in Nestlé's huge marketing campaign that my friends learned of the existence of such a machine, tried a sample, were seduced by its taste or design, spoke to me about it, etc.

Even if the efficient cause remains elusive – since it is generally the case that a combined bundle of impulses compels me to adopt a given behaviour – the introduction of a form, designed to circulate among us with the highest possible frequency, helps to explain how it is that our tastes and habits so often intersect with choices that are simultaneously free (since the action is not immediately forced upon them by an efficient cause) but nevertheless strongly conditioned (since they tend to be moulded spontaneously to the formal causes available in our environment). The formal causation lurking in every corner of our media echosystem incessantly feeds our ability to think – and it is quite suggestive to see this faculty which the Greeks referred to by the term *nous* (νοὑς) resonate with the very pronoun used in French for the first-person plural (*nous*). To say the same thing differently again: the media echosystem is structured by a FORMAL CAUSALITY based on *the power the forms circulating among us have to in-form our most intimate and spontaneous thoughts*.

We must set out from here if we are to challenge the individualist presuppositions that lead most discourses on the attention economy astray: before being a matter of individualized choices, attention is first of all structured (and spellbound) by collective enthralments, which are inextricably architectural and magnetic, and which are induced by media apparatuses circulating certain forms (rather than others) among and within us. It is based on this capacity to think collectively – the communal νοῦς from which *we* [*nous*] emerge as a community – that attention phenomena at the level of the mediasphere must be analysed.

Living in France and necessarily participating in the islamophobic enthralments currently resonating in the media sphere, I cannot fail to notice that a woman is wearing a veil – similarly, living in America and submerged in the long-term inertia of racist stereotypes haunting that country, it is difficult for a white person from a wealthy neighbourhood not to nurture feelings of fear and threat when passing a group of young African-Americans in the street late at night. The attention I pay to what surrounds me and to what I encounter is constrained, in the first instance at least, to follow paths opened by the images and discourses circulating among and within us. From which comes a PRINCIPLE OF TRANSINDIVIDUAL ATTENTIONALITY: *through 'me', it is always 'our' collective thinking and feeling* [νοῦς/ *nous*] *who is paying attention.*

Collective Attention

Even if the view down on Earth from above is misleading with respect to a deeper ecology, as it flattens out the social conflicts structuring the human world, the detour via Saturn will enable us to elaborate a few first basic principles with which we can begin to sketch out an ecology of attention.

POSTULATE OF LIMITED RESOURCE: *the total quantity of attention available to humans is limited at any given time.* As we will see, attention can intensify, concentrate or become more highly attuned over time, and we can very well admit that the aggregated quantity varies with the ages – as a function of attentional quality and not only as a function of the number of humans on the planet. We all know, moreover, that depending on the established habits of the person carrying it out, the same task requires very different efforts of attention. From Saturn, therefore, we can neither confirm that the limits of aggregated human attention are fixed once and for all, nor that a given task is out of range at a time t. We see, however, that each human only has a limited number of waking hours in the day, and that their attentional resources only allow them to focus on a very limited number of tasks at a given moment, based on a limited number of acquired abilities. So, seen from Saturn, the sum of the phenomena to which humans pay attention at a given moment represents a non-infinite quantity of attention. Here we touch on the principle of *eco* common to *economy* and *ecology*: human activities are only tenable if the limited resources available to them are taken into account.

From this follows a COROLLARY OF COMPETITION: *the amount of focused attention allocated to a certain phenomenon reduces the amount of focused attention available for considering other phenomena.* Whether we are concerned with mankind as a whole or with each person taken separately, the limited amount of focused attention available at a given moment introduces a principle of competition between the objects considered or in the quality of the consideration given to each. At the nano-economic level of the individual brain, neurobiologists suggest that we measure attention in terms of sampling quality: the more I observe a phenomenon in 'high definition', the more precisely I focus on it, the more intensely I watch it, the less available focused attention I have for other simultaneous phenomena. What we attribute to an ability to carry out several operations at the same time (multi-tasking) – like driving a car and talking about philosophy with a passenger, while at the same time scratching your leg and noticing an ad for a new film – in reality implies knowing how to modulate the sampling level at which we take in and deal with the information drawn from each of the spheres considered (the surrounding cars, the implications of the counter-argument that has been raised, the location of the itch, the names of the actors). What our attention gains quantitatively by considering several objects simultaneously, it loses qualitatively in intensity with each taken separately. At this first level – which we will need to question towards the end of this book – the distribution of attention is based, therefore, on a logic of competition: what is given on the one hand is no longer available to be simultaneously given on the other.

So, the telescope on Saturn helps us, in the first instance, to envisage the general distribution of the limited resource that is collective attention on the surface of planet Earth. This can't fail to raise certain questions: seen from such an elevated position – from where we clearly see polar and mountain ice melting at a pace that is much more terrifying than our so called 'terrorist threats' – are we making 'good use' of our collective attention when in our millions we plug our senses and our brains into moving images of a prince's marriage, a world cup football final, a television debate, a video game or an independent film? Are the formal causes that we circulate among ourselves (perfume and car brands, bearded jihadists, guilty confessions of weak politicians, sordid crimes) appropriate if we want to concentrate our attention on solving our most urgent problems?

It would be correct, but no doubt too easy, to settle for a negative answer to these kinds of questions.[6] By clearly illuminating the distraction effects brought about by today's media, the view from Saturn – as always when we look at Earth from the sky above[7] – only reveals broad aggregated tendencies by crushing the (conflictual) agencies on which they feed. If attention ecology must set a challenge for itself, it is to translate the too abstract truth, which makes the mass media into 'weapons of mass distraction' into terms which are much more precise, and which would help us understand the concrete logics by which our attention is led to 'spontaneously' take an interest in objects that are apparently without interest.

Anchoring the analysis in an awareness of our collective attention allows us to avoid the moralizing discourse which, from Pascal to the Frankfurt School, deplores the apparently hopeless effects of the temptations of 'entertainment' and its industries. On the one hand, it is difficult not to admit that humans, like sheep and certain fish, think for the most part in herds and shoals: we tend to look in the same direction as our fellows. This sheep-like behaviour leads to a whole series of irrational disruptions and inefficient configurations, as it organizes our behaviour around attractors that are stabilized in a partially chaotic way. We can express this phenomenon by way of a FORMAL PRINCIPLE OF COLLECTIVE ENTHRALMENT which summarizes the considerations of the preceding pages: *human attention tends to fall on objects whose forms it recognizes, under the spellbinding influence of the direction taken by the attention of others.* As we have seen, individual attention is orientated according to echo effects, which make certain forms present in the environment resonate in it, and according to transindividual dynamics identifiable from the end of the first year of life when the infant is compelled to direct its gaze according to its perception of the gaze of others (which we will study under the heading of 'joint attention'). Even so, we should not deplore this group behaviour, which is constitutive of subjectivity and human sociality.

For, on the other hand, speaking of 'collective' attention leads us to foreground the plurality of dynamics from which our common enthralments result. Attention carries a power of *collection* which ensures very complex modes of interaction between social groups and the individuals emanating from them. The etymology of *colligere* points to the action of 'gathering together' – which should be understood in two different, but intimately entangled, senses.

On the one hand, 'collection' unites objects selected within an environment in response to a common criterion. It therefore implies a labour of observation and analysis – the choosing and filtering that is central to the functioning of attention. Attention's task is to select, from among the phenomena surrounding us, those that are significant for our survival and for the satisfaction of our desires. All attention, therefore, is 'collective', in the sense in which it collects characteristics whose common feature is that they help us to prosper in our environment. Attention in this way gathers together, in an apparently egocentric way, the bouquet of goods which we are able to draw from our milieu in order to sustain our existence.

But, in doing this, attention proves to be collective in a second sense, which was suggested above. Even if I may think that I am only concerned with myself, the bouquet that I collect inscribes me in a collective, in a 'community', which is very obvious for an outside observer: it turns out that the colours and forms of the flowers I collect resemble very closely those of my neighbours. Even when I think I am gathering on my own, it turns out that we are gathering together: we apply criteria and favour forms which unite us in one community. In other words, our selective attention serves, in one same movement, to filter phenomena from our environment and to constitute communities of sensibility and action. From this we can draw a PRINCIPLE OF SELECTIVE COLLECTIVIZATION: *attention simultaneously ensures a certain adaptation of our behaviour to our environment (by selecting in it what interests us) and a certain collective composition of individual desires (by spontaneously aligning our sensibilities and our preferences with those of others).*

Rational Attention and Shared Clichés

We understand better now why we should in no way deplore attentional gregariousness. Even if our fervent individualism admits it grudgingly, we are only able to collectively develop communal powers that are incomparably superior to our isolated capabilities because our attention tends to align with the attention of others – albeit in sometimes contrary directions, which nevertheless implies orientation along the same axis. The evaluation of what deserves our interest and what is a distraction turns out to be quite complicated in this respect. Who is to say that the alignment of desires symbolized by a charismatic princess does not contribute to an increase in the communal strength of a population 'distracted' by the marriage of a prince? Why deny that a sporting exploit could, through an effect of formal causality, inspire among its spectators the belief that it is possible to surpass oneself? How can you close your eyes to the fact that a video game develops certain skills even as it distracts us from current problems? We will see in the third part of this book that all these distractions are far from equal but, in response to abstract and indiscriminate condemnations of the mass media, cultural industries or the society of the spectacle, it is important to recognize the complexity of the dynamics that are concretely at work in our collective attention.[8]

We find here another point of contact between the attention ecology and the economic ideology from which it must be liberated. Just as both are based on the recognition of the limited nature of our available resources, both are led – in typically 'liberal' fashion – to presuppose a capacity for rational intellection at the centre of the vast majority of our human behaviours. We can make this the object of a POSTULATE OF PRACTICAL RATIONALITY: *from the moment they are able to support their existence, agents every day show evidence of a certain practical rationality in the directing of their attention.* In the face of the countless dangers that continually threaten our physical existence (a poisonous plant, a falling rock, a distracted driver), a first proof of behavioural rationality may be found in the fact that all these dangers have been avoided and life maintained. Here we have the most basic definition of attention: *pay attention to anything that may harm you* (*Attenzione! Achtung! Watch out! Cuidado! Caute!*).

Of course, this elementary form of attention and rationality constitutes only a minimal modality, stemming from a *vigilance* situated on a level with the conditions of simple subsistence. While its importance must be recognized, it is also important to determine its threefold deficiency – which will provide us an opportunity to highlight a difference with the hypothesis of the rationality of agents inscribed in a neoliberal economic paradigm.

Firstly, we should temper any postulate of practical rationality with a COUNTER-POSTULATE OF INFORMATION DEFICIENCY. The rationality of our behaviour is constantly jeopardized by the deficiency of the information that we have about our environment. In other words: *we never have the means to pay enough attention.*

The peculiar work of attention consists in precisely this: paying *enough* attention – to still unnoticed details, to still overlooked nuances, to still unexpected implications. If our behaviour is always (a little) irrational, this is because our actions are always (a little) constrained (for lack of means or lack of time), a constraint which prevents us from collecting enough information to be certain about what we are doing. It is precisely here that we can gauge the unrealism of the neoliberal paradigm which, blinded by its 'liberal' ideology, systematically fails to take into account the consequences of the multiple forms of constraint which 'irrationalize' our behaviour – beginning with the most important among them: information deficiency.

Secondly, neither simple individual survival, nor even individual prosperity, can sufficiently establish the rationality of a behavioural mode. The second correction to the postulate of practical rationality comes into focus as the requirement for a HORIZON OF TRANSINDIVIDUAL CONSISTANCE: *an individual lifeform only deserves to be called rational to the extent that it incorporates attention to its transindividual sustainability.* Something is only truly desirable, says Nietzsche, if you would wish its eternal return. We touch here on a fundamental point of divergence between the currently dominant economic paradigm and its necessary ecological overcoming. When we build nuclear plants producing radioactive material that will be dangerous for hundreds of thousands of years, we foolishly sacrifice the vital interests of thousands of future generations for the sake of a few brief decades of ephemeral and irresponsible prosperity. This intergenerational carelessness is just one symptom of a deeper weakness [*inconsistance*] whereby we blind ourselves to the necessary reproduction of the communal on which the continuance of our life forms depends. In everything relating to the renewal of our environmental resources, to our social fabric or our cultural creativity, our collective attention as governed by the economic paradigm allows itself to be guided by metrics that systematically neglect what is necessary for the reproduction of the communal that nurtures our individuality. Our fervent individualism only pays attention (with great greed) to what supports our petty personal lives, without paying serious attention to either the sustainability or the validity of forms of life which we should embody (transitorily) without exhausting them at our death.

Thirdly, within the narrow limits of our dominant presentism and individualism, the abstract postulate of practical rationality constantly comes up against the EVIDENCE OF DISFIGURED LIVES: how can we fail to see that *the current existence of so many of our*

36

contemporaries manifestly lags behind what they have the potential to become. By underestimating the constraints of information deficiency, by claiming not to evaluate the ends for which agents use the means they are provided by capitalism, the neoliberal paradigm comes to confuse simple survival (at any price) with the 'good' life – as suggested by its tendency to analyse criminality in terms of profit and cost calculations. By asserting the inextricable entanglement, as well as the unified dynamic, that binds the determinism of ends to the composition of means, the attention ecology can, in contrast, recognize (without claiming to be able to measure it precisely) the gap separating the minimal threshold of a practical rationality assuring our simple survival and the desirable horizon of an existence that has the potential to blossom.[9]

So, what remains of the postulate of practical rationality once we come to look at it again in the light of our information deficiency, the blindness coming from our transindividual weakness and the disfigurement from which so many contemporary lives clearly suffer as they are knocked down to a subsistence threshold without being able to affirm their existence in the development of a way of life endowed with its own consistence? We are left with the essential: a dynamic process by which the pluralist labour of our disseminated attention continually adjusts and renews our collective intelligence.

As it collects the pertinent forms that constitute our communal enthralments, our collective attention provides each of us with a series of sensory filters which makes certain saliences appear in our environment. When they inherit these filters, each generation benefits from the accumulated beliefs and knowledge of previous generations.[10] We may characterize these already constituted forms as *clichés*, through which the modes of perception of the phenomena of our environment are articulated, along with the ways in which we react to them and our manner of referring to them in communication with our fellow human beings – Philippe Descola would speak here of 'schemas', and Lawrence Barsalou of 'simulators'.

These clichés supply the elementary instruments which our 'automatic' attention uses to quickly identify the objects that surround us as either sources of pleasure or danger. This is a lit pipe and that is a petrol pump: pay attention to the risk of explosion! It is the practical rationality inherent in these clichés taken as a whole that, one way or another, assures our daily survival. Our attention makes use of these clichés almost automatically, so long as the recognition of objects we encounter is accompanied by predictable effects. As soon as a source that we expect to be pleasurable actually brings pain, another

37

kind of attention – intentional, reflexive, critical, interpretive – intervenes to try to make the necessary corrections and adjustments so that a similar unpleasant surprise is not repeated.[11]

Both (identifying) automatic attention and (corrective) interpretive attention constitute factors of negentropy: as Paul Valéry emphasized in the notes he amassed between 1901 and 1943 for a book he never wrote, attention 'is connected to everything in life that struggles against Carnot's principle' (which is to say entropy, 'disorder'). 'Threading a needle is working against disorder. Writing a sonnet.' Attention 'increases the productivity of a certain given initial situation – the sensibility of a sense, the precision of an act – of a response. In general, the response goes by the shortest path.' It is in this respect that Valéry speaks of *economy*, since attention allows operations to be performed 'with minimal trial and error [. . .] and the substitution of a kind of "certitude" for a statistical process'.[12] If I bring the thread to the eye of the needle distractedly, it will probably take dozens of attempts before I get it through; by concentrating my attention briefly, I replace a statistical process with a kind of certitude. The seamstress will probably be able to carry out the same operation without thinking – habit will have developed in her a gestural cliché, allowing her to find the shortest path with her eyes closed. In both cases, attention is an economic factor, 'increasing the productivity of an initial situation'.

With these two superimposed levels – automatism of the cliché and corrective intentional concentration – attention is involved in AN ADVENTURE OF COLLECTIVE RATIONALIZATION, in both the (philosophical) sense of mastering phenomena by understanding their causes and the (economic) sense of improving efficiency: *our collective rational attention is nourished by the daily trials to which we subject the clichés we have inherited, as well as the corrective reorientations that we bring to them in the exceptional cases where they failed our expectations and we were obliged to make some changes.* It is this incessant sharing and recycling of clichés that constitutes the common ground of our collective intelligence – expressed and embodied in the infinite subtleties of our language in a state of permanent evolution. If 'I' can only be attentive to something to the extent that *we* pay attention to it – and if collective attention must be considered primary with respect to any effort at individual attention – this is precisely because this common ground of clichés in perpetual reprocessing conditions my ability to identify the phenomena encountered in my environment. The attention economy is in truth fundamentally *collectivist*.

Attention Regimes

The preceding pages have overly simplified matters by opposing the individual and the collective in a binary fashion, as though my singularity were only opposed by a 'common' language, society or environment (all conjugated in the singular). This illusory simplification should of course be corrected by making the study of multiple and diversified 'milieux' – within which we are called to identify sources of danger or opportunities for pleasure – the primary object of an attention ecology. Following Dominique Boullier, we may characterize these different milieux from the perspective of the types of 'attention regime' by which they appear to be defined. Even if each of us has a slightly different perception of them, these regimes very clearly belong to a collective level. Their markers are of a conventional type; the apparatuses that organize them constitute fields; the attentional modes that they bring about result from large-scale social relationships, which they help to renew or reconfigure locally.

Envisaging our various milieux as belonging to different attentional regimes implies adding a modal (and affective) dimension to what we have until now been considering only in a factual (and cognitive) framework. Attention is not only a matter of objects that have been perceived or identified more or less correctly, of a limited resource whose distribution puts objects in competition with each other. It is also characterized by a whole range of very different qualities and ways of being attentive to what is around us.

In addition to measures of duration and intensity, management and marketing specialists have put forward a series of dichotomies, associated with different milieux and giving rise to different capture techniques, to distinguish the different ways of being attentive – dichotomies largely inspired by categories established by experimental psychology over the last hundred years. We have just encountered one of these when we distinguished between *automatic* attention (back-of-mind) and *intentional* and reflexive attention (front-of-mind). This kind of distinction is to be found at multiple superimposed levels of analysis. It is not only the driver of a vehicle who will often switch to autopilot to discuss sport or philosophy with their passenger; society as a whole, dominated as it is by productivist capitalism, does the same thing when GDP growth is blindly taken as an indicator of prosperity. Universities and political institutions proceed on automatic attention when they are happy to collect data from which they can distil their trimestral growth index; they only switch to an intentional and reflexive regime in exceptional circumstances, when an unexpected crisis strikes and some Nobel prize winner is asked to write a (quickly forgotten) report on the limits and distortions inherent in the way GDP is calculated.

Attention may be *captive*, when spectators imprisoned in their seats have commercials forced on them before the start of a film, or *voluntary*, when I chose to read a book on the beach instead of sunbathing with my eyes closed. It may be *attractive*, when the prospect of pleasure or gain is dangled in front of me (lottery, discount, sales), or *aversive*, when a large brightly coloured sign informs me of a mortal danger. As they try to get consumers to spend more or workers to work more, marketing and management specialists generally develop tools that target individual behaviours, like the *attentionscape* graphics that help them to observe the changes in our 'attentional landscape' in real time. But they too think in terms of milieux when, for example, they try to locate *environmental attention gaps*, like airport concourses or subway carriages, in the spaces of our everyday lives – all those places where we rush to install television screens to cram with commercials. So they distinguish between technologies that aim to 'attract attention' (attention-getting technologies) using one-off hooks (like pop-up windows or puns) – which risk, however, limiting their own effectiveness through saturation – and technologies that aim to 'structure attention' (attention-structuring technologies), which work over time as they guide attention from one salient point to another (something PowerPoint presentations or the traditional 'parts of speech' arranged by rhetoricians aim at).[13]

Dominique Boullier has described with greater precision four attention regimes, which, he wisely clarifies, are only idealized poles with respect to which concrete attentional milieux always represent impure forms (Figure 6). This characterization nevertheless helps us to understand how 'my' attention finds itself overdetermined by supra-individual apparatuses within which it must be recontextualized by any approach that would claim to be ecological.

The first regime is characterized by a state of ALERTNESS: our milieu sends us signals warning of threats, pop-up windows flash up unexpected profitable opportunities, or a film increases the noises of explosions and plays with quick-fire editing and suspense effects. The warnings jump out at us, from unexpected places; we are struck by their salience, which it is physically impossible to ignore. This regime currently governs the way in which the mass media attune us to the world: 'The posture of permanent alertness we are made to adopt, where stock market prices provide the best example, makes

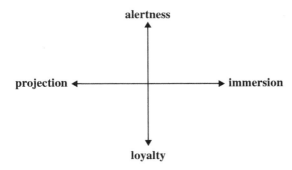

6. Attention regimes according to Dominque Boullier

any attentive development impossible over the long-term, because it is 'alert attention' that dominates, provoking and awakening without let up, without us ultimately being able to get a handle on it.'[14] This domination tends, however, to rapidly exhaust the wellspring of its functioning – too much alertness kills alertness: 'This alertness regime is today faced with a generalized channel-hopping and an "underlying reduction of the level of attention following an event", which undermines its foundations.'[15]

The second regime, which is at the opposing pole, involves creating LOYALTY. Instead of relying on the incessant interruption of unpredictable excitations maintaining a permanent state of tension and insecurity, loyalty creation aims to establish a relationship of trust, based on mutual listening over the long-term, so as to guarantee as far as possible the predictability of relations without surprise. We pay attention in advance to those that we trust, so that we no longer have to pay attention on each occasion to everything that we subsequently receive from them. 'The politics of creating loyalty consists in placing the receivers in an attentional condition which prevents them from differentiating between contents, which keeps them 'in-different' (don't channel hop, stay with this programme), so as to achieve a state of hypnosis.'[16]

The third regime is based on PROJECTION: wherever we go, we carry with us a certain sensibility, we filter stimuli through criteria which we tend to 'project' onto all our environments, both old and new. The projective regime allows me to feel at home everywhere, since I deny, in a sense, the diversity of places as I endeavour to find comparable features, wherever I may be. 'It is a question of establishing the highest level of immunity against external stimuli and of projecting your own frameworks and models onto the new world

41

without allowing yourself to be affected by it', along the lines of the 'projection of power' model practised today by Western countries, whose armies are organized so that they can 'leave their bases and go beyond their borders to act in foreign operational theatres'.[17]

Finally, the fourth and last attention regime suggested by Dominique Boullier is situated as the symmetrical reversal of this projection of power: in the IMMERSION framework, instead of recognizing the same familiar objects in each of the new environments I pass through, I find myself plunged into radically strange and exotic worlds, where I have to invent new evaluation and tracking criteria. Along with dark cinema theatres and the virtual worlds of video games, the immersion experience is like the first arrival in an unknown town or a country where you don't speak the language, where you don't know the customs and where you have to learn to manage on your own. Where the alertness regime brings threats into the heart of our own supposedly familiar space, immersion calls for a generally desirable attentive vigilance – whether because it takes place in the virtual space of a fictional universe or because it results from a choice for touristic disorientation.

These four attention regimes, whose more or less impure forms help to characterize the different milieux in which we develop, each constitute a different kind of enthralment, in the sense given to this term at the beginning of this chapter. Immersion fascinates us because of the exoticism of the novelties we are led to discover, while the efforts we exert to familiarize ourselves with this new environment risk producing addictive effects. Projection bedazzles us, as it leads us to daydream that every new milieu can be reduced to the frameworks of our familiar criteria. Loyalty creation hypnotizes us, deluding us with the hope of a perfectly reliable unifying relation. Finally, alertness puts us outside of ourselves as it feeds a state of permanent excitation which exhausts our lucidity by intensifying its mobilization.

We will understand nothing of the functioning of our individual attention if we do not re-situate it in the various attention regimes which structure our vital and communicational milieu. It is no good lamenting 'public stupidity', the 'spinelessness of journalists' or the 'occult power of lobbyists' – however real these may be – if we do not recognize the importance of those (invisible because environmental) factors that are attention regimes. From the moment our political life is condemned to pass through the mass media, our collective attention is inevitably structured by agenda-setting mechanisms governing the selection of themes serving as the attractors around which our daily conversations and social debates orbit.[18]

The attractions and distractions that presently occupy our media-sphere issue directly from the domination exercised by the alertness regime on our mass-media apparatuses, with a direct connection to the way in which they are financed. With its daily dose of scandals, catastrophes and 'crisis' discourses, the alertness mode is indeed the one through which our attention is most quickly and easily captured in the short-term horizon of audiences and advertisers. Behind the media enthralments and the attention regimes which bring them into being, we must, therefore, look for the environmental reasons for our collective attention and distraction in the very particular form of capitalism that governs the infrastructure of our communication networks. Better understanding of our attention ecology requires that we sketch out the anatomy of contemporary capitalism.

— 2 —

ATTENTIONAL CAPITALISM

While it is not sufficient to study the phenomena of collective attention solely through the prism of economic categories, it is nevertheless absolutely necessary to determine the extent to which the modes of production and subjectivation established by contemporary capitalism profoundly condition its functioning, along with the objects of our attention. Instead of taking inspiration from the 'new economy', as is the tendency for those who, following Michael Goldhaber, assume that it is not possible to get beyond the current neoliberal model, it would therefore be better to draw on more critical analyses discussing 'semiocapitalism' (Franco Berardi), 'hypercapitalism' (Jean-Paul Galibert), 'cognitive' capitalism (Yann Moulier Boutang), 'rent' capitalism (Carlo Vercellone), 'netarchy' (Michel Bauwens), 'artketing' (Martial Poirson), the 'parasitic' (Matteo Pasquinelli), or the 'mental' (Georg Franck) – each of these terms helping to clarify one of the multiple aspects of the same particularly complex object.

Putting questions of attention at the heart of the analysis of capitalism reintroduces a notion of conflict which had been overly attenuated by the 'digital' ideal of a digital realm living on thin air, de-monetised peer-to-peer exchanges and free access, on zero marginal costs and non-competing goods. As we have already seen, the attention ecology qualifies and reframes the dreams of 'immaterial' emancipation. Of course, with the reduction to zero of the marginal costs for the *transmission* of digital goods we are in the midst of the emergence of something absolutely novel with profoundly revolutionary implications. But, on the one hand, the costs of *production* of the material goods necessary for the existence and circulation among us of cultural goods are far from evaporating, remaining ecologically unsustainable at their current levels. While, on the other hand, and above all, when attention phenomena are taken into account, we find competition returning at the time of *reception* of cultural goods. This was certainly Herbert Simon's central message in 1969:

> In an information-rich world, most of the cost of information is the cost incurred by the recipient. [. . .] Human beings, like contemporary computers, are essentially serial devices. They can attend to only one thing at a time. This is just another way of saying that attention is scarce.[1]

The time has come to analyse in more detail the models outlined by the first attention economists to account for this competition that has been unduly occulted in digital imaginings. In order to try to synthesize as far as possible the main lessons to be drawn from these models, I will give them an axiomatic form which will tend, no doubt, to 'harden' the subtleties of the analyses put forward, but which will give us a better sense of the coherence of the proposed schemas – especially Georg Franck, whose pioneering works are only just beginning to be translated into French and whose two essential books remain unjustly unknown outside German culture.

Attention as the Hegemonic Form of Capital

AXIOM OF ATTENTIONAL CAPITALISM: *attention is in the process of becoming the hegemonic form of capitalism.* In the 1996 articles that brought the attention economy into the public domain, Michael Goldhaber suggested a concise equation: 'attention wealth = size x attentiveness of your past and present audiences'.[2] This attention wealth prevails as soon as it is recognized that 'money now flows along with attention':[3] people become rich *because* they have become famous (more often than they become famous because they are rich). Citing Thomas Mandel and Gerard Van der Leun who wrote in *Rules of the Net*[4] that 'attention is the hard currency of cyberspace', he predicted that, 'As the Net becomes an increasingly strong presence in the overall economy, the flow of attention will not only anticipate the flow of money, but eventually replace it altogether.'[5]

So here it is a question of 'wealth', 'money' or 'currency' (and not 'capital' strictly speaking) finding themselves superseded by attention, the new scarcity destined to become the benchmark of all value. This first equivalence, which is still very vague, is already sufficient for us to indicate the general area into which the question of value has been displaced. Indeed, everything rests on an ONTOLOGY OF VISIBILITY which *measures a being's level of existence by the quantity and quality of its perception by others*. An excellent recent book by Barbara Carnevali reconstitutes the whole tradition of thought (often haunted by guilt) which recognized the sociological applicability of the scandalous principle championed on an onto-logical and epistemological level by Berkeley – *esse est percipi*: we are only what we are perceived to be. Or, even more radically: we only exist (for ourselves) to the extent that we are perceived by others (and the more others there are to perceive us, the more we exist).

In contrast to the demands for authenticity coming from Rousseau, Romanticism or Sartrian existentialism, a number of philosophers and sociologists have sought to draw the consequences of this reversal that makes appearances into the first reality of our social interac-tions. It is in the context of this reflection that the ontology of vis-ibility, on which the analyses of the attention economy are based, should be situated. Barbara Carnevali has styled her work on social appearances as a 'philosophy of prestige' – a term whose etymology (*praestringere*), evoking a magical and seductive power for captur-ing attention, she emphasizes.[6] Georg Franck suggests a series of subtly nuanced terms to account for the different degrees of visibility characterizing notoriety, celebrity, prestige and, at the very top of his hierarchy, *prominence*: 'the undisputed common denominator of present-day élites is prominence – and prominence is nothing but the status of being a major earner of attention'[7]; ' the prominents are the capitalists of the attention economy; it is the class of people who are known by everyone'.[8]

This central role assigned to appearances in social dynamics trans-lates into four economic implications that form the backbone of attention capitalism. Firstly, a VITAL NEED FOR NOTORIETY means that *'we ceaselessly work to make ourselves attractive'*.[9] This is something entirely different from the banal dream everyone har-bours of becoming a rock star, an idolized footballer or a successful author. The generations of youth entering the job market are brought to understand that increased visibility (getting themselves known in certain networks, adding a line to their *curriculum vitae*) is their most precious income – which means that they can be underpaid in monetary terms for work dressed up as an internship. We find here a very concrete illustration of the principle stating that 'money now flows along with attention': in a whole range of professions, jobs (and therefore salaries) flow along paths of visibility, sometimes to the extent that it replaces monetary exchange.

It then becomes perfectly justifiable to make discretion into a fundamental principle of resistance to the development of attention capitalism. Beyond the sobering observation that, 'despite all the efforts of those who profit from this system, the people who are addicted to the image and to getting themselves noticed at any cost are largely in a minority', Pierre Zaoui remarks in a recent book that 'learning to leave the order of self-exhibition and generalized surveillance is already to engage in a certain form of dissidence. More generally, any serious or modest resistance will always have started with the acceptance of a certain concealment, which is to say, with the art of keeping a low profile and not getting yourself noticed, the art of discretion.'[10]

The desire for notoriety, however, has less to do with morality or ethics than with survival in a very particular economic system. The evolution of attention capitalism puts more and more pressure on economic agents as it pushes them to 'stand out' if they want to escape from the most alienating forms of communal exploitation. Few among us have the opportunity or the desire to make a radical choice for discretion – and this is no doubt why Pierre Zaoui describes 'the art of disappearing' as aspiring less to a maintainable ideal than an intermittent rhythm (allowing for the temporary retreat from the regime of visibility).

This (very effective) reign of appearances leads to a second, more surprising and more interesting, economic consequence, that brings to light a PRINCIPLE OF VALORIZATION THROUGH ATTENTION: *the simple fact of looking at an object represents a labour which increases the value of that object.* As was carefully analysed by Jonathan Beller in order to understand the productive nature of human attention, 'the value of our regard contributes to an increase in the value of the image':

> As we read [objects] (Coke bottles, sneakers, automobiles, whatever), we produce their signification. The image is perceived not only in and of itself, but as a consequence of the perception of others. The density of this perception of others is part of the quality of the image – its *caché*. [. . .] The perception that images pass through the perception of others increases their currency and hence their value. Vision adds value to visual objects, value that is often capitalized. [. . .] To "see" is already to "buy" (I'll buy that), to look is to labor.[11]

Let us return briefly to the Saturnian perspective of the last chapter: all those Earthlings who seem 'to be doing nothing' as they sit in front of their books, their computer screens or televisions, are in fact extraordinarily productive. Not only when they generate texts (information, plans, programmes, orders, laws) as they type on their keyboards, or when they accumulate information that will increase their future productivity, but also when they are doing absolutely nothing except ('passively') watching a mindless television series or a commercial. This validation through attention does not only relate to what is left behind in me by the perceptions I find myself exposed to: the philosophers of the Frankfurt School, Guy Debord, Vilém Flusser and Jonathan Beller have already characterized the mass media as factories charged with the industrial production of consumer subjectivities amenable to capitalist exploitation. In this, they are only taking up the intuition developed by Gabriel Tarde in *Economic Psychology*: 'the reproduction of wealth presupposes, before anything else, the psychological reproduction of consumer desires and the particular beliefs attached to these desires, without which a materially reproduced article would not be a source of wealth'.[12]

However, it is a question of something else again here. Independently of the way in which a painting, a television programme or a video game may affect my senses, my memory and my behaviour, I am 'working' when I look at it (*to look is to labour*) to the extent that my regard contributes to the value it draws from its visibility. Knowing that lots of people have seen a film makes me want to go and see it: when I bestow my attention, I work *de facto* to promote it to others (even if I can't stand the film).

We know that the value of a network or a technical protocol comes from the quantity of participants that it is able to attract. When I use Microsoft software, even if I access it for free, I am helping to support its dissemination, its market share, or, as it happens, its dominance. Producing and being able to read Word or Excel documents on my computer, I function as an agent of dissemination and effectively a promoter. I work *for* Microsoft whenever I work *with* Microsoft – with the additional ironic paradox that I have to pay a considerable amount for permission to work for them for free! This is the same phenomenon as described by Jonathan Beller when he notes that the value of an image increases in the view of others simply because I am looking at it. My attention actively participates in its *currency*, which is to say, its 'value', inasmuch as this depends on the reach of its 'circulation'.

We touch concretely here on the mechanism by which the attention economy is rooted in a CIRCULAR SELF-REINFORCING DYNAMIC: *attention attracts attention*. Attention accumulated in the past and the present supports the future accumulation of attention. It is because millions of tourists have come to see the Mona Lisa that millions of tourists rush to see the Mona Lisa. 'Nothing seems to attract attention like the accumulation of attention earnings,

48

nothing stimulates the media more than this capital, nothing increases the attractiveness of their advertising spaces more than the exhibition of the wealth of acquired attention.'[13] It is the past accumulation of collective attention concentrated on the prominent figure of George Clooney that enables him to concentrate our collective attention on Nespresso coffee machines. This is what Jean-Michel Espitallier expresses scathingly in his extraordinary little book *On Celebrity* [*De la célébrité*]: It is because I am renowned [*reconnu*] that I am known [*connu*]. It is because I am known [*connu*] that I am renowned [*reconnu*].'[14]

'The high technology of attraction works with this kind of self-reinforcing publicity. It works with known faces everybody wants to see because everybody knows that all the others also see them.'[15] We should think of prominent figures (film stars, sports stars, heads of state, television presenters) as 'the capitalists of the attention economy' since their celebrity is able to feed off its own movement: 'Prominence is that level of attentive wealth [*Beachtung*] where the affluence becomes conspicuous and itself turns into a source of attention income [*Aufmerksamkeit*]'[16]

The fourth element to identify at the heart of attentional capitalism further accentuates its appearance as a strange and troubling animal, seemingly striving to defy the laws of nature. Not only does it

celebrities who make television which makes celebrities who make television which
celebrities who make television which makes celebrities who make television which
celebrities who make television which makes celebrities who make television which
celebrities who make television which makes celebrities who make television which
celebrities who make television which makes celebrities who make television which
celebrities who make television which makes celebrities who make television which
celebrities who make television which makes celebrities who make television which
celebrities who make television which makes celebrities who make television which
celebrities who make television which makes celebrities who make television which
celebrities who make television which makes celebrities who make television which
celebrities who make television which makes celebrities who make television which
celebrities who make television which makes celebrities who make television which
celebrities who make television which makes celebrities who make television which
celebrities who make television which makes celebrities who make television which
celebrities who make television which makes celebrities who make television which
celebrities who make television which makes celebrities who make television which

7. Jean-Michel Espitallier, *De la célébrité*

transmute a simple look into work, after having transmuted visibility into salary; not only does it seem to feed off its own flesh, extracting from every accumulation the dynamic of a superior accumulation; but its limitless opportunism extends to treasuring those who attack it or despoil it – such is its ability to profit from their assaults and aggressions . . .

Our traditional understanding of social relations generally makes us feel the criticisms addressed to us as threats to our narcissism and as acts of hostility against our public self. In the same way, our attachment to private property, combined with our pride as an author worried about protecting his rights, makes us think of thieves and plagiarists as outlaws. The attention economy encourages us, however, to reverse these kinds of judgement: 'Anyone who copies you is turning their audience over to you, and thereby doing you a favour. Even anyone who tries to malign you or distort what you are saying calls attention to you in the process.'[17]

We can identify here a PROFIT FROM OPPORTUNIST VISIBILITY: from the moment we start living off visibility, *everything that lifts us out of obscurity is worth having*, even if the original intention is to do us harm. In other words, as the saying traditionally associated with Mae West goes, 'there is no such thing as bad publicity'. The most likely – and most humiliating – fate of any one of the six hundred novels published at the beginning of the literary year is to go unnoticed. A prominent critic may decide to take it to pieces, a paranoid celebrity may sue for libel, or a prudish censor may take pride in exposing it: its fate is immediately sealed. It will be the subject of debate and this will make it exist – *esse est percipi* – for those who attack and for those who defend it, and above all for those who are curious as to why people are fighting about it. From which comes a COROLLARY OF CRITICAL RENUNCIATION: *if you would like it to go away, don't talk about it.*

Based on the four principles evoked above – notoriety as a vital need and as a means of payment, valorization through attention, circular self-reinforcement of attention accumulation and the increase in visibility generated by negative criticism – we have the first elements with which to analyse attention capitalism. Despite starting with a fairly vague analogy between wealth, money, currency and attention, we see here the gradual emergence of a category that may be better characterized as a true form of capital. This assimilation of attention and capital seems, however, to come up against a problem which must now be explicitly confronted and resolved.

The Media as Attention Banks

Attention is a form of presence to oneself and to one's environment which is intrinsically linked to the flow of time. I can only be attentive to the present: you cannot ask me to be attentive (now) to what happened two days ago, or to what will happen in an hour. How, in these conditions, is it possible to speak of an 'accumulation' of attention – an unavoidable condition if we would like to consider attention in terms of *capital*, but which requires the persistence of the past in the present, contradicting the very nature of attention? Michael Goldhaber identified the problem in his first articles: 'Unlike the old matter-based wealth, the new wealth is nothing you can hope to put under lock and key.'[18]

Goldhaber himself outlined a first way of getting round the problem. Taking as an example the lecture he is giving at that moment to his listeners, he notes that their present attention retains within itself the contents of a past attention: it is because they have read certain articles of his, or have already heard about him, or because a friend has spoken to them about him, that they came out to listen to him. '[G]etting attention is not a momentary thing; you build on the stock you have every time you get any, and the larger your audience at one time, the larger your potential audience in the future.'[19] So, attention to past events accumulates in the memory of the individuals concerned, who constitute audiences depending on their attractions and their mutual affinities – following the model of the street musician who starts by charming passers-by, then the clientele of a local club, and who, following appearances in bigger and better venues, is able to build an international reputation.

In contrast to this bucolic vision of a traditional attention economy, Georg Franck seeks to understand more realistically, and more precisely, phenomena relating to the *industrial* production of audiences brought about by contemporary capitalism. So that he can seriously equate attention with a form of capitalism, he develops a systematic analogy between the role played by the mass media in the attention economy and that played by banks in the capitalist system. From the moment it comes into being at the industrial scale made possible by the technologies of mass communication established over the course of the twentieth century, the attention economy bases itself on a FINANCIAL INVESTMENT LOGIC: '*The currency system of attention relies on specialized financial services. This banking and stock-exchange function is performed by the mass media.*'[20]

When a large television channel can count on several million viewers each night, it commands an attraction capital that is inherent in this status. In the same way that a bank tries to balance its investments between safe bets and riskier start-ups, a television channel shows prominences, who are sure to bring in large attention revenues, alongside some less well-known figures to whom it loans its guaranteed pulling power. 'The reinvestment of the attraction return creates mental currency, in the same way that a credit bank creates money.'[21] While individuals benefit (at the time) from the huge visibility provided by a channel with a big audience – which is the wellspring of reality television shows – the media bank works to expand the quantity of attention currency, seeing to it that one of these individuals acquires sufficient celebrity to repay the original investment with profit:

> The media, within the attention economy, are what the financial sector is in money capitalism. The media are capitalizing attention: they receive attention with such regularity and certainty that they are able to offer it on credit as starting capital; they make use of fortunes by reinvesting attention wealth into attraction; they list the market value of fortunes by measuring their power of attraction. Just as banks are providing growing economies with an expanding money supply, the media are supplying expanding information markets with growing amounts of attention. Lastly, in the same way that financial markets have transposed the internal capitalization strategy of companies to the macroeconomic level, the media are transposing the capitalization of attention from the level of personal dexterity to that of an organized public sphere.[22]

We understand in this way how, thanks to a financial dynamic in which the media and celebrities accumulate significant attention capital in parallel, advances in attractiveness yield attention revenues: the (developing) star adds value to the Evening News who have invited them on, at the same time as the Evening News add value to the celebrity to whom they provide media presence. We are here at the heart of the mechanism so elegantly represented by Jean-Michel Espitallier when he evoked the 'celebrities who make television which makes celebrities who make television which . . .'

The analysis of mental capitalism developed by Georg Franck helps us, however, to notice a presupposition that is frequently obscured in the processes by which the attention economy is perfectly aligned with the logic of capitalist finance. The whole analogy between attention and capital, between visibility and profitability, between the media and banks is in fact based on a discrete and apparently insignificant operation which is nonetheless essential to the entire edifice. None of this would stay standing without a series of HOMOGENISING MEASURING OPERATIONS: *'attention only becomes a currency when it is measured in homogenous units and made to circulate via anonymous exchange acts.'*[23]

Just as attention cannot be spontaneously accumulated as such, requiring individual memories as well as media banks in order to behave as capital, it is in no way self-evident that it can be equated to a means of payment. A bank note provides a purely quantitative general equivalent which can be exchanged indifferently for a book, a few litres of benzene, a box of macaroons, a train ticket or a haircut. But you never have a 'general', purely quantitative, amount of attention available, which is indifferent to its object and which can be exchanged for an infinite range of heterogeneous experiences. You are always dealing with a particular person, endowed with a sensibility that is unique to them, paying attention to something precise, in determinate spatial and temporal circumstances.

Attention, which is always particular, only becomes a currency (*Währung*) – which may be exchanged on a market, accumulated as capital and invested according to the logics of finance – thanks to a translation operation which homogenizes and standardizes it so that it can enter into a system of equivalence. This operation is carried out by the various measuring devices involved in any kind of *rating*: print runs for hard-copy periodicals, ticket sales at the cinema, monitoring of radio and television audiences, visit counts on the internet. These measuring devices for standardized collective attention – which they transform into an *audience* – play an absolutely crucial role in contemporary society, since they are what, in concrete terms, enable us to treat attention as a form of capital, which can then enter fluidly into competitive, speculative, and exploitative games organized under the mastery of financial capitalism.[24]

Even if, impeding these translation operations, we managed in one go to block the submission of cultural life to the logic of the market, it would – unfortunately – be neither desirable nor possible purely and simply to prohibit these kinds of measurements, many of which are born of simple management necessity (counting the number of tickets sold at the entrance to a concert so as to pay for room rental). One can, on the other hand, support an IMPERATIVE OF POLITICAL RESISTANCE declaiming *the responsibility of everyone who works for the multiplication, the diffusion and above all the promotion of rating measures as criteria of evaluation for cultural goods*. Since the attention economy is governed by a dynamic of circular self-reinforcement, ratings apparatuses are much less *measuring* devices, that help to acquaint us with a reality on which we would like to act, than *capturing* devices that are completely enslaved to the financial logic by which they are instrumentalized. They are an integral part of the capitalist machinery which uses everything indifferently – petrol, images, animal bone meal, the affects – to maximize profit at the expense of those who work to produce the forms of our lives.

In the same way that, according to Georg Franck's wonderful phrase, 'The involuntary consumption of publicity amounts to a tax being levied on perception',[25] the propagation and invocation of audience measurements is equivalent to free advertising which reinforces the domination of those holding the largest quantities of attention capital, and so contributing to the oppression of the minority voices that ensure the vitality of a culture. The best way of nullifying these apparatuses would certainly be to not grant them any value (beyond pure practical management). But, since calls for responsibility rarely contribute to the reversal of an oppressive domination, it is doubtless desirable to supplement this imperative of political resistance with an INVITATION TO PREVENTATIVE SABOTAGE: *hackers of all countries, unite to paralyse the ratings machinery wherever you can!*

Tax Advertising in the Name of Unskewed Competition

An article by Josef Falkinger, which is not cited often enough, suggests, however, that even in the absence of any voluntary sabotage, attention capitalism is heading towards a mid-flight implosion simply because of its own internal logic – as this logic is presented in the models skilfully constructed by orthodox economists. After having put forward a NEOCLASSICAL DEFINITION OF THE ATTENTION ECONOMY as *'a family of senders, which employ costly signals to attract the attention of audiences and have an impact on them'*,[26] Josef Falkinger sets himself the task of formally modelling the costs and returns involved in sending these signals, which leads him to make an essential distinction between two very different kinds of economy.

'Economies that are information-poor' presuppose that economic agents (assumed to be rational) will be induced spontaneously to modulate their choices according to the signals that are available to them, so leading the totality of transactions towards an optimization coming out of their mutual gropings. This is the Hayekian model which governs the entire orthodox neoclassical economy. The situation is very different once it is attention, rather than information, that is fundamentally scarce. 'Economies that are information-rich' are characterized by the presence of THRESHOLDS, FILTERS, and PORTALS which effect a *preselection of the information taken on by economic agents, a preselection that is conditioned by the unequal broadcast power of costly signals designed to attract attention.*

A signal will not be noticed by a receiver unless it gets beyond a certain minimum threshold. This threshold may relate to a perceptive filter that is absolute (no human ear would be able to hear the sound of a falling grain of dust) or relative (a whisper that would be perceptible in a silent environment becomes inaudible in the noise of a crowd). It may also relate to access restrictions imposed by media intermediation (media gates): a notice published in a local fanzine constitutes a weaker signal than an advertisement showing on TF1 at primetime. The richer the economy is in information, the higher the thresholds relating to perceptibility rise, the more information is supressed by the filters, the bigger the determining role played by media portals and the more relatively expensive it is to send signals.

This raising of thresholds leads our economies to divert an increasing proportion of their activity away from the *production* of goods themselves and towards the *promotion* of merchandise (brands), which is to say, towards the work of capturing attention (in other words, to the artificial production of *demand*). Even if the absolute cost of disseminating information has continually gone down since the development of the printing press in the sixteenth century, of periodicals in the eighteenth century, audio-visual media in the twentieth and the internet in the twenty-first (it is relatively less expensive to post a blog in 2014 than to print a book in 1550 or launch a periodical in 1780), the threshold of commercial viability has required, since the industrial revolution in the nineteenth century, the investment of more and more resources in the promotion of the merchandise in question. In the marketplace, it was enough for the fishmonger to shout louder than his neighbour, or make his stand more brightly coloured, in order for his products to get beyond the perceptive threshold of potential buyers. Launching a new product today – whatever its intrinsic quality – means mobilizing considerable resources so that it can pass through the necessary media portals for consumers to become aware of its existence.

So an ATTENTION ARMS RACE is set up: *the more a market society becomes mediatized, the more it must dedicate a significant proportion of its activity to the production of demand, investing ever greater resources into the machinery of attention attraction.* Like military arms races, this attention arms race is in itself a tragic waste, thanks to a sub-optimal organization of inter-human relations. And in the same way that a peace treaty allows for a reduction in military expenditure, we may imagine economic mechanisms that would be capable of reducing the waste and pollution brought about by the dramatic growth in publicity activities. This is what Josef Falkinger outlines in the second half of his article.

He starts by noting that, despite their triviality and their obviousness, the attentional mechanisms that have just been recalled have considerable implications for the credibility of neoclassical economic modelling:

> In an information-poor economy every agent who has an economically viable idea or product can participate in the competition for buyers, since there are free entries on the buyers' mind. In contrast, in the information-rich economy entries on receiver minds are exhausted. Since there are so many and powerful potential information sources, attention necessarily focuses on a subset of potential sources. Since content can only be evaluated after an item has passed the perceptual filter, the selection of this subset cannot be based on content. [. . .] The presented analysis of limited attention as a scarce resource points out that economic competition is contingent on a perception filter and that the set of perceived items is a subset of the economically possible items. In an information-rich economy, there is no guarantee that the perceived items are the best possible items.[27]

The central postulate of the rationality of economic agents and the optimality of the equilibriums produced in a state of free competition is here threatened by the most banal observation of the attention economy in the context of a heavily mediatized regime. Consumers can only consider buying products whose existence they are aware of; but their awareness of this existence is based less on the inherent merit of the products than on the advertising budgets promoting them; so the economy as a whole does not find its equilibrium around the most useful or agreeable products, but around the products that are most aggressively promoted. Of course, these distortions relate more to cultural goods (films, books, music) than to everyday consumer products – but it is not unreasonable to think that they also effect, in advance, the selection of hydroponically grown tomatoes from Carrefour rather than the local products distributed by the associations supporting small-scale farming.[28]

Whatever the case may be, the (generally concealed) evidence of these distortions leads the orthodox economist – as soon as he takes the time to look into the attention economy with any seriousness – to call for measures whose consequences would be properly revolutionary:

> In an information-poor economy with no scarcity of attention, effi-ciency is achieved under laissez-faire. Intervention is required in the information-rich economy. [. . .] Whereas in the information-poor economy decentralized competition for attention and money leads to an efficient equilibrium, in an information-rich economy the decentral-ized equilibrium is inefficient. The reason is that there is wasteful com-petition for scarce attention. An efficient solution can be implemented by imposing a linear tax on attention-seeking activities and distributing the raised revenue to the buyers.[29]

If orthodox economic science, neoliberals and capitalism's apolo-gists really wanted to promote 'free and unskewed competition', they would start by putting an end to (or drastically taxing) advertising activities, where the unequal powers with respect to the propagation of costly signals constitutes a 'market distortion' that is much more sinister than any of the interventions for which the state is berated. The re-establishment of the market efficiency dreamed of by ortho-dox economists could then come about through the introduction of a TAX ON ADVERTISING EXPENDITURE *at a level (f) defined with respect to the strength of the advertising signal emitted, with profit-margin (θ), broadcast range (r), buyers' budget (y), cost of the signal (k) and a measure of the information wealth of the economy concerned (τ)* (Figure 8).

$$f = \frac{\theta\, r\, y\, /\, \kappa - \tau_0}{(1 - \theta)\, \tau_0}$$

8. Formula for a tax on the activities of attention attraction, according to Josef Falkinger

Parasitism, Asymmetries, Exploitations

There is of course very little chance that capitalism will implode mid-flight because of its formalist commitment to the claims to efficiency it espouses. Its nature has less to do with the optimal organization of the common good than with opportunist parasitism. In his book *Animal Spirit: A Bestiary of the Commons*, Matteo Pasquinelli condemns the 'digital ideology' that for a long time has represented the net as a horizontal network, made up of symmetrical and fundamentally democratic relationships, within which hubs/agents produce and exchange non-rival goods, freely and at no cost, on an egalitarian foundation whose general model is represented by *peer-to-peer*. Taking inspiration from the theory of the parasite formulated by Michel Serres in 1980, he emphasizes that it is only possible to understand the digital mutation of capitalism if we identify a *ternary* structure (not binary as in *peer-to-peer*), which is fundamentally *asymmetrical*, and where an *immaterial parasite* extracts an energy surplus (which may take the form of work, profit or libidinal investments) to allocate it to a *third party*, who in this way becomes the beneficiary of a monopoly *income*. He illustrates his analysis with the recent evolution of the music industry: 'P2P networks may have weakened the music industry, but the surplus has been re-allocated in favour of companies producing new forms of hardware [mp3 players, iPods] or controlling access to the internet [Verizon, Orange, Bouygues].'[30]

The models put forward to describe the attention economy present the same divisions as those observed by Matteo Pasquinelli in the sphere of digital cultures. In their manual for managers and marketers, John Beck and Thomas Davenport lure us with the promise of an inevitable ATTENTIONAL SYMMETRY: 'if you want *to get any attention, you've got to give attention*'.[31] The hypothesis is not baseless: in the framework of a face-to-face exchange, for example, during a dialogue between friends, a teaching situation or a live show, it is generally true that the attentions of those present are mutually reinforcing and feed off one another.

Even a digital apologist like Michael Goldhaber recognizes, however, that this kind of symmetry is frequently illusory. During a lecture, the speaker may well try to be attentive to those who have come to listen to him but, from him to them, there is only *'illusory* attention [. . .] that helps create an apparent equality of attention', when in fact an asymmetrical structure of interaction clearly prevails.[32] In the new economy, much more so than in the old, '[n]ot everyone can attract the same amount of attention. Some of us are stars, but most just fans.'[33]

These inequalities oppose the rich and the poor who are no longer (only) defined in terms of monetary revenue, but in terms of attention, differentiated according to the three nuances suggested by the German language – *Zuwendung*: in which direction are we looking? *Aufmerksamkeit*: whose presence and existence do we notice? *Beachtung*: whose needs and whose voice are we taking into consideration?

The kind of exploitation characteristic of mental capitalism works against those, of whom there is a huge number, who always give their attention and consideration, but who hardly receive any in return [*die der vielen, die immer achten, aber kaum beachtet werden*].[34]

Indeed, the problem should not be posed so much in terms of equality or un-respected reciprocity as in terms of disproportion and what Bernard Stiegler has called 'symbolic misery': 'Wealthy people in the new economy are those whose attention earnings are larger by orders of magnitude than their spending. The poor are those who do not get enough attention to keep their self-esteem intact. This wealth of some and the poverty of all the others are interrelated: the amount of recognition available for distribution is not unlimited. The attention circulating in society is finite.'[35]

As is symbolically illustrated by the periodic burning of the French suburbs, the NEW CLASS STRUGGLES *oppose 'those who appear in the media and those who do not'*. It is necessary for some cars to be burned (in greater numbers than usual) so that problems of discrimination and social misery can make their way – in an alarmist culture – onto the small screen. While the attention capitalists are eagerly invited to vent their narcissism in the intimate setting of an exclusive interview, the proletarians must put up their hoods and dress as hooligans to scrounge a few seconds of (immediately vilified) anonymous visibility.

It is at the level of the global distribution of our collective attention that current social conflicts must be considered. Despite its flattening effect, the telescope on Saturn reveals with perfect clarity the asymmetries of attention that characterize the new forms of exploitation: the aggregated quantity of the hours of televised programmes entering 'disadvantaged areas' is completely disproportionate with what comes out (so long as they are not shimmering in the fire of a conflagration). As well as providing an illustration of the new proletariat who 'always give their attention and consideration, but who hardly receive any in return' (a category that includes the youth of immigrant populations as well as the National Front's voters), this example clearly shows the harmful effects of the alarmist culture that conditions our current mass-media echosystem. Playing on the nuances of the German language, we might say that the media attention directed towards the suburbs (*Zuwendung*), besides its quantitative poverty, is qualitatively rooted only in *Aufmerksamkeit*: it is enough here to 'note' (*bermerken*) the signs of an imminent overflowing of the 'problems of the suburbs' into the well-off districts. Even in the extremely rare return-images, the proletarians receive just a very small amount of the *Beachtung* that a respectful (*achten*) consideration of the lived experiences of the inhabitants would grant them, with their fate of exclusion (from the labour market), (cultural) oppression and (sartorial) criminalization.

This same asymmetry can be found at the global level of GEOPOLITICAL ATTENTION EXPLOITATION: '*the most advanced – Western – cultures export information massively and import huge amounts of live attention for it, while the cultures of other regions export very modest amounts of information and accordingly earn little attention for it*'.[36] Also at this scale, the attention proletarians living in rich countries see those who they might consider to be similar to them appearing on their screens only as worrying 'terrorist' figures, whose existence they only notice as a threat, a warning and a danger, without feeling obliged to give the least consideration to their subjective experience.

Such asymmetries come much less from the bad will of agents than – as Marx noticed – from the very nature of the relations of information and attention production. Georg Franck pertinently insists on the fact that the source of these disproportions and distributive injustices is to be found in the effects brought about by the development of mass telecommunication technologies during the twentieth century. Alongside their use as weapons of mass distraction, the mass media are dangerous because of the ease with which a standardized, 'industrialized' message – produced, multiplied and automatically distributed at low cost – initiates a labour of reception in those to whom it is addressed that is still 'artisan' and costly in time and effort since it has to be performed by our old biological apparatus (eyes, ears, brain). As well as advertising, that 'tax levied on perception', there is a diffusion of automated cultural products, which is essentially a kind of spam:

> The relationship between the attention invested by the suppliers and that collected in return is strictly asymmetrical. The suppliers disseminate information in the form of technical reproductions, while the consumers pay with live attention for each copy. Only through this asymmetry is it possible to collect such masses of donated attention, which is what makes a medium attractive for those appearing in it and which allows the media their lavishness in conferring the modern peerage of prominence.[37]

A hacker only needs a few minutes to send a spam email to a mailing list that he has been able to parasite; in a flash the machine automatically does all the work of reproducing and sending it. Even if each of us only takes a few seconds to identify a message as spam or phishing, the time taken to receive these mailshots amounts collectively to millions of hours. It is this same disproportion that makes a technology like television into a constitutively exploitative machine from the perspective of attention economy.

So, at the heart of attention capitalism, it is necessary to identify a phenomenon of OVER-ECONOMY OF SCALE: *the effects of multiplication made possible by the technologies of mass communication exploit the living attention of the receiver by subjecting it to the dead attention of machines*. In a face-to-face dialogue, the attention time of the participants unfolds according to a common temporality in the present (at a 1 minute: 1 minute scale). In a talk given in a full lecture theatre, the preparation time invested beforehand by the presenter – a time that may be considered as the form of the attention that he gives to his listeners in advance – compensates to a degree for the structural asymmetry of the lecture situation (10 hours of preparation x 1 speaker equals 30 minutes of lecture x 30 listeners). Even if preparing TF1's or France 2's 'Journal de 20 heures' (the Evening News) mobilizes the attention of one hundred people for two days, and even if most of the six million viewers only watch it distractedly, the orders of magnitude lose all proportion as you move from one side of the camera to the other (1,600 production hours $\neq$ 3,000,000 reception hours). Even with a stage setting centred on the illusory attention of a journalist looking France directly in the eyes, we are clearly in the realm of spam.

When they collect gigantic quantities of live attention thanks to the multiplication of a small quantity of attention by technological automation devices, the cultural industries are the beneficiaries of an enormous surplus value, in the form of an ATTENTION APPRECIATION, resulting from *the difference between attention given and attention received*. Of course, there is nothing to be offended by here. The ability to broadcast information on a vast scale is in itself a very good thing. It is simply the case that, as was very well analysed by Vilém Flusser starting in the 1970s, this broadcasting produces programming effects that profoundly and dramatically alter our social relations.[38] What is gained with the ability to industrially broadcast programmes to millions of people, is lost in the brutal imposition of a unilateral and homogenising programming which necessarily mechanizes those who it treats in an automated way.

In other words: the quantitative appreciation, which assures the economic and political power of the mass media thanks to an over-economy of scale mechanism, risks the heavy price of a qualitative depreciation, which impoverishes and brutalizes the potential for individuation borne by human attention when it is equitably distributed. As has been well analysed by Bernard Stiegler in numerous recent publications, it is in no way the technological inventions themselves that are disfiguring, but their subjection to the tyranny of ratings. Our collective attention is currently being abused by the inertia of obsolete economic models, inspired by the logic of an industrial capitalism inherited from the twentieth century, which ignores the specificity and the properties of the attention ecology. Can we hope to see digital cultures overcome the impasses of an attention capitalism subjected to the financial logic of ratings? The question deserves a chapter to itself.

— 3 —

THE DIGITALIZATION
OF ATTENTION

As they add a new stratum of global, instantaneous and infinitely modular communications to the mediasphere, digital technologies have started to drastically restructure every level of the global economy. From the point of view that interests us here, this restructuring rests on the simple principle of ELECTRIFICATION OF ATTENTION: '*computers replace attentional energy with electrical energy*'. While the mass media introduce over-economies of scale as they take us from one-to-one discussion to the attentional aggregation of millions of individuals, the magic of search engines has enabled us to make attention hyper-savings, infinitely enriching our lives as they electrically execute searches in a fraction of a second which would have taken us days, months, and sometimes years of effort.

If, as we saw in the first chapter, the attention economy cannot be reduced to the 'new economy' that emerged in the 1990s with the development of the internet, we should not, for all that, underestimate the impact of digital technologies on the uses and distribution of our collective attention. Can we still hope, like Félix Guattari in 1990, 'that there will be a reorganization of the mass-media power that crushes contemporary subjectivity, and the entry into a post-media era consisting of a collective individual reappropriation and an interactive usage of information, communication, intelligence, art and culture machines'?[1] Even if emailing lists, blogs and social networks are added to the mass media inherited from the twentieth century, which they reconfigure without replacing them, the interactivity reinstated by digital technologies makes them the bearers of an emancipatory potential that remains to be discovered and tested. We will see over the coming chapters how these functions affect the ways in which we pay attention to one another. It is, however, already possible to identify, from the collective point of view, new possibilities for action and new modes of exploitation brought about by the electrification of our attention.

Free Labour and the Vectorialist Class

As Tiziana Terranova has been analysing for more than a decade, the internet today offers capitalism a vast hunting ground which is teeming with FREE LABOUR. It freely provides the labour for 'building websites, modifying software packages, reading and participating in mailing lists, and building virtual spaces': 'free labour is *the moment where this knowledgeable consumption of culture is translated into excess productive activities* that are pleasurably embraced and at the same time often shamelessly exploited'.[2] The magic of electrified attention presents us with boundless and virtually free riches; we work on these riches often with enchanted and generous jubilation; businesses have learned how to take advantage of this, profiting financially from our enchantment.

Of course, just because we work for free, it is not necessarily the case that we find ourselves in a position of exploitation. There are a great many set-ups where everyone can benefit from an attention that increases the collective power of the commons, even if the work is not directly remunerated in the framework of a salaried job. One of the most suggestive symbols of this productive free labour is CAPTCHA (completely automated public Turing test to tell computers and humans apart), invented by Luis von Ahn in 2000 when he was barely twenty-two years old. When you want to pay for something online or download certain files, you will sometimes see several distorted letters appear which you have to re-transcribe to identify yourself as human (or someone using in good faith), since software intended to clog up free services with paralysing requests is currently unable to identify these deformed characters. While each of us uses CAPTCHA as a key for gaining access to a restricted service, the programme is using us in turn to build a character recognition software that is more powerful than those that exist today: as we mobilize our live attention to humanly decipher the distorted letters, we are working to teach the machine to refine its own deciphering ability. With two hundred million words handled in this way every day on the internet, the software coming out of this programme (RECAPTCHA) has been able to make considerable progress from which we are all set to benefit through a more precise digitalization of scanned texts.[3]

As this example illustrates, when we interact on the internet, our attention constitutes a constant source as well as an enormous power of distributed communal intelligence – that can sometimes be made surprisingly productive by a well thought out algorithm. The emergence of the digital is first of all the (often passionate and playful) eruption of this distributed intelligence, whose liberating and culturally enriching power has been wonderfully increased by real-time networking.

And yet, contemporary capitalism is organized around the parasitic capture of the (more or less distributed) productivity of this free labour: 'Free labor is a desire of labor immanent to late capitalism, and late capitalism is the field that both sustains free labor and exhausts it.'[4] Fans, bloggers, contributors to collective sites or email lists, even reality television participants: so many forms of unpaid labour which may be classed as *PLAYBOR, an inextricable combination of playful pleasure and productive labour, making the internet into an unstable and disconcerting mixture of playground and factory.*

The most suggestive way of characterizing the power relations established by attention capitalism has been developed by Ken McKenzie Wark who, starting with his *Hacker Manifesto* in 2004,[5] has put forward a socio-economic analysis which opposes the two collective entities structuring a new form of class struggle in the digital age. The HACKER CLASS, engaging in various kinds of (technological, conceptual, aesthetic, political) improvisations, *dedicates its attention to the production of new knowledge and new cultures – a surplus of 'information' in other words – but without having the means by which to realize the value of what it creates.* On the other side, 'the *vectoralist class* does not produce anything new. Its function is to make everything equivalent, as it transforms novelty into merchandise. It is able to do this because it possesses the means by which the value of the new can be realized.' Because 'information is never immaterial. Information cannot *not* be embodied. It has no existence outside of the material.'[6] The vectors are precisely the cables, disks, and servers, but also the software, the businesses and the flow of investments which information requires in order to be materialized, stored, classed, retrieved, and so that it can circulate in the space and time between humans.

VECTORALIST POWER consists, therefore, in '*the power to move information from one place to another. It is the power to move and combine anything and everything as a resource.*'[7] So, the vectoralist class is made up of all those who control and profit from the necessary material vectoralization of information – whether that be through the industrial production of iPads, cables and microprocessors (Foxconn, Sony, Apple), through the extension of communications networks monopolized by private multinationals (Orange, Free, Verizon, Google, Facebook), through the commodification of information, images and sounds by the legal fictions of intellectual property (Microsoft, Universal, TF1, Mediaset, Fox), or through the control of the vectors along which the financing of the investments that irrigate all these businesses passes (Goldman Sachs).

This characterization of class relationships in the digital age allows us to summarise what we discovered about attention capitalism over the course of the preceding chapter. The first axiom, which makes attention into a new form of money or capital, finds justification in the superimposition of the creative (and more or less playful) labour carried out by the attention of hackers on the one hand, and the material and financial structures over which the vectoralist class exercises its control on the other. The description of the media as fulfilling a banking function based on the reduction of living attention to a homogenized ratings metric corresponds perfectly with the distinctive operation of the vectoralist class: 'make everything equivalent, by transforming novelty into merchandise'. By 'moving information from one place to another' and 'arranging anything and everything as a resource', the media not only benefit from the capital gain generated by over-economies of scale but, above all, they profit from a (parasitic) unearned income, coming from the fact that they alone 'possess the means by which to realize the value of the new'.

Vectoralist power is based firmly on an ontology of visibility: 'If capitalist power reduced being to having, then vectoralist power reduces having to appearing. The actual qualities of things become secondary to the logistics and poetics that decorate the commodity.'[8] It is the accumulation of gazes and attention that constitutes value. The vector has no proper substance: like media apparatuses, it only exists through those who pass through it – and from whom it makes every effort to profit. What is true for TV *channels* is even more so for digital vectors like Facebook and Google.

The Mechanical Pre-configuration of Attention

Whether they are television transmitters, fibre-optic cables, social networks or flows of financial investment, vectors condition our regimes of visibility along with the processes of valorization connected with them. In order to understand how the digitalization of these vectors today structures our collective attention, we need to look in more detail at the technical mechanisms on which this digitalization is based – whether it is a question of the general procedure of digitalization or the particular functioning of a search engine.

Attention and valorization have always gone hand in hand – in a close connection whose essential stakes have yet to be sufficiently determined. As we have already had occasion to note, it is only possible to value something whose existence we have noticed by an effort of attention; reciprocally, we tend to pay attention to what we have learned to value. So, there is nothing particularly new about the circular self-reinforcing dynamic between attention and valorization evoked in the preceding chapter. The development of (quicker, more inclusive, more widely shared) new vectors nevertheless induces quantitative effects that qualitatively alter the orientation of our digitalized attention – and which therefore over-determine the collective valorizations with respect to which our social behaviour is calibrated. This qualitative alteration is grounded in at least three mechanisms.

First of all, the fundamental procedure of digitalization tends to short-circuit the selections that humanity had until its arrival carried out through the analogue phenomena of *Gestalt*. For millennia, we learned to pay attention to forms rooted in the imagination (*imagos, Gestalt, patterns*); the new digital apparatuses analyse these forms into discrete data (*data, bits, digits*), which are rooted in symbolic logics. Where the segmentation of the sensory continuum (the colours of the rainbow, the notes of the musical scale) was carried out by individual subjectivities – each infinitesimally different, even if they intersect collectively within the culture that they determine – this segmentation is now carried out at the level of the machines that vectoralize sensory perception.

However high the definition of a digital image, however refined the computer's soundcard, colours and sounds are today reduced to standardized sampling units which are predetermined by the system of digitalization on which the operation of the apparatus being used is based. We may, with Sylvain Auroux and Bernard Stiegler, speak of GRAMMATIZATION to refer to this *reduction of the sensory continuum to which we are attentive to discrete units susceptible to logical manipulation.* 'Digitalization' properly speaking consists in the assignation of a 'number' (which may ultimately be decomposed into a sequence of 0s and 1s) to each of the discrete units resulting from this analytical process.

Even if the difference between an analogue image or sound (a film photograph, a vinyl or tape recording) and their digital equivalent is generally beyond our consciousness, or even our perceptive ability, it is nevertheless necessary to note here a completely fundamental anthropological and ontological change, whose importance was highlighted by Vilém Flusser as early as the 1970s. Flusser summarized this change in a dense but enlightening formula: 'the old images are subjective abstractions drawn from phenomena, while technical images realize objective abstractions'.[9] When I look at a field of poppies, it is in my mind that the sensory continuum is segmented into forms and colours whose contrasts and oppositions I comprehend: my mental image is a 'subjective abstraction' that I draw from phenomena through the collective perceptive schemas that define my culture. When I look at a digital photograph of this field, a whole series of 'objective abstractions' have preconfigured what is submitted to my attention (depending on choices relating to the sampling rate, the contrast setting, the focal length, the exposure time, etc.). The core of the concrete perception that I receive of this field is structured (and haunted) by a certain abstract 'logic' – in the strong sense of a human language (*logos*) determining certain relationships among a finite stock of discrete units, which is to say, by a certain 'protocol' which introduces a filter between my personal attention and that to which it is applied.

Digitalization does not only, therefore, effect a grammatization of the sensory continuum (reduced to more or less nuanced samples of the reality represented). It also participates in a PROGRAMMING procedure, which is to say, in *a protocol which, by determining the input of the concrete continuum as abstract data, materially (and not just culturally) preconfigures our perception of reality.* In other words: every grammatization implies a certain grammar which is imposed through it. This is the fundamental intuition animating all of Vilém Flusser's thought, which we have hardly begun to evaluate: the programming of our perceptions by our technical devices necessarily leads to the programming of our behaviour, because our attention is preconfigured.

The digitalization of our attention subjects it to programming effects inherent in the vectors, which allow it to circulate more quickly, more broadly and more intensely than ever before. The passage by these vectors imposes – in a rigidly mechanical, and no longer only cultural, way – the subjection to certain protocols that function as conditions of access.[10] Vectoralist power is exercised at the fundamental (and generally hidden) level of the preconfiguration choices inherent in the protocols of grammatization used by devices. The selection of a given sampling rate (generally conditioned by economic calculations directed by sales profit) leads to the mechanical obliteration of certain nuances that are considered to be negligible – by whom? For what reason? By what measures? By what sensitivities?

A third effect of the digitalization of attention results from the increasing tendency of our different kinds of programming to extend across the whole of the planet. At the same time that digitalization puts forward thousands of texts, images, pieces of music and videos for my attention, giving me access to a variety that is absolutely without precedent in the whole history of humanity, it imposes inevitable effects of STANDARDIZATION, because *a data flow can only circulate in a vector if it submits to the configurations and homogenising norms defined by its protocol.* In the first years of YouTube's existence, you could make (almost) anything and everything free access – so long as you cut it up into ten-minute sections. You can communicate any kind of writing to anyone anywhere in the world – on condition that it can be input by a keyboard (which makes it graphologically dumb) or a scanner (which wipes out any texture in the original paper). You can transfer any kind of music to mp3 – on condition that it complies with a level of compression that muffles the intensity of high quality recordings. A certain degree of standardization (that may be more or less damaging) is the price we pay to benefit from the ease of transmission offered by a vector.

In the near future, when the majority of the world's population will be connected to the internet, we foresee (still not clearly enough) the homogenising effects brought about by the importance of certain major interfaces, which are for the most part on the point of becoming quasi-monopolies (YouTube, Microsoft Word, Facebook, iTunes, Amazon, Alibaba). As they pre-format our collective attention, their protocols have global effects that may contribute just as much to the homogenization and synchronization of our behaviour as to its diversification – depending on whether we favour, contain or neutralize certain of their effects. Electrification is in the process of reconfiguring our collective attention, at a global level, according to self-reinforcing dynamics that profoundly restructure the way in which we perceive and evaluate our lived experiences. There is no phenomenon that better illustrates this reconfiguration of our collective attention than the history and recent development of a search engine like Google.

PageRank: Attention Aggregation Machine

As a first approximation, a search engine may be described as an attention machine tasked with pre-filtering the immense quantity of information made available to us on the internet. Google is therefore illustrative of the ATTENTION CONDENSERS called for by Herbert Simon in his pioneering 1969 article: 'An information-processing sub-system (a computer or a new organization unit) will reduce the net demand on the rest of the organization's attention only if it *absorbs more information previously received by others than it produces* – that is, if it listens and thinks more than it speaks.'[11] As highlighted by Dominique Cardon, these condensers profoundly alter our relationship to knowledge. Those who know how to hack them are able to offer ways of accessing enormous quantities of data (*big data*) in such a way that we can visualize millions of heterogeneous behaviour types reduced to a few modular parameters. In this way, we may be led to believe that the data 'speak for themselves', short-circuiting traditional intermediaries like theories, explanatory models and other interpretative schema. It is these visualized condensations 'that we must examine to begin with, before interpreting'.[12] Our attention is thus brought to bear on absolutely new cognitive and visual objects, whose possibilities, pitfalls and promises we are only just beginning to glimpse.

Looking more closely at the very particular condenser that is Google, it is apparent that it only *directs* our attention by *following* our attention – according to a recursive loop which feeds on the attention of others. The PageRank algorithm, on which Google's success rests, is in fact based on bibliometric impact ratings established in the academic world to evaluate the quality of a scientific article measured by the number of articles that make reference to it: the more an article is cited by other articles, the higher its score, and the further it rises in the rankings. So, it is a question of establishing a hierarchy (of importance, seriousness, reliability, prestige, prominence) according to the degree of attention bestowed on entities considered within a community.[13]

Even if we have moved from the narrow sphere of the university (with its articles woven of citations) to the vast world of the internet (populated by sites connected with hyperlinks), a similar principle of HIERARCHIZATION BY ATTENTION AGGREGATION is applied by the condenser which made Google's fortune: *you are valued at the value of the attention you are given.* So we come back here to the principle of valorization through attention that we encountered in the preceding chapter. Although it is calculated from around a hundred criteria, your PageRank score is principally a function of (1) the number of links that lead to your page, (2) the score of the pages that lead to yours (the higher their prestige, the more they confer on you), (3) the traffic passing through your page, (4) the likelihood that

9. Illustration of PageRank by Felipe Micaroni Lalli on Wikipedia

internet users will click on it from a list of search results, and (5) the likelihood that they will linger there (Figure 9). These five criteria quantify different parameters of the attention accorded to the page in question: it has attracted and caught someone's attention sufficiently for them to refer to it by hyperlink; this reference is that much more significant if it comes from someone who themselves attracts more attention; the page is visited by net users whose attention it has grabbed; it is able to retain this attention by persuading them to stay longer than the average 10 seconds spent on a web page.

When we use Google to find information on the internet, we are, therefore, using an ATTENTION MACHINE TO THE SECOND POWER (or third or *n*th power), which *directs our attention depending on the way in which other net users have directed their attention.* Four aspects of this attention aggregation machine should be brought to light.

The first appears when we compare the kind of selective filtering performed by Google with that practised by a vector like the French Radio/Television Agency[14] in the 1960s. The state monopoly effectively acted as a (particularly narrow) filter, since these channels selected the only televisual images that were then available to a French household. Google, on the other hand, performs a ranking operation rather than a selection operation. Most searches offer up thousands, or even millions, of results for anyone who has the patience to go to the end of the listed pages. But the point is that no one has this kind of patience. Except in what are ultimately quite rare cases of censorship, nothing is strictly speaking excluded from these channels. What counts, however, is not whether something gets included (or not): it is being at the height of visibility, right at the top of the first page of search results. The new proletarians are not so much the 'excluded' as the 'relegated'. The organization of our collective digital attention by Google structures our field of visibility on the basis of a PRINCIPLE OF PRIORITIZATION: *the power of the vectoralist class consists in the organization of priorities, rather than the inclusion or exclusion from the field of visibility* – which is why it is difficult to condemn what are in fact very effective forms of censorship: everything is allowed, everything is available, but only a very small minority is really visible and decisive (if not properly decision making).

It is thanks to this prioritization that Larry Page's and Sergey Brin's invention is able to perform its daily wonders for us. Using their search engine gives us an incomparable power to extend, intensify, clarify, and inform our attention, as it augments our individual attention energy through the magic of electrical energy. These wonders are, however, based on a PRINCIPLE OF ALIGNMENT which should give us cause for concern: *PageRank only finds what we are looking for because it aligns our individual attention with the dominant directions of our collective attention.* I am led to see what the greater proportion of my fellows have seen, there where they have chosen to look (click).

This is not a problem in itself, as long as one postulates that each of us is endowed with practical rationality. Google would then, as we have already noted, be the perfect symbol of the distributed productivity of our collective intelligence: it is our curiosity, our intuition, our informed choices, our personal knowledge and our considered experiences that go to nourish this empty condenser that is the PageRank algorithm with a power of communal thought. In this sense, we can only berate Google for having exploited the free labour that we invest in it with each of our clicks, allowing the company shareholders to profit from a return that should by rights come back to the commons – once Messrs Page and Brin have been handsomely remunerated for their brilliant invention, for their initial investment (financed in part by Stanford University and the National Science Foundation) and for the upkeep of the servers that they have concealed all over the planet.

To be the astounding condenser of collective attention that daily produces miracles in a fraction of a second, PageRank nevertheless relies on a dynamic of attention convergence, which is spread in a quasi-monopolistic way over the whole surface of the globe and which is at great risk of resembling, if viewed from Saturn, the mimetic group behaviour of a school of fish. Far from being the remedy to media aggregation hoped for by the prophets of a post-media age, the internet ruled over by Google, YouTube and Co. resembles (more) desperately the *synopticon* described by Thomas Mathiesen and Vilém Flusser:[15] a world in which everyone allows himself to be hypnotized, in front of his little screen, by the same continuous surge of insignificant sounds and images – the song 'Gangnam Style' did not necessarily herald, either in its content or the way in which it was broadcast, a much more promising media future than 'Billie Jean'.

Automated Valorization

If there is a danger that herd behaviour is intensifying, this probably isn't happening as a result of this or that algorithm, but as a result of the narrowly mercantile logic in which the development of the internet is allowing itself to become entangled. Even if our petty individual narcissism dreams of placing us at the centre of the media world, the phenomena of alignment, convergence, synchronization and concentration of attention brought about by PageRank would remain innocent enough if the attention economy wasn't completely overdetermined by the quest for a financial profit that has now been elevated to a condition of survival.

The third aspect of this machine for aggregating collective attention that is Google can be located, therefore, in the PRINCIPLE OF COMMODIFICATION which *seeks to submit attentional flows to needs and desires that will maximize financial returns*. If, as an attention condenser, PageRank exemplifies the extraordinary power of the digitalization of our minds, as a capitalist enterprise, Google exemplifies the most harmful control that it is possible to imagine the vectoralist class exercising over our collective attention. Not content with taking an enormous income from its quasi-monopoly over our access to the internet, with AdWords the firm has developed an advertising capture machine that is destined, it would seem, to impinge more and more on the supposed transparency of their algorithm. Once the margins have been filled with small commercial notices, paid links come to occupy the top lines of page results – in that position of priority visibility where in principle we should only find the pages that are most pertinent from the point of view of their contents.

From the moment the ranking logic automated by PageRank comes to determine almost all the paths by which we access the internet – Google, YouTube, Amazon, etc. – the whole web finds itself besieged by the omnipresence of mini local audience ratings, pre-orienting all my choices in accordance with our combined sheep-like behaviour. Many digital-culture pioneers miss the 'good old days' before Google when you could still truly 'navigate' or 'surf' the internet, with all the unseen reefs, unexpected deviations and minor shipwrecks that that entailed. The serendipity[16] inherent in this kind of navigation largely vanished from practices as soon as the implacable efficiency of our search engines started to direct us with diabolical pertinence and precision to what we wanted to find. By enabling us to find straight away that for which the aggregating machine helps us search, while discreetly slanting the results so as to maximize the financial return of its monopoly income, Google contributes to a reduction in the emancipatory promise inherent in the dynamics of the internet, bringing instead new forms of exploitation, which are different in nature but not necessarily less disfiguring than the old ones. Even if, thanks to the ubiquity of cookies, the singular history of my searches and previous responses personalizes (and 'improves') what the machine shows on my screen, how could I not feel smothered by the weight of an ever-present audience rating which pre-vectoralizes each of my search directions – each cookie only noting my singularity so as to better place it on the standardized measure of a consumer profile?

At the root of this growing commercialization of the internet, we find the emergence of the fourth aspect of the aggregation of attention operated by the machine – the automatic quantification of the values put into circulation in a global attention economy.[17] Matteo Pasquinelli presents this process of automated evaluation with particular lucidity:

> PageRank specifically describes the attention value of any object to a such extent that it has become the most important source of visibility and authority even outside the digital sphere. Eventually PageRank gives a formula of value accumulation that is hegemonic and compatible across different media domains: an effective diagram to describe the *attention economy* and the *cognitive economy* in general. [. . .] Before the internet this process was described as a generic collective drive – after the internet, the structure of the network relations around a given object can be easily traced and measured. PageRank is the first mathematical formula to calculate the *attention value* of each node in a complex network and the general *attention capital* of the whole network [. . .] This *rank value* set by Google is unofficially recognized as the currency of the global attention economy and crucially influences the online visibility of individuals and companies and subsequently their prestige and business. This *attention value* is then transformed into monetary value in different ways.[18]

We are very close here to the core of the reactor that powers the attention economy – in that it is (sadly still) an 'economy', oriented towards financial profit, and not an 'ecology', understood as an eco-system which we must urgently take care of if we wish to develop forms of life that are collectively sustainable and individually desir-able. As we noted with Georg Franck in the preceding chapter, it is only possible to speak of an attention economy to the extent that the infinite diversity of what we pay attention to can be reduced to a quantifiable homogenous substance. It is precisely this reduction that is carried out by PageRank. If this algorithm is able to prioritize the information we are offered, if it can align our gaze and com-mercialize our curiosity, then this is thanks to a PRINCIPLE OF QUANTIFICATION which constitutes the fourth and final aspect to be noted here: *the machinic aggregation of attention carried out by PageRank produces a figure which assigns an attention value to every entity at a time t.*

We are truly dealing here with a Taylorization of the mind: the magic of Google rests on the automation of the collective process through which we attribute value to the things that make up our world. Matteo Pasquinelli inscribes PageRank in the perspective of four valorization models that we have glimpsed already over the course of the preceding pages: the economy of bibliographic refer-ences governing the academic world, the economy of attention reconfigured by the internet, the prestige economy that organizes the art-world and the credit economy administered by ratings agencies. These different valorization mechanisms represent 'a new form of biopolitical control and production of new subjectivities and social competition [which] replace the traditional discipline of the era of the Fordist industrial metropolis': 'these measuring systems do not invent anything new, but they occupy and map a network of pre-existing social relations and behaviours'[19] – of which they enable an ever more fully automated valorization.

These four models – constituting four still partially distinct spheres within the attention economy, which are, however, currently being integrated by Google – are in fact a site of competition between two different kinds of operation which should be carefully distinguished. In the academic, artistic and financial worlds, a *RATINGS* logic still seems to dominate, which is to say, *the positioning 'along a scale according to a system of subjective assessments,* based on recogni-tion, trust and support by persons with whom a complex network of relations has been established'. PageRank, on the other hand, is illustrative of a *RANKING* logic, which is to say, *the positioning 'in a certain range according to an objective procedure, a method, an algorithm* (as happens in the evaluation of academic journals, in the results of the Google search engine or in the calculation of the number of followers on Facebook and Twitter)'.[20]

In most spheres, mechanized – electrified, digitalized – attention is tending to substitute for human attention, essentially because of cost: everything is set to push us from rating to ranking. Putting a list of publications through a programme to find a factor H (the 'impact' factor measuring the number of times an article has been cited by another article) or counting the citations on Web of Science (a private company which maps out scientific publications by formatting them for bibliometric analysis) requires less attention (and so fewer resources) than finding a colleague inclined to read it and discuss the contents. Taking advantage of split-second pricing differentials by plugging in computers programmed for speed trading guarantees greater profits than trying to measure the value of a company's shares – not to mention its social value.

As they 'replace attentional energy with electrical energy', computers certainly render us a huge service, illustrated by the speed and pertinence with which Google's nets gather in the most unlikely fish that we could send them out to look for. This automation, based on circular self-reinforcement dynamics nevertheless becomes worrying when we are no longer content to mobilize machinic devices to help us find what we value, but when we abandon to them the very work of valorization. But it is precisely this threshold that is now being crossed from all quarters – with the risk that we will see the nets thrown into the web turn us all into schools of fish to be enmeshed in inextricable tangles.

Vectors versus Scalars

Doom-laden anxiety about the pernicious effects of new media is as old as the world: from Plato proclaiming the degradation of our memory under the effects of writing to Nicholas Carr decrying the erosion of our attention with the distractive temptations of the internet – all of these critiques are simultaneously wrong to prophesy the apocalypse and right to bring to light certain dangers inherent in the introduction and distribution of new technologies. The digitalization of our attention is as rich in its promise as it is threatening in its commercialization. Whatever the power of an entity like Google, its profits and its survival depend on us, just as much as our access to information, email, videos and books is today under its control. The emergence of rival search engines, the introduction of new tax regimes, the establishment of a politics that legally protects common intellectual goods, a boycott, a few bad public relations decisions: any of these may put a dent in, undermine, even blow away in a matter of months the profit harnessing model on which its current hegemony is based. Because it is immanent to our very attention – which it sharpens and intensifies as it orientates and exploits it – the control exercised by Google relies on our inalienable ability to redeploy our attention in the directions that seem the most promising to us.

At the conclusion of these considerations of the way in which contemporary capitalism and its new digital technologies restructure our collective attention, it is perhaps appropriate to take a step to one side so as to note a suggestive cross-over between the characterization recently proposed by McKenzie Wark of a 'vectoralist' capitalism and the observations amassed by Paul Valéry at the beginning of the twentieth century on the 'vectoral' nature of any effort of attention:

> Attention is vector and potential.
> The gaze could be analysed as a vectoral property – which incidentally is true of any attention inasmuch as it is directional.
> It is also a direction of effort.
> Attention is the effort of prolongation, of continuity, in clarity.
> Thought is always formed in vectoral mode and then puts itself into scalar form.[21]

To characterize attention as a 'vector' is, for Valéry, to insist that it is by nature pressure, prolongation, effort, conatus – or, to be even more precise, 'direction of effort' (the *Zuwendung*-attention already encountered above). If attention selects, filters or prioritizes, it does so starting from a principle of orientation. Attention cannot be reduced to a simple given, a static number: it is much less (countable) reality than (unpredictable) 'potential'. In other words, as it relates to thought, attention 'is always formed in vectoral mode' (like an arrow), and it is only when it *stops* to think and develop that it can be grasped 'in scalar form' (like a number).

This *scalarization* – which is to say, the operation that translates arrows into numbers – denies the fundamental nature of attention, in the same way that putting a bird in a cage denies its nature as a flying creature. But, as we have seen, it is precisely to a ubiquitous scalarization that we are condemned by the financial logic of capitalism. Everything must be reduced to figures (audience ratings, market segments, impact in citations, market pricing, GDP,

PageRank) – everything has to be. . . *digitalized*! The 'digitalization of attention' is marked by a fundamental ambivalence since attention is by nature vectoral while digitalization is by nature scalar.

Even as we note that our attention depends on the vectors that orientate and channel it – which is perfectly true and which is what subjects it to the now disproportionate power of the vectoralist class – we should not lose sight of the fact that *attention is itself a vector*: pressure, orientation, 'direction of effort', *Zuwendung*. According to its etymology (*ad-tendere*), attention 'tends towards' something: it calls for an exit from oneself, a broadening of horizons. It indicates a 'potential' in *excedence* over any predefined and preconfigured identity.[22] To recognize the vectoral nature of attention is, on the one hand, to assess what determines it: like its representation as an arrow, it has a certain size, a certain orientation and a certain direction, which can only be understood and explained within a certain field of forces in which it reacts to exterior constraints (flows, channels, pressures). But this also requires that we emphasize, on the other hand, that it is not a simple line, measurable in centimetres and reducible to a scalar number: the point of its arrow serves as a reminder that it aims at something other than what it is at present.

The digitalization that 'replaces attentional energy with electrical energy' opens magnificent perspectives for future developments as it multiplies the powers of our live attention – on condition, however, that it is not imprisoned in the cage of the short-term profit calculations that characterize financial capitalism. The vectoralist class is not exploitative because of its 'power to move anything and everything', but because of its requirement that 'value be realized' in countable terms. Such is THE TRUE CHALLENGE OF THE DIGITAL CULTURES now emerging: *how can you take advantage of the vectoral power of the digital without allowing yourself to be imprisoned in the scalar cages of digitalization?* Only the art of interference, the elusive strength of hackers, can rise to such a challenge – which is at the heart of the attention ecology in the age of its electrification.

Seen from the planet Saturn, the collective attention which circulates among us and which nourishes our spirits (*noûs*) takes the form of a composition of forces, where each look, instance of listening and click simultaneously conforms to a communal vectoralization of our efforts and contributes to a reinforcement or inflection of the course. Two kinds of discourse and reasoning – both equally valid and necessary – can, therefore, be held in parallel, despite their apparent contradictions. It is true that, as we have tried to show throughout the preceding chapters, my individual attention finds itself constantly and thoroughly overdetermined by the collective structures by which it is channelled, be they cultural or technological. Which is why it was important to start by gaining an inevitably brief and simplifying insight into the transindividual forces that animate and constrain every expression of our attention capacity.

It is nevertheless equally true, as will be examined in the following chapters, that the use we make of our attention capabilities opens up margins of agency where we actively contribute to *making* the (inextricably individual and collective) *attention* which orients our behaviour.[23] It is not contradictory to accept that my attention is entirely conditioned by the collective structures whose principle dynamics we have just looked over, while asserting that the great flows that carry us all along are only constituted through the aggregation of each of our infinitesimal gestures. So as to better understand the nature of these infinitesimal gestures, we need, however, to come down from Saturn to get as close as possible to the concrete micro-situations in which we pay attention to one thing rather than another. The time has come to trade the interplanetary telescope for the noological microscope, which alone is able to grasp what happens in us when we maintain an attentional relation with one object or another in our milieu. As Arne Naess emphasized, ecology is in fact more a question of relationality than environment: attention is a certain kind of connection between that which I am, that which surrounds me, and that which may result from the relation that unites these interested parties.

Part II

Joint Attention

— 4 —

PRESENTIAL ATTENTION

We are always attentive in a particular situation. The vast majority of scientific research dedicated to attention makes every effort to simplify this situation to the extreme. A subject is asked to follow the trajectory of a basketball, or concentrate on letters or images passing over a screen, and to recall them after being distracted for a few minutes. The social situation which nevertheless structures (and over-determines) the psychological experiment is rarely taken into account. But the subject whose attention capacity is being quantified is himself the object of a certain attention from the person doing the experiment. And he knows it. The attention he gives to the letters or basketball is a function of the attention he imagines the scientist is in the process of giving to his behaviour.

The assertion that I never pay attention alone can, therefore, be understood in two very different ways. It may indicate, as we saw in the preceding chapters, that even when I seem to be alone looking at the page of a book, newspaper or website, which is absorbing my attention, this is the result of a very complex inter-play of media enthralments, selective alignments, vectoralist strategies, profit-hunger and the will to resist – which together imply a vast array of social relations within the apparently isolated relationship that my eyes maintain with the page or screen. But it may also designate a collection of more specific, localized situations, where I know that I am not alone in the place in which I find myself, and where my consciousness of the attention of others affects the orientation of my own attention. In this case, we are dealing with situations of *joint attention* – to which the second part of this book will be devoted.

Joint Attention

In developmental psychology, people speak of joint attention to refer to the fact that, from nine months onwards, when a parental figure directs their gaze to look at an object other than the infant, the infant directs its own gaze towards the object in question.[1] The attention of several subjects is therefore 'joined' in the sense in which, because they are attentive to one another, the direction taken by the attention of one of them pushes the attention of the other in the same direction.

Under the influence of fame and visibility, which is becoming more extensive and more intensive in step with the media developments that have punctuated modernity, it would certainly be justifiable to consider every form of attention to be (at least virtually) 'joint'. Without going back to the role that La Rochefoucauld attributed to *amour-propre*, Sartre to being-for-the-other or Honneth to recognition – which all indicate that the conception I have of myself is a function of how I perceive myself to be regarded by others – the extent to which the attention of others interferes with our own is apparent at virtually every instant of our daily existence. When surveillance cameras record my gestures and actions or a friend puts them up on Facebook, when a government agency gathers metadata on my telephone calls and internet connections, when PageRank keeps a record of my clicks or Amazon computes my purchases so as to suggest to other clients that they will like Mary Halvorson's new CD because they like Tim Berne's latest release – in every case of this kind, we suspect our attention to be the object of the attention of a more or less determinate other. So, way beyond psychologists, intelligence agencies or children and their parents, we are all immersed in tightly bound networks of interwoven attention. When we choose a CD, a film or a website under the influence of another's choice, our attention is effectively bound with theirs in the fashion characteristic of joint attention: I turn my gaze in this direction as a consequence of the fact that someone else in my environment has previously turned theirs in this same direction.

Attention ecology would nevertheless benefit from a more precise definition of joint attention. In order to distinguish joint attention from collective attention, the following pages will concentrate on situations of PRESENTIAL CO-ATTENTION, characterized by the fact that *several people, conscious of the presence of others, interact in real-time depending on their perception of the attention of the other participants*. This excludes all forms of influence between anonymous individuals mediated by algorithms, trends or media broadcast, and it restricts the effects of group convergence to situations of co-presence limited in space, time and by the number of participants involved. It is (in part) through the mechanisms of joint attention that schools of fish or stadia of spectators turn the direction in which they are looking and their bodies with remarkable homogeneity and synchrony one way or another – sometimes producing a feeling of fusional co-agency that is celebrated in the ritual of the Mexican wave.

Whether two lovers look in the same direction together or a crowd of tens of thousands of participants mimics the movement of a wave on the terraces of a stadium, joint attention involves the shared feeling of a co-presence that is sensitive to the emotional variations of the individuals involved. The simplest example no doubt being when two people face each other and periodically check on the face and in the look of the other how they are reacting to the development of their relationship (during a conversation, for example). If sensitivity to the emotions of the other participants passes through an apparatus like Skype, rather than taking place in the immediacy of physical co-presence, this does not make a great difference (so long as image freezes do not overly hamper the connection). The 'presence' shared in these situations is therefore more temporal and sensitive than strictly spatial and physical, since the participants are not obstructed by the telesthetic apparatuses.

Besides co-presence, situations of joint attention seem to be characterized by three phenomena. The first is a PRINCIPLE OF RECIPROCITY: *attention must be able to circulate bidirectionally between the parties involved.* The infant learns to follow the parents' gaze in a relationship where the parents also endeavour to follow the gaze of the infant. The model here is provided by the conversation situation, whose etymology suggests that it is precisely a matter of knowing whether 'to turn together the one towards the other' (*convertere*). There is conversation (rather than peroration) to the extent that a principle of reciprocity invites an alternation of roles between those speaking and those listening. This requirement for reciprocity does not necessarily imply a perfectly equal relation, any more than it implies an equitable division of speaking time. A master may converse with his pupil without renouncing his superior status, just as a laconic person may be content with a few words to maintain position in a debate.

It is in light of this principle of reciprocity that Vilém Flusser distinguished two great models of communication systems:

85

With the radio system, the central transmitter is connected in a single ('univocal') direction to a multiplicity of peripheral receivers. The communicational process is 'discourse'. In a network system, multiple participants are connected among themselves in a ('biunivocal') way that enables them all to transmit and receive; the process of communication is 'dialogue'. The aim of the first system is to broadcast pre-existing information; [. . .] the aim of the second system is to synthesize pre-existing partial information; [. . .] in the second, the level of information is raised; in the first, information is simply stored up. The post and the telephone are more or less pure examples of the network system, the radio and the press are more or less pure examples of the radio system.[2]

As Georg Franck highlighted, the massive forms of exploitation characteristic of our current attention economy are rooted in the non-reciprocity introduced by mass-media apparatuses organized in accordance with the 'radio system'. Before the hope of a post-media future kindled by the arrival of the 'network system' in the form of the internet – anticipated by Flusser who wrote these lines in 1974 – the cultural industries based their profit and their authority on a regime of unequal exchange, which broadcast electrified attention (reproducible at low cost) to collect living attention (much rarer and costlier). When we pass from the analysis of collective attention, organized by the profoundly asymmetrical apparatuses characterizing the mass media, to joint attention whose model is the reciprocal conversation supported by the telephone or the post, we are therefore doing something very different to simply changing scale with respect to the number of participants involved. Most importantly, we are changing the structure of relations. Environments that are favourable to joint attention are characterized by the mode of interaction more than by their size. The reciprocity inherent in situations of joint attention represents a kind of antidote to the asymmetries structuring our media attention economy.

The second characteristic phenomenon of joint attention is the STRIVING FOR AFFECTIVE HARMONIZATION that constantly underpins it: *you cannot be truly attentive to the other without being considerate towards them.*[3] This condition for the success of any conversation demands a continual work of reciprocal adjustment between speech on one side and listening on the other. A 'discourse' can be broadcast and remain largely indifferent to the reactions it engenders in its listeners, as is the case with radio systems which generally do not allow any direct return to them. On the other hand, a 'dialogue' only moves forward thanks to micro-gestures of encouragement, sympathy, prevention, precaution or reassurance – thanks, in other words, to the many different kinds of 'attention' – that each participant directs to the other so as to maintain a good emotional resonance between them, which is much more important for the continuation of their exchange than the rigour of argumentative reasoning.

The importance of this delicate and generally spontaneous work of emotional harmonization becomes clear in communication conditions where it is painfully lacking. Who hasn't been caught up in the absurd disputes that are so frequent on emailing lists, where a minor disagreement gets out of hand, degenerating into insults of epic proportions? If the same arguments were formulated in a dialogue in which everyone can observe the effects of their words on the face of the other, and correct slippages in real time, these disputes would generally be resolved through a knowing wink of the eye, a mischievous smile, an immediate corrective or a pacifying gesture forestalling the development of a conflict. Because email correspondents, who are always temporally out of sync, can neither see facial micromovements nor hear subtle vocal intonations, the confrontation of discourses deteriorates and intensifies even with words that the protagonists hope will be appeasing, which are always misinterpreted because they are not embedded in a true dialogue situation. The recent spread of emoticons (☺, LOL), the first occurrence of which seems to date back to the 1840s, is only a very frustrated substitute to compensate for the infinite finesse of looks, facial expressions, attitudes and tonalities that several millennia of conversational practice have taught us to develop so that we can adjust our speech and listening with consideration for our interlocutors.

As was so well demonstrated by Daniel Bougnoux when he emphasized 'the primacy of communication over information', this emotional attention assures the maintenance of a fundamental connection between the participants in a dialogue, 'the weaving of the bond, the prolongation of contact', which are the preconditions for any exchange of argument.[4] Before worrying about 'information' (true or false, pertinent or not), you must start by establishing, and above all maintaining, the connection which enables those in dialogue to stay on the same emotional wavelength.

Since it depends on affective singularities whose reactions are very difficult to predict, this work of reciprocal adjustment and harmonization can never be completely prepared in advance. The third characteristic phenomenon of joint attention situations is therefore to be found in the IMPROVISATION PRACTICES that they necessarily call for: *showing yourself to be attentive to the attention of the*

87

other requires learning to get out of pre-programmed routines, so you can open yourself to the risks (and techniques) of improvisation. Everyone knows how to improvise, because everyone has learned to participate in a conversation – where no one knows in advance what their interlocutors are going to say. Apart from in the very rare cases in which we recite ritual formulas or play roles that have been written in advance, we never start a sentence without exposing ourselves to the risks of the micro-improvisation which will bring it to its completion – if everything goes well because, in reality, we often sacrifice syntactical rigour to the instincts of expressivity.

On this point as well, situations of joint attention rooted in the network system and exemplified by dialogue should be contrasted with situations observed in the radio system characteristic of the mass media. Apart from a few extremely rare examples, everything that comes to us through the television, if it has not been edited in advance with the comfort of a temporal delay has, when it is broadcast live, been meticulously pre-scripted. Here too, the main difference is to be found less in the size of audiences than in the means of communication: mass-media discourse broadcasts a pre-programmed message in one direction, even in talk shows or reality TV shows which are supposedly based on the 'spontaneous' performances of 'real' people. Everything is done to guard as much as possible against those improvised surprises that constitute the charm and vitality of the living dialogical structures in which joint attention takes place.

These considerations bring us to the heart of what must be analysed as an attention *ecology*. The three phenomena evoked above concern less the properties of certain acts than the defining characteristics of certain milieux. In this chapter we are interested in human environments as they are structured by the presential attention of others. The principle of reciprocity, striving for affective harmonization and improvisation practices are connected together within an ecosystem that has enabled humans to 'communicate' over the millennia – in the strong sense of this word, often highlighted by Daniel Bougnoux, which has much more to do with communion and care for the community than with the simple transfer of information.

Without being so arrogant as to blame parents for the attention deficit disorders experienced by their children – since the etiologies are still badly understood and in any case relate to multiple levels of causality – we may note that most of the treatments considered for ADDs involve, when they go beyond the short-circuit of simple medication, what therapists refer to as 'environmental methods'. Whatever the biochemical processes involved at the neurological level, ADDs are at least in part symptoms of the asymmetries, affective disagreements and communicational rigidness that make our family, school and media ecosystems so precarious and unstable. It is right that distracted or hyperactive children are sometimes presented as canaries in the mine whose distress indicates that our attentional environment is at risk of becoming unbreathable.

In the hope of clarifying and deepening the analysis of what is at stake in joint attention, where the balances are so fragile and the failures so harmful, the rest of this chapter will be dedicated to two scenarios that are at once very distinctive and very suggestive of the difficulties and promise implied by presential co-attention – the teaching situation and the experience of live performance.

Teaching Situations

After several decades of pedagogical experience and reflection, Robert Caron, director of the Centre Paris Lecture, recently positioned himself in opposition to many of the grievances concerning 'children's lack of attention, their restlessness, manic channel-hopping, their lack of inclination to listen to the sacred word of adults'. Rather than jump on the bandwagon of medicalized solutions or blame the internet, understood as a distraction machine, he suggested turning the problem back on teachers: children 'don't listen because there is nothing to hear' in many of the words they are offered.[5]

Cathy Davidson, a professor of education specializing in digital studies at Duke University in North Carolina and an advisor to President Obama, says the same: if many children have lamentable results in the standardized tests to which certain timid and reactionary educational systems are increasingly retreating, it is less because the children are not able to do what we expect of them than because the schools that have come down to us from the industrial revolution underestimate and hinder the development of their intelligence, which has been nourished on digital experimentation: 'Kids aren't failing because school is too hard but because it doesn't interest them. It does not capture their attention.'[6] Trapped between technological innovation and pedagogical inertia, teaching situations would doubtless benefit considerably from being analysed from an attention ecology perspective.

Like every speaking subject, teachers intuitively sense the necessity of capturing the attention of their audience (in accordance with the *captatio benevolentiae* of classical rhetoric). The people writing syllabuses bend over backwards to lure 'the young' towards 'serious' subjects by sprinkling them with supposedly attractive sparkles (introducing a philosophical subject through a reference to something in the news, playing a piece of rap to attune them to poetic metre). And the insults fly between those who accuse them of trivializing knowledge and those who berate them for teaching dry and drying subjects. Thinking of teaching situations in the context of the three dimensions of joint attention mentioned above will perhaps help us to supercede these pointless debates.

Indeed, from the nursery school to a professor's seminar, a classroom represents a situation of presential co-attention whose structure and methods may support or inhibit didactic interaction. The categorizations suggested by Vilém Flusser prove to be particularly enlightening here for distinguishing two poles of pedagogical practice. At the first (MASTERLY) POLE, *the classroom is structured in accordance with the 'radio system'*, with a 'central transmitter' (the teacher) 'connected in a single ('univocal') direction to a multiplicity of peripheral receivers' (the pupils). The teacher arrives in the classroom having prepared a '(dis)course', the aim of which is to 'broadcast pre-existing information', which has been 'stored up' and which he seeks to transmit with minimal loss – the best marks go to the student who is able to regurgitate what the teacher has taught. At the other (INTERACTIVE) POLE, *the classroom may be structured as a 'network system'*, connecting the participants in 'a ('biunivocal') way that enables them all to transmit and receive' in a 'dialogue' whose goal is 'to synthesize pre-existing partial information'[7] (and not only transmit it).

Even if all teaching practices are situated somewhere between these two extreme poles, their positioning on this axis helps to identify the kind of attentional ecosystem on which their dynamic is based. When Robert Caron suggests that if pupils are distracted this is because we are telling them things that they know already, he decries something inherent in the masterly pole: if the aim is to transmit information, the fact that I already have that information (or that it seems to me to be completely irrelevant) undermines the *raison d'être* of the communication. In an interactive apparatus, however, the fact that my interlocutor has stated a platitude makes me raise the general information level by responding with a more salient suggestion. So that we may frustrate the simplistic opposition between the autistic declamation of a teacher full of his own self-importance and inept collective barroom chatter, the three dimensions of co-attention in the present will enable us to clarify the criteria according to which masterly speech and interactive pedagogy can both constitute stimulating attention ecosystems. Radio or network – the two in any case tend to alternate within most teaching structures – the important thing is to be sensitive to the three following principles:

THE NECESSITY OF ATTENDING TO RETURN ATTENTION: *enunciative asymmetry does not excuse the obligation to maintain a symmetry of attention between speakers and listeners (even if this symmetry is diluted according to the number of participants).* What John Beck and Thomas Davenport state as a law of marketing (but which was invalidated a long time ago with the industrialization of our media apparatuses) fully applies in the classroom: 'if you want to get any attention, you've got to give attention'.[8] Masterly speech will be better accepted the more the teacher endeavours to be sensitive to the feedback he can read on the faces of his listeners (surprised looks, frowns, sighs, yawns). Even if this feedback is more difficult to grasp and interpret in a lecture hall of five hundred students than in the intimacy of an Oxford tutorial, the work of any discourser also consists in cultivating what Michael Goldhaber called an *'illusory attention* [. . .] that helps create an apparent equality of attention'.[9] The advantage of 'personalized' teaching situations, like those permitted by Oxford's traditions (and wealth), comes from the fact that 'to get a person to pay attention to your information, the information has to be about that person'.[10] The illusion that the teacher must aim at producing is rooted in the ideally symmetrical model of conversation: 'turning' to each listener as though the words were personally addressed to them.

THE NECESSITY OF AN EMOTIONAL CONNECTION: *inasmuch as a certain affective communion is the indispensable substrate of any communication, it is first of all on an emotional level that teachers must connect with their students.* When she makes herself attentive to the variations of attention that can be observed in her students, the teacher should not only try to identify what they do not understand: above all, she should endeavour to measure the emotional reactions provoked by the words exchanged, so as to perform the delicate work of emotional harmonization at the heart of any situation of joint attention. As was so well brought to light by Gilbert Simondon,[11] our emotions express the state of the transindividual relation that unites us with our environment: they serve as a thermometer for measuring the state of our attentional ecosystem. Contrary to the cliché which idealizes the teacher, particularly at higher levels, as a paragon of rationality, and contrary to the method of competitive selection which, in French establishments, favours disciplined knowledge without granting the least pertinence to emotional sensitivity, the fate of teaching is in play at a more fundamental level than that of information transmission and reasoning: in the ability of each participant to know how to pay attention to their affects, which are always necessarily shared since they emanate from the relations established between the preindividual portions of their personalities. To establish an environment favourable to the dynamics of joint attention, the teacher must, therefore, learn to feel, recognize and modulate the (harmonious and dissonant) affective resonances structuring the classroom. This necessarily means, however, that they will have to constantly readjust not only the content, but also the methods of their teaching.

From which we derive the third principle, relating to a NECESSITY FOR INVENTION: *the classroom only offers an ecosystem supportive of joint attention if it is the place of a process of collective invention in action.* It is not only at the level of the university that we should speak of 'teacher-researchers'. Even if the contents of a course in elementary geometry has, apparently, been fixed since Euclid, what is done in the classroom has a lot less to do with 'transmission' (modelled on the baton passed from hand to hand by relay runners) than with continual reinterpretation: even if the formulation of the theorems has hardly changed, in every group each learner comes to it with singular knowledge, imagination, sensitivity and attitude. Paying attention to their return attention and their emotional disposition will therefore lead every teacher to look for words, images, analogies, and new examples so as to help each of them grasp it as best they can. In most subjects – literature, philosophy, human sciences, of course, but certainly biology and physics as well – this continual reinvention of the methods of presenting knowledge is intimately connected with a renewal of their content: describing matter in terms of wave/particle duality does not pass on the same baton as describing it in the Newtonian imagery of billiard balls or in the Cartesian vocabulary of vortexes.

Conceiving the classroom, at every level, as an attentional ecosystem effects a convergence of the etymologies of invention (*in-venire*) and attention (*ad-tendere*) into the same GROWTH OF OUR FACULTY FOR NOTICING. The slightly silly cliché that defines love by the fact of looking together in the same direction may be recycled as we imagine – inextricably joined – teaching and research as *processes aiming at making viewpoints converge on the discovery of remarkable, and until then unanticipated, facts.* In a classroom we learn to look where the other is looking – so that we may come to notice aspects that we had not yet ourselves caught sight of.

In the course and writings that Husserl dedicated to the phenom-enology of attention, he discusses at length the theory of Carl Stumpf (1843–1936) which placed a 'pleasure taken in noticing' (*Lust am Bemerken*) at the heart of its definition of attention. While Husserl rejects the idea that every act of attention aims at pleasure, he seems, however, to take up the central importance, emphasized by the German language, of the effort made towards *noticing* (*bemerken*) at the heart of attention (*Aufmerksamkeit*).[12] The essence of attention consists in a labour undertaken to augment our ability to notice that which is noticeable in what is in sight (or in another sense). It is this ability to notice what is there – which is important but which we have until then neglected – that Joseph Jacotot and Jacques Rancière have made into the resource of a pedagogy directed towards intellectual emancipation. The essential function of their (potentially ignorant) master is not to explain contents, but to train the pupils' attention, whether that be through a demand made on their will or through the stimulation of their desire.[13] It is towards 'a habit of, and a pleasure taken in, noticing' that every teaching experience should tend.

Learning to look there where the other is looking does not only describe, however, the labour of the learner who is invited to follow the look of the teacher, but also the task of the latter, to the extent that she knows how to draw on the surprises, difficulties, misunder-standings and flashes of insight coming from her students to extend, clarify, deepen, or complicate her own understanding of the problem. On both sides, we 'invent': we find a new path to 'arrive in' (*in-venir*) an unexpected landscape (even if this is only a new way of looking at a place that we thought was familiar). On both sides, this invention happens through an effort to 'tend towards' (*ad-tendere*) something new: the students are called to extend [*tendre*] their look towards what their teacher is showing them, while the teacher should take the opportunity provided by their resistance to attempt [*tender*] to align her look with theirs, gaining in this way a means of extending her own understanding of the subject. So, the object of a lesson is not so much a datum to be transmitted (a theorem, piece of knowledge, a figure understood 'in scalar form'), but, taking up the terms in which Paul Valéry defined attention, a 'direction', an 'effort of prolonga-tion, of continuity, in clarity', to be conceived 'in vectorial mode' (an arrow).[14] It is a question of seeing more 'clearly' what there is to be seen, but which we did not see – that which we come to by sharing our points of view: we see *better* because we endeavour to see *with*.

Being attentive to what the other pays attention to – a minimal definition of joint attention – naturally leads, therefore, to *inventing together*. Even if the micro-community engaged in this activity is in no way constituted of equals (from the point of view of the knowledge accumulated by each as well as that of institutional status), it is always this singular assembly of individuals that reinvents a distinctive approach to communal knowledge, not without introducing on each occasion some slight innovations. As much as it is viewed in terms of 'a master' facing 'students', the classroom should be seen in terms of a group of researchers in the process of inventing a new way of making sense of a sphere of knowledge – a group in which it is the collective attentional ecosystem, more than the teacher, that is in the positon of agency.

Even though his discourse is much more general than teaching situations and joint attention, Bernard Aspe admirably weaves together the different principles evoked above (reciprocity, affective harmonization, improvisation) in the description he gives of the 'transindividual' as understood by Gilbert Simondon:

> It is only in a community that emotion can take place as such. And the fact that it can take place signifies that it can be extended in an *action* on the world. Emotion does not call for an outpouring, but an overturning of individuated structures, which can only be performed communally. [. . .] The transindividual relation passes through individuals, incorporating them into a reality that is larger than them: a system of resonance. Before individuals, there is the preindividual; but beyond, there is the system of resonance. It is when it gives rise to a particular consistence that the transindividual relation configures itself as it gives birth to this new being: the group of interiority, or the *transindividual collective*. This can be understood as a 'unified system of reciprocal beings', and it is this reciprocity that enables the resonance effect. [. . .] The paradigm of the transindividual collective for Simondon is the group of researchers or rather inventors – because it is in invention that the transindividual relation best reveals its fecundity.[15]

The Promise and Limits of MOOCs

It is more important than ever to reflect on the mode of existence and the attentional ecosystem of the very particular transindividual community that inhabits the classroom. France has discovered rather late a great wave of innovation which, with the onslaught of free courses offered online to tens of thousands (and potentially millions) of participants under the title of MOOCs (massive open online courses), is currently overturning the world of education at a planetary level.

A survey of a hundred MOOCs published in 2013 by *The Chronical of Higher Education* found that a professor will spend a hundred hours preparing the videos, web pages, interactive exercises and multiple choice questions that are put online to provide net users with what she considers to be the essential contents of her course. She then spends around eight hours per week on an online platform where she reads the participants' messages, responds to some of their questions and makes some clarifications, corrections or provides additional information. On average, there is just one assistant to help her with her teaching duties – even when 33,000 students signed up to a course of this kind, 2,600 of whom completed it with a satisfactory mark. Seventy-four per cent of teachers used automatic procedures to assign marks (which 97 per cent of them found to be relatively reliable), 34 per cent used a system which encouraged participants to correct and mark their work among themselves (with the same level of assurance). Even though a third of the professors questioned were originally sceptical about online courses, more than 90 per cent said they were (relatively) 'enthusiastic' at the end of the experience. Despite these rapturous figures, a little more than a half do not believe their MOOC to be as academically rigorous as the version of their course given in person.[16]

The promise of MOOCs shines out. You no longer need to go to Harvard or Oxford to receive a top level education: once Bruno Latour at Sciences Po in Paris or MIT professors are offering their courses free-access in the form of MOOCs, the poorest student in Dakar or Mumbai can benefit from teaching that has until now been reserved for the most privileged sections of the global elites. All of us, throughout our lives, can educate ourselves from the best sources, creating the cocktail of courses that best suits us, without having to worry about registration fees, geographical location, timetable, academic prerequisites or disciplinary barriers. Ultimately, MOOCs shimmer with the light of what could be a truly democratised education on a global scale – and of course, we should be delighted by this 'thrilling' prospect.

We may also be delighted to see MOOCs give rise – by the very fact of their deterritorialization – to forms of connectivity, reciprocity, peer-to-peer exchange and alternative evaluation practices which until now had only featured in the marginal experiments typical of the mutual school [*l'école mutuelle*].[17] Even if the primary motivation is financial, having students mark each other's work has its own pedagogical virtue, as it alternates the positions of teacher and learner. Both through the opening of these courses to whoever is interested and through the horizontal exchanges they encourage – since, when they live in the same town, students tend to get together informally to prepare for exams together – we can also see a liberation from the constraints that still too often imprison studies (in France and the United Kingdom) in frontal and strictly hierarchical set ups and in overly narrow and hermetically sealed disciplines.

Finally, we can easily imagine the impressive economies of scale that administrators and governments hope to achieve from MOOCs. After several decades of dramatic rises in enrolment fees – which have made North American student debt the next financial bubble threatening the global economy – and in an era in which states are desperately trying to reduce their public spending, MOOCs seem to proclaim the ideal solution for reducing the 'unsustainable' proportion of our household and communal budgets taken up by education. Even if the vast majority of students hardly go beyond the first two or three lessons, being able to enrol 33,000 students and pass 2,600 of them with a satisfactory grade, while only paying for a single professor and a single assistant, verges on an economic miracle.

Courses by correspondence have of course been around since the end of the nineteenth century, and teaching through the television and radio for several decades – without a revolution in the field of education, as we have not failed to proclaim on each occasion. It would nevertheless be absurd (and sad) not to assess the perspectives opened by the development of MOOCs. Something new is being set up, which warrants close attention and better organization. As was rightly highlighted by Christopher Newfield over the course of the articles collected on the site he has dedicated to this question,[18] it would nevertheless be extremely dangerous to see here *the* solution to the current problems associated with financing higher education.

You can imagine the anxiety the surge of MOOCs must be producing in teachers hoping to defend their corporatist interests. It is doubtless not by chance that the gain in momentum of online teaching has been accompanied in the United States by an unprecedented erosion in the appointment of tenured positions. The administrator's ideal economic model would ring-fence a few large outlays (more than 50,000 dollars) to enable an eminent professor to put together a high-level course, destined for distribution to hundreds of thousands of students – a course where the work of 'servicing' relations with students is undertaken by a small army of deputies (all duly equipped with a doctorate) working without job security, who are saved from poverty by being allowed to look after the course discussion list, respond to emails and correct homework by hand (and by assembly line), since, in certain subjects at least, the attention of a human marker is more highly valued than automated processing or peer-to-peer evaluation.[19]

Apart from the multiple gains promised by the emergence of MOOCs, a reflection on attention ecology may nevertheless help to articulate more precisely what is lost when teaching passes from the collective classroom to a personal screen. From the point of view of the economic history of attentional apparatuses, MOOCs are situated in direct line with the development of the mass media. A series of technological innovations enabling advantage to be taken from an asymmetry swapping dead attention (videos, texts, documents, online questionnaires) for live attention (the students'), with an over-economy of scale that is synonymous with huge profits (as we saw in the second chapter) thrown into the bargain. Even if the courses remain free (open), which will certainly not be the case generally, new models of exploitation, exemplified by Google, enable the monetization of the attention of a net user that has been invested in a free-access site, according to the logic already mentioned where, in the end, if a service is offered to me for free, it is because I am myself the truly valuable merchandise.

If more than half of MOOC teachers recognize, despite their 'enthusiasm', that their online teaching is less 'academically rigorous' than the version given in person, this is doubtless due, at least in part, to the inertia of habit and a corporatist reflex – it is difficult to ignore the extent to which this innovation weakens the status of the universities. But it is perhaps also because they sense more or less clearly the extent to which the sharing of presential attention represents an essential dimension of the pedagogical experience. Once we are submerged in technologies which make information available at a click in a fraction of a second, the proficiency training taking place in our educational institutions can no longer be organized around the transmission of content. Of course, as Nicholas Carr rightly notes, memorization of content is in no way obsolete in itself: it is an integral part of the mental processes structuring our orientation in the world, and no one could simply externalize their memory onto a hard drive or into a cloud or search engine connected to the internet without paralysing the operation of their intelligence.[20]

While instruction may bear on contents, a portion of which will always call for a certain effort of familiarization, meaning that they are committed to memory, the essential aim is now predominantly *showing how to research*. And because the formalization of methodological rules is always infinitely inferior to the practices it seeks to summarize, inculcation through example and intuitive imitation of research gestures remains the most appropriate way of transmitting the most precious expertise required by a human life. From which comes a first MAXIM OF GESTURAL IMITATION: *the best way of showing another how to research is still to research together.*

As we have just seen, teaching's essential task consists in heightening the ability to notice what is remarkable and important in what we are looking at (but which we cannot see alone). If, faced with a text, a chemistry experiment, or a psychological or sociological observation the teacher indicates in advance what should be noted, the students will perhaps acquire a better understanding of the object under consideration – but they will not learn to look more attentively, which is to say to notice (*bemerken*) autonomously what warrants being retained in a sensory datum. The instruction made possible by a pedagogical situation teaches us how to research for ourselves, as we watch and imitate a teacher researching in front of, and along with, us – 'for real', since pretending to look for something that we have already found usually only makes for an absurd and ridiculous parody. In short, it is *by making authentic research gestures* that participants in the pedagogical interaction can raise it to its full potential.[21]

It is this 'researching-together' that is described in the quotation from Bernard Aspe summarizing Gilbert Simondon's theses on the 'transindividual community', whose paradigm was precisely 'the group of researchers or rather inventors – because it is in invention that the transindividual relation best reveals its fecundity'. This relation, he clarifies, 'passes through individuals, incorporating them into a reality that is larger than them: a system of resonance'. It is neither the teacher-researcher nor the students alone researching in a classroom, but the ensemble that they form through the confrontations and exchanges between the knowledge and the ignorance of each of them, through the interlacings, the mutual enrichments, the convergences and the divergences characterizing their plural interacting attention. It is by researching together that they form 'a unified system of reciprocal beings', and 'it is this reciprocity that enables the resonance effect'.

But this resonance effect can only be realized in the synchrony necessary to the correct working of affective harmonization and collective improvisation. From which comes a second MAXIM OF CORPORAL PRESENCE: *only presential interaction directly uniting resonant bodies can optimize pedagogical practice.* We saw why in the preceding paragraphs: in the same way that email disfigures the subtlety of the interpersonal modifications that come about in face-to-face conversation, research gestures are reduced to caricatures of themselves when one tries to distribute them preserved in videos, theoretical formalizations or methodological principles.

Sensory immersion in a community of interacting bodies represents an indispensable experience for the constitution of subjectivity. Only this enables us to take charge of the affective dimension of our relationships with others: as Bernard Aspe further highlighted, 'it is only in a community that emotion can take place as such. And the fact that it can take place signifies that it can be extended in an *action* on the world.' Contrary to what is often asserted, it is probably not video games that make otherwise calm and disciplined boys commit school massacres, but rather their isolation behind screens, without this inimitable (and indispensable) form of communion that is bodily communication.

The best MOOCs may, therefore, provide a commendable service: if they are well put together, they may contribute to giving certain kinds of knowledge and gesture an absolutely new and very welcome distribution. They cannot, however, *substitute* for presential teaching, any more than a video of a pizza (even high-definition) can substitute for a real pizza in the eyes of a hungry person. As well as information and research methods, we all hunger for irreplaceable affective resonances that only an ecosystem of reciprocal attention experienced in the immediacy of co-presence can bring.

In reality, the restriction imposed by this demand for synchronization and immediacy is not so much of a spatial order – since here too, we might imagine a very near future in which telesthetic apparatuses make the presence of a distant partner 'almost immediate' – than a limit pertaining to the number of subjects implied in the transindividual community communicating through effects of resonance. So long as it takes place in good technological conditions, a teleconference with three people sitting at their desks doubtless provides a more convivial attention ecosystem than the physical co-presence of a teacher facing five hundred students in a lecture hall under sterile flourescent light. From which comes a third MAXIM OF SIZE APPROPRIATENESS: *every kind of teaching determines an upper size-limit for a convivial environment, beyond which it becomes impossible to constitute a 'unified system of reciprocal beings'.*

With their current average of 33,000 registrations and 2,600 students passing the course, the MOOCs studied in 2012 are a long way beyond this size-limit – however excellent the material uploaded by the professor may be, and however dedicated to their task the poor assistant responsible for managing interaction with other participants may be. We may certainly hope that effects of resonance make sub-groups of students exchanging emails or meeting regularly in a café into 'unified systems of reciprocal beings'. But the wealth of interaction made possible by daily or weekly meetings bringing together fifteen or so participants in a classroom will have been sacrificed by the institution. If the latter is serious enough about its didactic calling to multiply the number of assistant posts and give them the concrete means to undertake research with groups of students limited to an appropriate size, *alongside* the courses put online by eminent professors, then so much the better! But in this case, we are talking about a system that is almost as expensive as current setups – and, as soon as only a few teachers are authorized to distribute their conception of their discipline to several tens of thousands of anonymous consumers, in accordance with a process of Taylorization reproducing in people's spirits the homogenization undergone by manufactured goods over the last two hundred years, then we will have sacrificed pluralism, diversity, and therefore the dynamism of the research.

Without in any way condemning MOOCs, a consideration sensitive to attention ecology leads us to put the promises of budgetary economy into perspective, and above all to situate them in a logic of expanding teaching supply, rather than a logic of contracting pedagogical services. MOOCs certainly represent a thrilling opportunity to distribute documents and procedures more broadly than ever, helping higher education to penetrate regions and layers of the global population that did not previously have access to them. But, far from replacing functions currently ascribed to teachers, they instead call for the multiplication of convivial small-size ecosystems, within which more humans may learn – in relations of reciprocity – to research together, to improvise individual and collective gestures of invention, to train their attention and to structure their subjectivity.

The Live Performance

Even if some of my university colleagues would prefer not to admit it, it is perhaps in the fields of the performing arts and sporting performance that we may locate the main difference between MOOCs and the classroom experience. Why do we brave the cold, the heat, the crowds, the often uncomfortable seats, the often sub-standard acoustic and visibility conditions, sometimes paying a lot of money, to go and listen to music at a concert or watch matches in a stadium which are available to us at home for free, with the quality provided by our stereo or high-definition screen?

I will respond with the help of four basic principles rooted in the analysis of joint attention. The first is the FASCINATION OF GESTURAL SUSPENSE: *nothing excites our attention more than experiencing a gesture live as it is happening.* If sport is so enthralling for some of us – to the great displeasure of the rationalist censors who denigrate as a distraction the concentration of our attention on twenty players chasing after a ball to send it between two posts – it is because it remains one of the rare spheres in which we can witness irreversible gestures in real time. Whatever the role played by preparation and the monotonous repetition of the same bodily gestures over the course of thousands of hours of training, performance is always a moment in which the gesture must exceed all the efforts of programming that made it possible. Because the body's abilities are pushed to the extreme without our knowing when it will have gone too far (as in athletics), because it is not possible to predict an opponent's reactions (as in tennis), because collective gestures are coordinated in real time, relying on the intuition of collaborators (as in football), sports fascinate our attention as they stage our relationship with time. Their suspense comes from the risk taken in an attempt at exceptional performance surrendered to the context of an irreversible temporality – that we otherwise only encounter in the traumatic episodes of accident, illness or the death of a loved one.

Theatrical, musical and dance performances also draw some of their force from this performative dimension. The risk of forgetting a line, hitting a wrong note, or falling, establishes a subtext of tension that intensifies the artist's and the spectator's attention: before any aesthetic value, the simple fact of having maintained the role of the performer without failing is always already something of an exploit. The beauty of a live performance comes (among other things) from the unpredictable – and so improvisational – element characteristic of every gesture, inasmuch as it always exceeds or falls a little short of its programming. In the same way, a teacher always experiences a touch of stage fright before entering the classroom: and you can bet that the best performers are those who are ready to take the most risks, who manage to capture better the attention of their students.

This gestural suspense, however, does not only come from a relation to time. If we stopped there, watching a match, listening to a concert or following a course live on the television at home would be as fascinating as being present in the stadium or the audience. But, the intensity of a live performance does not only come from this *live* temporality, but also from the sharing of the same space which puts spectators in the localized presence of the performers. To take

101

up the distinction suggested by Gabriel Tarde at the end of the nine-teenth century, while the collective attention characteristic of media apparatuses, where all members read the same newspaper or listen to the same radio broadcast without directly interacting with each other, synchronizes the reactions of a 'public', the joint attention charac-teristic of live performances brings about 'CROWD' EFFECTS, as it encourages *unpredictable contagions of mood that spread directly from a spectator to his neighbours.*

As well as being immersed in a story, the theatre or dance specta-tor is plunged into a collective body where, as Bernard Aspe was just saying, 'the transindividual relation passes through individuals, incorporating them into a reality that is larger than them: a system of resonance'. When a laugh starts up at the back of the room, inducing hilarity through a waterfall effect, a comic tonality which had gone unnoticed the previous evening will be actualized for the whole of that day's performance; when a fan applauds at the end of the first saxophone solo, encouraging his neighbours to express their appreciation, the whole of the rest of the concert will be energised. Even when television channels introduce canned laughter to mark the punchlines of their comedies, the viewer's experience is one of individual attention, while the experience of a live performance belongs to joint attention: everyone orientates what they listen to, where they look and their reactions according to the orientation of the listening, look and reactions of the other spectators. The thrill peculiar to the experience of the theatre or stadium comes at least in part from the resonances that immersion in a crowd makes resonate in me – which is celebrated symbolically in the joyful elation of the Mexican wave.

The relation to space is nevertheless more complex than the simple immersion in a group of resonant bodies. The attentional ecosystem of the theatre and the stadium is in fact structured by the centrality of the performers, on which the concentration of gazes bestows an aura of exception. The inside of this space is therefore organized around a PROXIMITY STATUS: *the closer to the performer we find ourselves, the more our attention tends to be energized (above all if they are also a media star).* Seeing a close-up of a tennis star or an actress honoured with an Oscar on the television is not particularly stimulating – our screens are constantly saturated with this. The prospect of finding ourselves two (even ten or twenty) metres from her is enough to make us brave bad weather, traffic jams and queues. This attention is all emotion: we cannot hope to 'learn' anything from it, but we cannot stop our heart from beating faster and harder.

As was rightly noted by Isabelle Barbéris and Martial Poirson, 'the attention economy impacts on performances, which increasingly involve an aesthetic of astonishment and an overloading of effects', attesting to the integration of live performance into the larger sphere of 'media society'.[22] A particularly noticeable effect of this integration is evident in the way in which the ecosystem of the stage comes to be structured by the mediatized constitution of 'prominence', to take up the term Georg Franck uses to indicate the summit of fame in the attentional asymmetry brought about by the mass media. Every stage performance has a sacred dimension, no doubt because of the symbolic death that performers risk if their gesture (which for artists and sportsmen is intrinsically fragile) does not measure up to expectations. As Edgar Morin remarked as early as 1950,[23] the media prominence which makes the stars' aura shine gives the impression that a living god is descending to Earth into the sacred space of the stage or the stadium, before our bedazzled eyes, within our view, sometimes our reach, even (supreme blessing) close enough for an autograph.

It is to frustrate the effects of this aura which augment, sanctify and deify the occupants of the stage – creating an intimidating and paralysing disproportion with the obscure anonymous people making up the audience – that Olivier Bosson has suggested the maxim *1:1 scale* [*l'échelle 1:1*].

This maxim indicates the relationship that we want to establish with the public: we want to be at the same scale as them. [. . .] At scale 1, you maintain a certain continuity in relationships. In other words 1:1 is a magic formula for warding off the aura that quickly surrounds people on the stage, which shatters the relationship, making it exaggeratedly asymmetrical [. . .]. By approaching these places at a 1:1 scale (with our maxim, our tool), you ask yourself on each occasion about the auras that are at work, the codes, the playacting, the 1,000 biases which mean that where you should see a person, you don't see them, or hardly, as though they were more or less absent. We are going to try to crack these codes, to see them for what they are, for their artifice. And as a by-product, we'll see people, beings, and objects too in their clear existence. We will see the two side by side, simultaneously. In short, 1:1 has to do with presence, itself being partly connected with sincerity and, even more, with the places where we locate sincerity.[24]

Reacting against a certain (mediatized, capitalist) attention economy which disproportionately increases the visibility of certain prominent beings through the mechanical concentration of an enormous quantity of attention, 1:1 scale endeavours to establish an attention ecology which maintains 'a certain continuity in relationships' and which clears a privileged space of sincerity and authenticity. But an ecology of this kind is in a certain sense inherent in the basic coordinates of the live performance. Despite all the media glamour that deifies the status of stars, a theatre stage, a rock club or a basketball court allow us to see bodies, in all of their vulnerability and frailty. However doped the athlete, however self-important the star, there is a certain form of 'sincerity' established by bodily proximity. The peculiar intensity of encountering a celebrity in the street or on the stage comes precisely from the fact that we discover them in their human dimensions, at the scale of their biological body, through the aura of their media exaltation (in which they nevertheless continue to glow in our bedazzled eyes).

A fourth and final principle to help us understand the peculiar properties of the attention ecosystem that make the live performance attractive. The ADVANTAGE OF 1:1 SCALE *allows us to benefit simultaneously from the attentional asymmetries established by the media apparatuses, and to resize them to the scale of bodily presence in a situation of proximity.*

After having observed Earth from Saturn to understand the global flows of collective attention, after having analysed how the asymmetries of the capitalist attention economy inflate some of us beyond all human size, the study of attention in the present brings us back to a 1:1 scale. In order to construct itself, our subjectivity needs the sensitive proximity of attentive bodies experienced in physical presence: it is in intimate relation with their objects of attention, their emotional tones, their attractions and their repulsions – in that they traverse us and inhabit us through the effects of affective resonance – that we structure, orientate and sustain our personality. The attentional ecosystems offered by situations of dialogue, teaching or live performance owe their richness, among other things, to the very peculiar intensity that comes from setups establishing presence. Witnessing a gesture as it is happening in the fragility of its necessary improvisation, strengthening our affects thanks to crowd effects that carry what we feel beyond what we know, sensing the shine of the auratic stature of a performer while encountering them in the continuity of 1:1 scale – all of that, which contributes to the richness of conversation, of the classroom or theatre, is lost when we try to distribute its dried out skeleton in the form of MOOCs or televised theatre.

The joint attention described in this chapter establishes effects of PRESENTIAL ENTHRALMENT which *weave our affectivity through the inter-fertilization of crossed attention communicating in a relation of immediate bodily presence.* This presential enthralment is

104

different in nature to the media enthralment that channels our collective attention, since it takes shape at a scale that is necessarily limited by the number of participants. This is why MOOCs will help to supplement presential teaching without substituting for it. This is why, as our online communications increase, we must learn to reconstitute convivial spaces of presential attention – in the classroom, in the computer room, in the theatre, at the museum, at the café, in cultural and religious places. We are hopelessly in need of vaults [voûtes][25] where we can resonate and reason together: it is for us to protect and invent those which will help us to think and act better together, and be more present to ourselves as we harmonize better with the attention of others. Our most urgent need may be to RE-VAULT!

— 5 —

THE MICRO-POLITICS
OF ATTENTION

From the age of nine months, the human subject is not only attentive to the objects that appear in its sensory field: above all, it is attentive *with other humans* that are attentive around it. Speaking of 'joint' [*conjointe*] attention evokes associations with marriage, which is not so ridiculous since we find ourselves to be very intimately united with the people with whom we share the same objects of attention – with whom 'we look in the same direction'.

Joint attention connects us. It does so through the play of surfaces, whose lustre attracts the gaze of some, which in turn attracts the gaze of others. But it also connects us more deeply: it is because the attention of others touches our 'innermost being' that we are so sensitive to its slightest variations. What is at stake with these simultaneously superficial and profound connections? How is it that we are only 'human' to the extent that we can do justice to them? In what way do we risk being trapped by them, if we do not know how to momentarily suspend their hold? What forms of detachment are the essential corollary to everything that connects us to one another?

Responding to these questions means reconsidering our social relationships from the perspective of the different attention ecosystems in which they participate. This will provide an opportunity to clarify how attention and ecology are intimately connected – and to try to redefine each of them on the basis of their reciprocal relations.

The War of the Ecologies

It is less and less tenable to conjugate ecology in the singular – as though everyone claiming to 'pay attention to the environment' were

106

paddling in the same direction. More and more disputes pit ecologists against one another – not only because their small groupings show strong tendencies towards division and sectarian drift, but also, more fundamentally, because there are today (at least) two very different ways in which you may claim to be ecologically minded.

For MANAGERIAL ECOLOGY, environmental concerns amount to *economizing our resources so as to sustainably reproduce the ways of life that we have enjoyed since the take-off of industrial development*. The green economy, sustainable development, carbon tax, compensation, incentives and markets for trading in the right to pollute are foremost in the arsenal put forward for 'saving the planet', which is generally seen from above (or observed from Saturn), in terms of statistics, flows, programmes, plans and regulations.[1] For RADICAL (OR DEEP) ECOLOGY, on the other hand, it is only starting from concrete collective alternatives that other forms of life will emerge – out of the political activism of grassroots organizations (organized from the bottom up) – such that we may *revaluate the relationships that connect us to one another and to our environment, which implies fighting against our current addiction to the fetishes of consumer growth*. So, degradation, standardization, inequality, eco-fascism and the patenting of organisms are all condemned – while occupation movements, slow movements, local-sourcing movements, the commons and/or degrowth movements are promoted.

Besides the fact that they consider environmental questions either statistically from above or from the roots of collective action, these two great currents are opposed on the status of the economy. For the managers, the (orthodox, capitalist, neoliberal) economy constitutes an insurmountable frame of reference, at least in the medium term, for conceiving and promoting realistic measures likely to bring the material prosperity initiated by the modernization of Western societies at the end of the eighteenth century to the whole of humanity. For the radicals, the concepts, percepts, and the affects generated in the framework of the capitalist economy constitute the primary cause of the not only unsustainable, but above all undesirable, character of a means of development which results in the 'manufacturing of unhappiness' [*fabrique de l'infélicité*].[2]

Even if they occasionally agree on certain recommendations (against the current wastage of energy resources, against climate-change denial, or nuclear insanity), each current 'pays attention' to things that are actually quite different. An emblematic example of the opposition between the attentional regimes constituted by each of them is provided by the Jardin des Lentillères, established on the edge of the Tanneries squat in

107

Dijon. Since 2010, a heterogeneous association of young radicals and gardening-loving retirees have occupied a vast wasteland of the Dijon conglomeration, whose inhabitants have been kept informed over the past fifteen years about a series of redevelopment projects that have never come to fruition (a TGV station, a private hospital, and, most recently, a green neighbourhood). A collective formed, the Pot'Col'Le, to plant and cultivate an urban market garden. Between the Tanneries and the Lentillères, an entire social existence was transplanted to the site, with squatters reoccupying some of the abandoned dwellings, a concert area, a centre of political resources, meeting places, a migrant and asylum-seeker refuge, and the distribution of freely priced vegetables from the beds of the collective garden.

Even if, as I write these lines, the authorities have not (yet) used force to expel the occupants of the Lentillères, they have done their best to throw a spanner in the works (destroying still inhabitable houses, digging huge holes to make the terrain uncultivable) – all in the name of what is destined to be a green project, christened, not without irony, 'Jardin de Maraîchers' [*Market Garden*], and pushed by a town council that is quick to show off its ecological leanings. The eminent Parisian architect-urbanist Nicolas Michelin, head of the agency ANMA, who was awarded the project by the town council, also claims to be proud to 'rely on strong ecological convictions: urban projects inspired by the spirit of the place, specifically designed for the context, bespoke buildings, and a constant desire to use natural energy'.[3]

This war between ecologies brings two very different attention ecosystems face-to-face. The attention of the urbanist and the town council who awarded him the project is focused on plans, models, flow calculations, anticipated returns on investment. It is starting from these basic parameters, and within their constraints, that green spaces, places for socializing, or the placement of solar panels are conceived. The territory is analysed from above, it is arranged in the light of abstract concepts ensuring that it is articulated according to an economic reality determined by financial profitability – and this is done on the basis of a reduction in scale, necessary for the architect and urbanist, which translates a metre of the real world into a few millimetres of paper (or screen).

The attention of the occupiers is by no means devoid of abstract analyses, also based in overarching concerns – it is 'globally' minded since it turns on questions at a planetary scale, like climate imbalance. In their promotion of urban gardens, they are trying to inscribe this place in an alternative economy of local flows, and slow, convivial

108

and singular methods of production. But, above all, their attention is based in proximate collective practices, rooted in the materiality and the lived history of a territory, woven from the concrete invention of alternative social bonds. We are here at 1:1 scale. Their attention is 'radical' because it is rooted in the vegetables and the social relations that they cultivate from day to day.

The contrast between these two forms of attention towards ecology is clear to see in the recontextualization of the declarations of the green architect undertaken by the radicals of the Pot'Col'Le in a publication introducing their action:

> This little local paper, published at irregular intervals, is titled *The Spirit of the Place*. The expression does not come from us, but from the urbanist Nicolas Michelin, who, for several years has been planning the destruction of this neighbourhood. In rousing tones, he asserts that: 'The spirit of the place is the impression, the air, the atmosphere . . . [. . .] We must, before building, immerse ourselves in what exists – in the history – of people. This is the foundation of our urbanist occupation. I do not understand people who invent complex systems without considering the existent' (*Le Journal du Palais, 26 September–2 October, 2011*). We are the existent, an existent participating in the life of this neighbourhood that we have renamed Lentillères. We will not be fooled by their fine words, and we will defend everything that we have built here, far from their sterile and pre-fabricated urbanist concepts.[4]

Aligning yourself with an 'attention ecology' (still to come) is therefore deceptive so long as you have not clarified which ecology you are talking about. More than a simple question of scale, what separates the two forms of ecology, demonstrated exaggeratedly by this example from Dijon, is the *rooting of an environmental sensitivity in social practices inventing concrete alternatives to the ravages of capitalism* – in the name of which we would do well to state the PRIMACY OF ROOTED ATTENTION. As a good manager, concerned with sustainability, the urbanist is of course right to pay attention to the environmental impact of the projects he designs. We may be grateful to him, and the show of strength of a few radical activists should not condemn his work. When a conflict breaks out between a distant architects' office, duly integrated into the global game of the capitalist marketplace, and a grassroots collective struggling to defend or establish an alternative sociality, heterogeneous to this game – as is the case here, but also with certain dam projects and in the struggles of native populations – the primacy of rooted attention encourages us to invest *a priori* a higher degree of trust in the radicals than in the managers.

This follows from the very nature of the presential attention analysed in the preceding chapter, since the collectives conducting radical ecology's struggles on the ground remain extremely close to the principles of organizational reciprocity, emotional connection and improvisation that characterize joint attention. In closer harmony with their territory and each other, they often embody better than anyone the force that comes from human subjectivities enriching their intelligence through the interweaving of their attention. It is to the conditions and difficulties of the embodiment of this force of joint attention that the rest of this chapter is dedicated.

Before continuing, we should nevertheless avoid some of the pitfalls of this 'war of ecologies'. The worst would be to oppose them monolithically and to demand that we take sides *for* one and *against* the other, as though they were in a static conflict. Along with the primacy of rooted attention, we should assert the DYNAMIC COMPLEMENTARITY OF MANAGEMENT AND RADICALITY: through the same conflicts that set them against each other, *the radicals and the managers together extend the boundaries of our collective attention with respect to ecological questions.* The 'defenders' [*zadistes*] who occupy the zones for development [*zones d'aménagement différé (ZAD)*] by setting up zones for defence [*zones à défendre*] – as in the famous example of the land intended for the construction of an airport at Notre-Dame-des-Landes, near Nantes – push against productivist inertia, which is at once essential to a radical reorientation of our modes of development, and yet profoundly insufficient given the scale of the problems that we face. It is thanks to the pressure of radicals that managers become translators (who are themselves also essential), spreading 'best practices' – concretely, even if slowly and in watered down form – through the (political, economic, legal) institutions that govern our collective behaviour and constitute an absolutely inescapable level of mediation. As we will see at the end of this chapter, it is in the *dynamic articulation* (rather than the static opposition) of the managerial and the radical that we must seek a possible corrective to our current erring.

Attention as Care

From the start of this work, an important dimension of attention has been almost completely overlooked – the very one that is expressed by the substantive when it becomes an exclamation: *Attention!* A bar-room ethology may see in this use of the word the vestige of its most elementary signification. Maybe, we were originally only attentive to a phenomenon because we thought we had something to fear. *Caute!*, *Cuidado!*, *Achtung!*, *Watch Out!*, *Sta attento!*, *Fais attention!*, such would be the first recommendations of a good sense, a prudence and an intelligence whose goal was maximizing our persistence in being by helping us to avoid for as long as possible the potential causes of our destruction. The primary motivation and instinct of joint attention would be found in a survival reflex: if my interlocutor diverts his eyes to look at something behind me, it is perhaps because he has just noticed a danger – and I had better turn around straight away to look in the same direction. No love to be found here, but just generation upon generation of natural selection by the cruel law of survival of the most prudent, in a world of prey and predator.

A properly conceived Darwinism would not exclude this survival instinct leading to a transindividual solidarity rooted in ASSOCIATIVE VIGILANCE: *in facing the external dangers threatening our life and well-being, we are better equipped, stronger, and more prudent as a group than we are alone.* Four, six, eight, or ten eyes are better than two for keeping track of dangers in all directions at once. Each of us will be better protected if we are 'attentive together' – to use a slogan that stinks of the current security hysteria.[5]

Despite its survivalist character, this situation provides us with a point of departure for examining five forms of joint attention. At the same time that each anticipates a different kind of danger, these five forms together suggest five ways of binding attention and ecology to one another – once the latter is understood to relate to an effort to protect the living conditions that are indispensable to our well-being. This brief overview will take us from external dangers to increasingly internal (even intimate) dangers, while providing us with an opportunity to situate attention ecology in the context of the ethics and politics of *care*.

As soon as we come to live mostly in towns, and no longer on savannas populated by tigers and snakes, associative vigilance takes the 'political' form of defensive collectives. Capitalist rapaciousness sets up a factory which maximizes profits as it minimizes spending on salaries and devastates the environment: associative vigilance pushes for the creation of unions, residents' associations, resistance groups and other non-governmental organizations. In every instance, it is a question of mobilizing the power of a collective to *impose the obligation to pay attention* (to the living conditions of the workers, to the availability of resources, to the rights of interested parties, and to the value of affected phenomena). In the industrialized, urban milieu, the original collective reflexes and defence mechanisms against dangers coming from the environment are transformed into defensive strategies to counter the harm imposed on the environment by the short-term heedlessness structurally promoted by capitalist logic.

The processes by which this collective vigilance is neutralized are excellently related in Jean-Baptiste Fressoz's *L'Apocalpse joyeuse* [*The Joyful Apocalypse*], which contributes to a reversal of our historicization of ecological attention.[6] We often imagine that ecological sentiment comes as a reaction to industrial pollution, that we should therefore date its emergence from the beginning of the 19th century, and that previous populations did not need to pay attention to the environment since they did not have the means with which to damage it as dramatically as us. The historian shows, to the contrary, that a whole series of reflexes and collective defence mechanisms were already in place under the *Ancien Régime,* and that the developments of industrial capitalism (like, incidentally, those of the later communist electrification) had to instigate a programme of 'minor disinhibitions' to bypass, deactivate, and invalidate the self-defensive perceptions, legislations, and practices that hampered the maximization of profits. Our sensitivities, our communities and our institutions have actively learned *not to pay attention* to the different modes of pollution that have devastated our vital milieux – largely by invoking a 'modernizing' science and an economic rationality that considers the Earth from the lofty perspective of statistical aggregations. It is under the effect of these multiple 'minor disinhibitions' that our society has been able to overcome the instinctive ('backward-looking', 'retrograde', 'primitive', 'Luddite') resistance and the associative vigilance that hampers the triumphant advance towards development and growth.

A second type of environmental attention relates to what we may call PREVENTATIVE MAINTENANCE: *to assure the maintenance of our living conditions, we must take care to assure the reproduction of our natural and human resources*. It is here no longer a question of facing up together to an external danger (the tiger, the establishment of a factory), as with associative vigilance, but of taking care of the inner functioning of our ways of life – of their sustainability. We must pay attention not to exhaust what sustains us, be that the water of a phreatic table, the work of a certain social group or our own motivation to work. In order to do this, we must together become attentive to the precursory signs of a coming exhaustion (the level of the wells gets lower, the poorest can no longer cope with the increase in the price of water, stress keeps me up at night). While this preventative

112

maintenance of course benefits from a (scientific) overview that helps to 'monitor' and anticipate developments that are either too vast or too slow to be seen by the naked eye (the level of radioactivity, climate warming), it is also based on joint attention. Indeed, we enter here into the sphere of *care*, which is to say, of a constellation of sensitivities and practices that English groups together into a single term and which French distributes between the words 'attention' [*attention*], 'concern' [*souci*], 'preoccupation' [*preoccupation*], 'compassion' [*sollicitude*] and 'consideration' [*soin*]. Preventative maintenance takes into consideration our life forms, worries about what makes life possible and is concerned with identifying [*repérer*], and repairing [*réparer*], what threatens these forms from the inside.

Now, the thinking of *care* – coming out of American feminist reflections denouncing the epistemological bias internal to the overarching universalism adopted a-critically by dominant theories of justice[7] – has made us sensitive to the fact that this constellation of sensibilities and practices must always be re-situated in the daily dithering of contextualized intersubjective relations. The essence of *care* is fundamentally rooted in joint attention: be attentive to what preoccupies others.

We can therefore identify at the common heart of joint attention, *care* and ecology the same RELATIONAL CONCERN: as soon as we are conscious of being not so much autonomous 'individuals' as a certain 'relation' to a certain (physico-biological and social) environment, then *the quality of our existence depends on our consideration of the quality of the relations that simultaneously weave our environment and our being.* This relational concern marks the difference between what Arne Naess called 'deep' ecology in opposition to 'superficial' ecology. The latter considers the environment as an external resource from which we draw elements that are useful to our well-being. We are only concerned with protecting the resources in question, which are considered separately and discontinuously (drinkable water, petrol, wood, bauxite) – an approach encouraged by a dominant conception of scientific 'analysis'. 'Deep' ecology (or 'ecosophy'), on the contrary, is 'relationalist': entities do not exist outside of the relations that constitute them. As soon as we distinguish between an individual and their environment (which is rich in various resources), we are practising a form of 'environmentalism' that betrays the deep truth of ecology – which is, on the contrary, rooted in a concern for the relation as such and does not permit us to speak of an 'environment' as something that could be distinguished from the being that inhabits it.[8]

This relational concern – which is itself of extremely general significance, even if it encourages us to consider only singular and concrete instances – resonates intimately with phenomena of joint attention. As we have seen, it is almost never an isolated individual who directs their attention towards this or that object, except at the level of reactions belonging to pure physiological reflex. It is my relation to the other – mediatized or presential – which makes me look here rather than there. But, inasmuch as it is a 'concern', and not only a disengaged observation, this relation implies that I seek to take it into 'consideration'. Indeed, the virtue of *care*, in its ethical dimension, is that it assures a fluid continuity between the registers of sensitivity (attention, preoccupation), motivation (concern, compassion) and practical action (the work of consideration).

As we saw in the preceding chapter when we evoked the micro-practices of affective harmonization necessary to the successful unfolding of our conversations, joint attention is the site of an intense relational concern and a constant consideration. This consideration is generally spontaneous: most of the time, my gestures of approval, smiles and other facial movements take place in me – through the force belonging to the relation uniting me with my interlocutor – without my needing to make them the object of a conscious and considered effort.

The ethics of *care* nevertheless suggests at least three injunctions thanks to which we will benefit from a tentative consideration of the joint attention that unites us to one another. We here enter the sphere of group micro-politics,[9] which is of crucial importance to ecological movements. Indeed, radical political groups of the past and present are typified by a calamitous relational ecosystem (chronically unstable, sectarian, and prone to division) – that a more sustained attention to the three principles of concern mentioned below might help to improve.

Relational concern first leads to a concrete effort at ATTENTIVE LISTENING: *you shall do your best to make yourself attentive to what preoccupies the attention of the other, and to concretely rectify what is concerning them (without judging its abstract validity)*. As with compassion, *care* assures the passage from attentive sensitivity to attentive action. It is a matter here of suspending any overarching judgement as to the value (the legitimacy, rationality, insignificance or sentimentality) of a concern, a demand or a complaint. If, within a small group where joint attention is the primary force, someone is suffering as a result of some behaviour or some negligence, the vital concern for this joint attention requires that everything possible be done to eliminate or ease the causes of this suffering. Faced with the danger of splintering, attentive listening is indispensable to assuring the minimal cohesion of the transindividual community.

According to a movement which would seem to go against the preceding point, but which is in fact complementary, relational concern then encourages us to value a PLURALIST CONCERN: *you shall try even harder to value a sensibility if it is foreign to you and initially incomprehensible.* Indeed, a double danger threatens the dynamism of activist groups: the torpor of consensual alignment is often not much better than the splintering of dissension. Too much cohesion is as deadly as too little. As was highlighted at the beginning of this section, the strength of the group comes from its capacity for associative vigilance, which itself is based on the fact that its members do not all look in the same direction (or the danger will surprise them all at the same time). It is here that the analogy of a school of fish is limited: human associations are that much stronger if they learn to take advantage of their inherent pluralism, which in the last analysis results from the fact that everyone perceives the world from a particular point of view and that our gazes are therefore destined to cross one another. The ideal conjoining of our attention requires us to be concerned for the relations that connect us, while being just as attentively concerned for what makes each member within the group individual – which implies disconnecting ourselves not only from the other, but from ourselves, so we can learn to accommodate ourselves to the differences that initially bothered us.

The two preceding injunctions are in fact based on a more essential third, which requires from each member of a community a certain ADVANCE OF TRUST to the others: *you shall listen to others starting from the principle that they are doing their best and that they generally have good reasons for feeling, thinking and acting as they do.* (We see that here we are dealing with a corollary to the postulate of practical rationality discussed in the first chapter.) If someone seems to feel, think or do something aberrant, it is probably, therefore, because we do not see the good reasons that have led them to behave in that way – in the same way that we do not see the tiger or the snake coming up behind us. Far from being at odds with our initial vigilance, and pertaining to naivety, this advance of trust within the group extends the distrust (of its *own* blind spots) which explained the very foundation of joint attention.

So we find here the formation of a path leading from protection against external dangers (rooted in the attentional regime of 'alertness') to an effort to maintain internal relations against the risk of fracture (rooted in the regime of 'loyalty creation'), and then to guidelines

115

aiming at the neutralization of the internal dangers coming from an excess of cohesion (crossing the regimes of 'immersion' and 'projection'). This brief overview of the virtues and problems inherent in eco-systems formed by joint attention has only studied the ways in which attention connects us so that we can get a sense of how this attention also requires that we are able to *disconnect* – from those closest to us, starting with ourselves. It is this need for detachment that we are going to analyse at the end of this chapter and second section.

For a Political Ecology of Free-Floating Attention

Freudian psychoanalysis has formalized a surprising attentional practice, which is actually of considerable significance well beyond the psychotherapists' couches and consulting-rooms. The PARADOX OF FREE-FLOATING ATTENTION suggests that *by not paying attention to what someone is trying to tell us we will better understand the meaning of their message.* There is paradox to the extent that we usually define speech as a communicational practice aiming at the intentional transmission of a message from a transmitter to a receiver. For this practice to be successful normally requires that two conditions are met: on the one hand, the said receiver must make himself attentive to the words of the transmitter, rather than the weather or the colour of his socks; on the other hand, he must seek to reconstitute what the speaker means by way of his words, rather than the origin of his accent. The paradox comes from the fact that while the psychoanalyst is certainly interested in what the patient wants to express, he thinks he is better able to discover this by *not* paying attention to what the latter 'thinks he is saying'. The knowledge and practice coming from Freud postulate that unconscious desires haunt our words like spectres, and that it is by allowing our attention to float around the patient's formulations that we can better grasp these apparitions.

The psychoanalyst responds to the free-association of the patient, who is invited to say everything that passes through his head, with a free-association of his own, which has the same goal: producing disassociations and reassociations between the memories, images and words that haunt our minds, making us prisoners of pre-established schema of thought. Free-floating attention essentially consists in the suspension of the traditional constraints of reasoning so as to allow oneself to be carried by effects of resonance. Of course, this takes place in the highly asymmetrical framework of the cure, where one person speaks without really knowing what they are saying, while the other listens, asking himself what there is to be heard: it is because the patient attributes a supposedly superior power of elucidation to the silent attention of the psychoanalyst that the apparatus enables until now evanescent truths to coalesce.

It is worth returning to the double justification that Freud gave for this attentional ecosystem in the framework of the cure: 'we spare ourselves a strain on our attention which could not in any case be kept up for several hours daily, and we avoid a danger which is insep-arable from the exercise of deliberate attention. For as soon as anyone deliberately concentrates his attention to a certain degree, he begins to select from the material before him'.[10] Everything seems to begin with a problem of attention economy: the psychoanalyst would suffer an unbearable attention overload if he had to continue to concentrate on what his patients want to tell him for eight hours a day. This is truly a case of what is often denounced today as an insufficiency of attention capacity for the tasks that need doing. This lack of resources is however transformed into an asset (less is more), holding out the promise of an EMANCIPATORY DISTRACTION: if we cannot be attentive enough, let us be attentive differently – and *make our dis-traction into an opportunity for a detachment which, freeing us from our voluntarist blinkers, will allow us to reconsider the problem in an entirely new way.*

By allowing him to avoid 'selecting [what is most significant] from the material before him' – which is to say, what conforms best to already familiar configurations of meaning – the free-floating lis-tening advocated by Freud helps to free attention from the precon-figurations inherent in any expectation [*attente*]: 'it is a matter of suspending or putting in parenthesis what you know about the world, about yourself and the other, so as to be receptive to what you do not know about it', writes Didier Houzel in a summary of Wilfred Bion's work.[11] In order better to grasp the most profound significance of certain words and signs, it is important to know how to separate yourself from an attachment to their first, obvious and intentional meaning. As was rightly suggested by Peter Szendy in the apparently very different sphere of musical listening: 'Is not a *certain* distraction just as necessary a condition for an *active* listening as total, structural and functional attention?'[12] André Carpentier for his part character-izes this attitude as that of the *flâneur*:

> So, the flâneur's approach consists in introducing himself into the midst of beings while maintaining a free-floating vigilance with respect to everyday things. I mean a kind of vigilance that suspends programmed

thinking and leaves the flâneur available to the surrounding world, generally without the resources of a specialized analysis, as he puts himself in the presence of things and allows sensation to open up. This requires a form of detachment that is close to letting go, combined with a laying bare of the senses, normally sight and hearing in the first instance. Of course, the flâneur is never completely detached from any exploratory ambition, but he refuses to sacrifice to it his freedom to procrastinate. In fact, the flâneur is always torn between grasping the factual as closely as possible and practising a form of critical detachment, which are the two attracting poles of his sensible presence.[13]

It is this same principle that motivates a whole field of literary practice and study which, since the time of the surrealists, has mobilized the effects of diffraction and polysemy peculiar to linguistic signifiers, so as to find a signification in the text that exceeds both what the author wanted to put there and what readers believed they had found as they sought to reconstitute the author's intentions. Indeed, in contrast to historical analysis, LITERARY INTERPRETATION is distinguished by an *effort to make oneself attentive to what signs can say, beyond what the author may have wanted to say.* The most obvious meaning does not require interpretation. The hidden dimension of what motivated or caused the use of words is the resource of historical enquiry, which helps us to grasp the complexity of the linguistic, ethical and political choices made by authors. Our relation to the literature of the past and present (and to art more generally) is, however, overdetermined by a whole series of resonances situated beyond the obvious meaning and before the (conscious or unconscious) intentions that produced the work. It is attention to this beyond and before which is the specificity of literary listening. Work that is inspired by this does not seek to understand causes, because the schema of causality presupposes the reduction of phenomena to categories that are already known. Literary work aims, on the contrary, to adumbrate forms in becoming, which are always a little spectral, and which still remain irreducible to any pre-existing, clear and distinct knowledge. It endeavours to make nuances apparent which evade already identified contrasts.

Psychoanalytical hermeneutic and literary hermeneutic share the same presupposition of INTER-ATTENTIONAL ADDED VALUE: *the interlacing of joint but free-floating attentions (which are concerned, therefore, with separating themselves from one another), produces new sensibilities and forms of understanding that are superior to the sum of the knowledge brought by each.* The ecosystem that valorizes free-floating attention – whether asymmetrical as in psychoanalytic cure or literary communication, or symmetrical as in interpretative debate[14] – functions in the same way as the conversations Vilém Flusser used to illustrate 'network systems': the interplay of attention leads to a 'raising of the level of information'.

The elementary situation of joint attention, as a situation of associative vigilance, only brings about a transfer of information between the members of the group: by making myself attentive to the gaze of someone who can see a tiger approaching from behind me, I gather information which saves my life, but which was already present within our community. In an ecosystem where the attention of each remains attached to the attention of others, we are dealing with a multitude of radios univocally broadcasting information to listeners who use it to complete their individual vision of the world. Information circulates and tends to level out.

The detachment brought about by free-floating attention – whether it is rooted in a voluntary effort or in simple distraction through a lack of attentional resources – allows our joint (but unstuck) attention to discover forms, properties and potentialities that were not previously available to any of the individuals in the group. The emergence of an inter-attentional added value enables the raising of the general level of information as it introduces entirely new discoveries. Such is the case in a psychoanalytical cure when what is said by one, un-tied and re-tied by the free-floating attention of the other, comes back to him in a form capable of elucidating the fantasies that had until then remained unconscious to the patient and unknown to the therapist. And such is the case in literary interpretation when, for example, by detaching himself from the grand political themes developed in depth in Sartre's work so as to focus his free-floating attention on apparently insignificant details (bananas, cars, hands, ends), a critic reconfigures the problematics of engagement in a way that neither Sartre, nor the critic before he read Sartre, nor we before having read the critic, would have been capable of formulating.[15]

Apart from psychoanalysis and literature, the practice of free-floating attention has further implications in the sphere of political ecology, with which I will conclude this chapter. As we saw at the end of the preceding section, political organizations are just as likely to collapse from a lack of cohesion, leading to fracturing, as from an excess of unanimity, bringing about lethargy. Maintaining an ecosystem of joint attention that is simultaneously vigilant, coherent, attentive and pluralist is without doubt the major challenge to which very few organizations are able to rise over the long-term.

119

The emancipatory distraction discussed above may be able to help us fail less often in this difficult squaring of the circle.

Indeed, cultivating free-floating attention helps to bring about two movements that are capable of neutralizing many internal conflicts (if we may not hope to resolve them). A certain distraction goes together with a certain *stepping back*, which leads to a putting into perspective of the true importance of (the often insignificant) points around which conflicts form. Even if these details are not really conflicts, we know that the devil is in them, and their inflation by a hyper-focused attention often produces scissions. Listening to these conflicts from a little distance while thinking of something else allows us to keep a better sense of proportion, and to see that it is more important to agree on what is essential than to differ on a point which, if not insignificant, is at least secondary.

A certain distraction may also be emancipatory precisely because it allows us to 'think about something else' while debate is focused on the contentious question. As well as giving some distance, free-floating attention helps to produce a STEP TO THE SIDE, allowing for *the invention of an excluded third, to overcome the dead end of situations where the argument is caught up in a strictly binary alternative.* We know that for Gilles Deleuze, inspired in this by Gilbert Simondon, the political gesture *par excellence* consisted precisely in rejecting the binary choices in which our attention allows itself to be imprisoned (*for* or *against* this colonial-humanitarian military campaign?) – and proposing diagonals which, instead of making us choose between two contradictory evils, open the space of a superior dimension where the oppositions appear complementary to one another (how can we work *elsewhere* to prevent the next conflict *before* it requires a military intervention?).

Emancipatory distraction, stepping back and stepping to one side encourage a POLITICS OF CONVIVIAL DISSENSUS, where *the attentional ecosystem happily welcomes conflicts for their stimulating effects of pluralism, without allowing minor differences to obscure the general direction in which the whole is heading.* How is it possible not to agree (while continuing to stay) with one another? Such is the challenge of political organization which reflection on joint attention may help us to take up – given that the strength of its 'conjunction' comes precisely from the fact that not everyone is looking in the same direction. Learning to be attentive to what preoccupies the other, being concerned for it so as to maintain the collective dynamic, without for all that allowing oneself to become obsessed by details or allowing emotions to get carried away – this requires an ability to reconcile the apparently contradictory demands of an attachment based in *care* and a detachment based in free-floating attention. This is the arbitration towards which the politics of convivial dissent must work, in such a way that the dynamic complementarity of the managerial and the radical may be exploited.

Of course, the disarray of movements of resistance to capitalism in recent decades arises from the play of planetary forces, where economic interest, the protection of privilege, political rivalries and the appropriation of media dynamics by the logic of financial profitability are much more decisive factors than the clan divisions of statistically insignificant small groups. A little more 'conviviality' among activists will not, therefore, be enough to provoke an assault on the new Winter Palaces. And yet, how can we ignore that the fragmentation and/or hyper-localization of collectives putting forward (concrete or theoretical) alternatives to capitalism are at least in part responsible for its disastrous victory at the present time?

Increasingly, partisans of a radical ecology are trying to get out of the binary alternatives that have been such a burden over the last decades as they impose an exclusive choice between potentially brilliant but strictly local concrete alternative experiments, and vague attempts at macropolitical association that are doomed to end in disavowal. At a time when, despite all the local initiatives, global and irreversible threats are already starting to affect our immediate environment, an *ecology of attention to ecology* absolutely must come up with an excluded third that will build a bridge between the joint attention of collective movements and the collective attention of media flows. National and supranational macropolitics cannot be abandoned to domination by economic powers and political apparatuses that are completely subsumed in the continuance of vested interests.

The radical ecology that decries the harmful effects of capitalism has to develop a *political attention echology* that is capable of making its claims and experiments resonate in a social and media web thirsting for promising innovations – despite the way in which it is at present crushed by the dominant media.[16] This echology will have to endeavour to repeat step by step the lessons to be drawn from the concrete alternatives that abound at a local level. It will also have to make use of the discrepancies that affect every echo (temporal delay, variation of volume, change of tone). While our attentional apparatuses must be periodically re-energized by 1:1 scale, jumps in scale are indispensable to an echology based on stepping back and stepping to one side. It is because of a lack of collective attention that our most desirable lifestyles are being crushed by modes of production that can only ever be modes of pollution.

Calling for a return to attentional modes that are better focused on the real problems affecting us (as opposed to the entertainments that distract us from them), on the books that will enable us to understand them better (rather than the internet by which we are doomed to distraction) or on authentic, present, human relations (removed from all those mediations that cut us off from our roots) – all this may seem a little too nostalgic and moralizing not to be suspicious. Developing a political echology of *free-floating attention* may on the contrary encourage us to take note of the relational and technological transformations that structure our current epoch, whether we like it or not. Making a certain distraction into an emancipatory force, recognizing the place and the inescapable virtues of mediation in our social relations, looking, even in entertainments, for what may help us to redirect our attention – all this is perhaps more promising for transforming the future than trying to reconstruct it on the past.

How can we practise this free-floating attention, attuning it to populations of net users and surfers? How can we modulate its rhythms so that we are able to intensify it when it is appropriate to do so, while leaving its levity free for serendipitous encounters? This is what the third part of this book will attempt to clarify. After having looked down from Saturn on the flows of our collective attention and after having attempted to approach joint attention at 1:1 scale, it is now fitting that we should enter into the functioning of attention as we experience it most immediately, in our innermost personality. How can we benefit from the attentional buffeting that our media systems and relational situations produce in us? This is something that we can only discover, ultimately, in our daily individuation.

Part III

Individuating Attention

— 6 —

ATTENTION IN LABORATORIES

We have now arrived at the place where other books on attention start: what happens in me when *I* pay attention to *something*? In the experience that we have of it, attention is indeed immediately an individual affair, connecting a subject with an object. Which explains the success of William James's 1890 definition, appearing as a matter of course in the first pages of a large proportion of books on attention:

> Millions of items of the outward order are present to my senses which never properly enter into my experience. Why? Because they have no interest for me. My experience is what I agree to attend to. Only those items which I notice shape my mind – without selective interest, experience is an utter chaos. [. . .] Everyone knows what attention is. It is the taking possession by the mind, in clear and vivid form, of one out of what seem several simultaneously possible objects or trains of thought. Focalization, concentration, of consciousness are of its essence. It implies withdrawal from some things in order to deal effectively with others, and is a condition which has a real opposite in the confused, dazed, scatterbrained state which in French is called *distraction*, and *Zerstreutheit* in German.[1]

As a selective principle, animated by certain forms of interest, individual attention serves as a filter not only for what I 'notice', but also for what I *am*: it is the interface through which 'my mind takes possession' of certain objects that it notices in the world, and through which these objects in turn 'form my mind' as they constitute 'my experience' of the world. At the same time as it fills me with the world that I take possession of, from the moment that 'my experience is what *I agree to attend to*', this interface is the place of a fundamental form of liberty.

125

Even if multiple relays (media, educational, publicity) have contributed to getting this book into your hands, only *you*, reader, can decide whether or not to continue reading beyond the fifth chapter. Now that Pierre Bayard has taught us how to talk about books that we have not read (completely), you may very well stop here, without any harmful consequences for your reputation, your career or your exams. If you have got this far, and if you continue to read, it is because you have chosen – 'freely' – to give it your attention and your precious time (thank you for that!). Instead of picking up a telescope in order to ask ourselves from the perspective of Saturn what has conditioned you to read me, instead of asking how our attention is joined across time as you read, the following pages will borrow the neuroscientist's microscope in order to understand what happens between the pages of this worldly object that is the book, on the one hand, and the neurones thanks to which, by way of your hands and your eyes, your mind gives its attention to it, on the other.

Automatic Attention

Even if, as we have already highlighted, the history of the theories of individual attention remains largely to be written, it would seem that we can identify two major scansions situated in the middle of the eighteenth and nineteenth centuries. Where Locke and the sensualist tradition produced subjects conceived of as wax tablets, obliged to 'submit' to the impressions of sensory stimuli, philosophical and scientific works published after 1750 (and, to an even greater extent, Romanticism) largely thought of attention as something that individuals actively 'give' to this or that object in their environment – on the model of an investor who directs his capital towards this or that promising enterprise. So, we read in Jean-François Marmontel that attention 'is an action of the mind that fixes thought on an object and attaches it to it', while the *Encyclopaedia* defines it as 'an operation of our soul which, attaching itself to a part of a composite object, considers it in such a way that it will gain a more distinct idea of it than of the other parts.'[2] Lorraine Daston has clearly demonstrated how, for researchers like the Genevan naturalist Charles Bonnet (1720–93), scientific attention is a demanding, even ascetic practice, requiring mental, bodily and existential discipline.[3]

After 1850, however, attention appeared less as the faculty of a mind that was active and master of itself, than as a bodily reaction liable to be seized by capturing apparatuses. From that point on, we began busily measuring and exploiting the capturing alternatives, as exemplified by the new machines invented by experimental psychology (around Fechner, Wundt and their colleagues), the new media which were the allure of cities and world fairs (*Kaiserpanoramas* and other kinetoscopes), and practices like hypnosis. So, it is in this period that we move from an economic model (of investment) to an ecological model (of the relation to the milieu).

In reality, we realize that most analyses of attention have from time immemorial situated it across two levels, illustrated in Condillac's fable of the statue whose senses are reduced to the sense of smell and who then has various flowers passed under its nose: 'passive attention, coming from the sense of smell, will be all about the present smell of the rose, and active attention, coming from memory, will be split between the memory that remains of the smells of the rose and the carnation'.[4] From Condillac's 'passive' and 'active' attention to Daniel Kahneman's systems 1 (intuitive) and 2 (reasoned), the categorizations have varied widely, but we find a similar distribution of attention over two spheres, with one relating to automatic functions and the other to intentional efforts.

More broadly, from the mediasphere to the many different intercerebral dynamics, attentional phenomena seem to be characterized by a MULTI-LAYERED STRUCTURE: speaking of ecosystems, as we did in the preceding chapters, conceals the fact that *attention should be conceived as a superimposition of mechanisms operating on multiple entangled levels and in ways that are very different to one another.* The schema given in Figure 10 attempts to provide a representation of the most important strata (which are themselves composed of multiple internal layers) structuring the way in which a subject pays attention to an object at a time *t* of their existence:

Collective Attention	media enthralments	publics
Joint Attention	relational situations	groups
Individual Attention	things/experiences	individuals

reflexive	values	*evaluations*	subjects
voluntary	objects	*focusing*	executive system
automatic	saliences	*captivations*	perceptive system

10. The multiple layers of attention

Over the course of the last century, experimental psychology revealed a series of processes deep down in this entanglement through which our brain deals with a huge quantity of information without our being aware of it. The classic example is the *cocktail party effect*: in the middle of a party with loud music and lots of people, while you are in conversation with an old friend, you suddenly hear someone mention your name in a nearby discussion. In the second half of the twentieth century, psychology laboratories conducted many different experiments aimed at understanding the level at which the filtering of information revealed by the cocktail party effect takes place.[5] If you have been able to recognize your name in the surrounding noise, this is because something, in you, was not only hearing but 'listening' to nearby discussions, with sufficient attention to notice that they were speaking about you (or someone with the same name). So, we can pay attention [*prêter attention*] to something without giving it our attention [*sans y faire attention*]. . .

From which comes the necessity of identifying a first stratum of AUTOMATIC ATTENTION within which – in a complex relationship of suggestion, attenuation, reinforcement, and filtering with the other cerebral systems – *a 'perceptive system' engages in an initial labour of identification without intention, without consciousness and without apparent effort from the subject.* Once we have a whole series of cognitive processes taking place in us without our knowledge, it becomes problematic to determine who is (or is not) attentive to what. Even if I take advantage of an ad break to telephone a friend, do brands not print their message in me without my realizing it, from the moment they have worked out how to introduce the equivalent of my name?[6] Are the 'young' absorbed in their mobile phones really absorbed? If our brain is much less distracted than us, if we know more than we know, then judgements relating to our states of attention or distraction prove to be much more complicated than we might have thought.

The study of this automatic attention allows us to bring to light at least four kinds of phenomena. Firstly, we learn the mechanisms by which our perceptive system continually collects data on our immediate environment, thanks to a 'saccadic' movement through which our gaze constantly sweeps across our visual field, returning very frequently to certain privileged points (the eyes and mouth on a human face). The general principle seems to be that 'left to itself, attention cannot stay still'[7]: our sensory apparatus and our nervous system are always moving and looking to move, the greatest challenge for them is to stay fixed on something that does not move or change.

Consequently, we may characterize different ATTENTIONAL GESTURES consisting of certain *motor schema, carried out automatically by our sensory apparatus in its quest for information, and fitted to certain types of operation.* Frédéric Kaplan gives a striking example of this, contrasting the ocular saccades produced during the reading of a school textbook with those produced by manuscript annotations added to the printed text: the two form 'two distinct 'clouds' with particular sensorimotor characteristics'.

> There is a family of behaviours that externally resembles what we usually refer to as 'reading', but which in fact, when we analyse them from the perspective of the attentional gesture, turn out to be very different. We do not 'read' a magazine in the same way that we 'read' a novel, an instruction book like a dictionary or, in this case, a textbook and the surrounding annotations. In each case, our eyes dance very differently.[8]

Secondly, the incessant collection of information by the saccades of an attention that cannot stay still accounts for the multiple PRIMING EFFECTS that psychological experiments often reveal to our great surprise. Indeed, they seem to contradict the premise of William James's reasoning, according to which 'Millions of items of the outward order are present to my senses which never properly enter into my experience.' In reality, it turns out that *the presence of a thing in our sensory field affects our way of thinking, speaking and acting, without our being aware of it.*

We can see how this works with words: if I showed you the word *eat* and asked you to put in the letter missing from _read, you would be inclined to write a *b* rather than a *d* or a *t*. The same goes for bodily movements: subjects who have been made to hold a pencil between their teeth for a few seconds (so forcing them mechanically to make a smiling gesture) then find a series of comic drawings to be funnier than they are considered to be by the control group. We can of course see the same thing with images and sounds (in which we are immersed by advertising): an honesty box where office workers are supposed to put money to pay for the coffee, tea and sugar consumed during their break received very different amounts depending on whether the poster above it showed flowers or someone watching (Figure 11). The posters were changed each week, and the weeks with someone watching received three times more money on average than the weeks with flowers[9]. . .

The study of automatic attention also confirms, thirdly, that our perceptual field is organized according to CAPTURE BY SALIENCE – passed down collectively from generation to generation or inculcated

11. The effect of *priming* on the honesty box

individually through repeated experience – that induce the sudden emergence of '*impressions to which we cannot stop ourselves from paying attention*'.[10] So, in Figure 12, for people who are used to reading printed pages, the *m* in bold and black is much more salient than the *w* lost in the mass of grey letters. However 'constructed' (from a socio-historical perspective) and however 'subjective' our individual attention may be, certain phenomena impose themselves on it because of the inherent properties of sensory stimuli, independently of our tastes or current interests. In the same way that the violence of certain sounds, at certain frequencies and above a certain decibel level, cannot not affect us, certain visual forms are bound to catch our attention. In this way, certain stimuli impose themselves as 'distractors' – something that is illustrated by the Stroop test, where we struggle to quickly name the colour (black, grey, or white) of printed words because their verbal signification imposes itself, and unavoidably interferes with the assigned task (Figure 13). In the first line, we are induced to reply 'grey' because the word *grey* is imposed on us in the first instance, even if the colour that we are being asked to identify is really black.

The fourth phenomenon, which is intimately connected to the preceding one, relates to the effects of inertia brought about by habits inscribed in our automatic attentional reflexes. If we are able to deal with so much information so quickly, this is because our nervous system has developed sensorimotor schemas which are triggered

m m m m m m m m m m m m m m m m
m m m m m m m m m m m m m m m m
m m m m m m m m m m m m m m m m
m m m m m m m m m m m m m m m m
m m m m m m m m m m m **m** m m m
m m m m m m m m m m m m m m m m
m m m m m m m m m m m m m m m m
m m m m m m m m m m m m m m m m
m m w m m m m m m m m m m m m m
m m m m m m m m m m m m m m m m
m m m m m m m m m m m m m m m m
m m m m m m m m m m m m m m m m

12. Salience

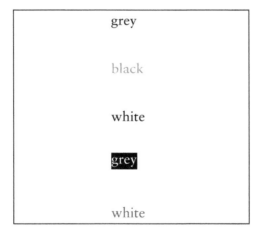

13. The Stroop Test

as soon as it is affected by certain stimuli. Jean-Philippe Lachaux has distinguished the immediate 'capture' of our attention by salient factors, from its 'CAPTIVATION' by *processes that absorb us in motor or emotional schemas that take a certain time to develop.*[11] Certain images (of sex or horror) cannot not produce certain emotions in us (of excitation, disgust, or anxiety) which resonate in our psyche for several seconds. In the same way, certain perceptions trigger motor schemas which prevent us from being attentive to something else: if an object seems to be approaching my face at high speed, I will instinctively close my eyes and move my head to dodge it.

These captivation mechanisms help us to determine better the somatic dimension of attentional phenomena. For a number of years Richard Shusterman has been elaborating a pragmatist philosophy of 'somaesthetics' aimed at making us more (and better) attentive to the intermediation role played by our body with respect to our environment.[12] As essential as this 'embodiment' of attention may be, it poses fundamental problems with respect to the determination of the limits of what constitutes our individualized attentional body. When Condillac spoke of 'passive' attention to designate the impressions that we receive from external objects, he justified the term by emphasizing that 'a being is active or passive depending on whether the cause of the effect produced in it is internal or external'.[13] The statue is passive when it smells an odour, because the cause of the sensation is external (in the rose). The phenomena of salience seem to confirm this passivity: certain objects impose certain reactions on my body, almost in spite of myself. We find, however, that not only does this passivity closely resemble activity, since it is at the root of a good many of our emotions and gestures but, above all, that the borders between the inside and the outside, activity and passivity, are scrambled as soon as phenomena relating to automatic attention are *historicized*.

Indeed, what is an apprenticeship, an education, a training, if not a process of habituation which is able to automate the linking of a certain perception with a certain motor reaction? From a very young age, our individuation develops through a labour of INCORPORATION which *shifts the effort of attention originally required to accomplish certain gestures to an automatic level*. The Stroop test (Figure 13) illustrates the power of the captivations that we have incorporated over the course of our development: if the signification of words did not irresistibly impose itself on me – interfering on this occasion with the colours in which a perverse psychologist has printed them – it would take us hours to read the least page. The automatic attention mobilized by reading had to be incorporated by the efforts of an apprenticeship. When the letters g-r-e-y 'impose' on me today from the outside – condemning my person to passivity according to Condillac's reasoning – we may equally reverse the argument and say that 'the cause of the effect produced' comes from 'me', inasmuch as it is me who has learned to read (or play ping-pong, or sense when a tiny tension in the face of my interlocutor is signalling that he has been offended by the word I have just used).

In the same way that it is more difficult than we thought to determine what we are attentive to and what we are not (like with the surprises of the cocktail-party effect), we are unable to exclude automatic attention from the field of attention properly speaking (under the pretext that it does not require intention, consciousness or effort), since it often represents past, sedimented, and embodied attention in the form of habit. A good attention ecology requires that we recognize its particular contribution to our processes of individuation at each of its multiple strata.

The Neuronal Economy and Voluntary Attention

The reorganization of the relations between activity and passivity, freedom and alienation, continues as we move up towards the second stratum of multi-layered attention (Figure 10) – the stratum of voluntary attention that individualist philosophers consider the core of our being, since 'the cause of the effects produced' seems to be situated 'in us': in the 'free choice' of our will. If my experiences are defined by 'what I agree to attend to', as was asserted by William James, what do those who are studying with MRI (magnetic resonance imaging) how this agreement takes place tell us from the depths of their laboratories?

While the terms and the nuances vary – some speak of 'priority management' or 'attentional supervision' and others of 'strategic' functions – the currently accepted psychological models submit the functioning of our attention to an 'EXECUTIVE SYSTEM' which, with its balancing mechanisms organized simultaneously into competing stimulations and hierarchical structure, *has the function of judging between the different possible courses of action.* These mechanisms come into play 'when there is a decision to be taken or a project to set up; when an error has to be corrected; when new responses need to be produced; in dangerous or difficult situations; or again when it is question of overcoming a habit or resisting a temptation'.[14]

The spectacular development of the neurosciences has led to a modelling in which the old *homunculus* of traditional psychology takes on the new form of a CHEMICAL ECONOMY OF ATTENTION: indeed, everything happens *as though our 'free choices' were controlled by levels of neurotransmitters present in the brain, with our behaviour shifting depending on one or other of our neuronal networks.* Jean-Philippe Lachaux gives the example of the neurones of the cingulate gyrus or the *nucleus accumbens* (NAc) whose sensitivity to dopamine (a chemical neurotransmitter) affects our tendency to make choices that are oriented towards the long or the short term.

> The NAc is subject to the influence of the prefrontal cortex and the complex formed by the amygdala and the hippocampus. When the level of dopamine in the NAc is lowered, the prefrontal dominates and behaviour is mainly directed by long-term considerations. When the level goes beyond a certain threshold, [. . .] the amygdala and the hippocampus take control of the NAc, and predominantly drive the behaviour and the attention of the individual towards short-term reward. [. . .] Voluntary control of attention is above all a control of attention according to long-term objectives. The orbitofrontal cortex and the anterior cingulate gyrus belong to the frontal regions that are able to take the long term into account and resist immediate distractions. They intervene continually to resist the power of our environment and our thoughts to captivate us.[15]

This then is attention, along with the 'force of will', reduced to a quantitative factor in an *input-output* matrix: increase the dopamine and the individual is oriented towards stereotypical sources of pleasure, without worrying about more long-term harmful consequences; reduce the level, and they suddenly become attentive (again) to finding the best means by which to assure their long-term well-being. We are here very much at the decisional heart of a chemical attention economy, which apparently leaves little room for our classical categories of intention, will, responsibility and free choice.

The economic treatment of attention in fact began independently of neuroscientific discoveries, when Daniel Kahneman and his team believed they could accurately measure our attentional effort by observing the level of our pupil dilation (and our heartbeat). The future winner of the Nobel Prize for economics developed a model from this at the beginning of the 1970s – so at the same time that Herbert Simon was placing the scarcity of attention at the centre of our civilizational preoccupations – that subjected questions of structure and functional pathways, which had previously occupied experimental psychology, to a 'theory of resources', fixing a genuine ENERGY ECONOMY OF ATTENTION in our brain: *defined as a mental effort, voluntary attention should be considered a scarce resource, limited both in its absolute quantity and its possible allocations.* It is, of course, the economic vocabulary of scarcity, allocation of resources, and supply and demand that structures this approach:

Different mental activities impose different demands on the limited capacity. An easy task demands little effort, and a difficult task demands much. When the supply of attention does not meet the demands, performance falters, or fails entirely. According to the model, an activity can fail, either because there is altogether not enough capacity to meet its demands or because the allocation policy channels available capacity to other activities.[16]

This analytical framework – expressed today by Kahneman in terms of 'budget', to account for expressions like 'to pay attention' – has four consequences which underpin the research into attention conducted by our neuroscientific and experimental psychology laboratories. In the first place, the theory of attentional resources confirms, despite appearances to the contrary, the PRINCIPLE OF SEQUENTIALITY formulated by Herbert Simon[17]: *our executive attentional system can, at each moment, only direct itself towards one object at a time.* Even as he notes that 'attention is divisible', Daniel Kahneman immediately clarifies that: 'at high levels of task load, attention becomes more nearly unitary'.[18]

While it is fashionable to speak of multi-tasking (or of divided attention), as though we were able to carry out two or three activities in parallel, the laboratories bring to light a PRINCIPLE OF INTERMITTENCE by which we *divide our attention by moving very quickly between tasks, only dealing with one at a time.* 'Someone may give the impression that they are paying attention to two things at once, when in fact their attention is shifting from one to the other. In this instance, their ability to carry out several activities simultaneously depends on an efficient executive system capable of an optimal temporal organization of attention so that it can move from one task to the other.'[19]

The central question of the neuronal attention economy is to be posed, therefore, in terms of SAMPLING MODULATION: *from the moment our different tasks no longer demand constant attention, our freedom consists in modulating the frequency with which we redirect our attention to them to make sure they go well.* The notion of sampling is particularly interesting because of the continuity it establishes between the analysis of neuronal processes and the functioning of digital technologies. Indeed, digitalization consists, we saw, in the translation of minimal discrete units cut from our perception of reality into digitalized data. The sampling rate determines the pixel density variation (high or low definition) for images or the compression variation for musical files (mp3).

As Jean-Philippe Lachaux highlights, boiling a pan of water (in

135

a few minutes), monitoring a baby's sleep (during a nap of several hours), or watering the plants (every week) involve different tempos, which generally allow us to sample with relative ease compatible portions of time when we can intervene: there is no need to keep our eyes fixed on the plants 24 hours a day to make sure that they are growing well, it is enough to look once a day to detect a potential problem.

> Whatever task you are undertaking, there is always a period during which you can stop paying attention to it without harming your performance. I call this the 'average period of free attention'. For a day-to-day activity, the AVERAGE PERIOD OF FREE ATTENTION *is the average period during which you can stop paying attention to it without something unexpected and potentially catastrophic happening.* It is the maximum period beyond which you cannot predict what will happen.[20]

In the same way that the undersampling inherent in the mp3 format (in comparison with the sound quality of a CD) allows for a more 'economical' distribution of music over the internet, the undersampling of multi-tasking allows us to 'gain time' by watching a television show (with one eye) while eating a meal. The 'average period of free attention' authorized by each activity means that some of them can be carried out seemingly in parallel, like listening to the radio and preparing a meal – when, in reality, this is thanks to a constant oscillation from one to the other. It is because this period is limited by certain irreducible thresholds that it is difficult or dangerous to look at your emails while driving a car.

Finally, and this is the fourth point, we understand that sampling variations are connected to different DEGREES OF FOCALIZATION: *the effort of concentrating attentional resources on a specific activity brings about a proportional reduction in the ability to perform other tasks at the same time.* The most famous example being the attentional blindness illustrated by Daniel Simons' gorilla experiment.[21] In a video lasting about one minute, you are asked to count how many times a basketball is passed between the three players of a team in white tee-shirts, while an opposing team of three players in black tee-shirts passes their own ball in the same space. Most people who watch it have little difficulty in counting fifteen passes.

When asked if they saw the gorilla, half of them are surprised and reply that they did not. When you watch the video again, however, it is clear that someone disguised as a (black) gorilla very slowly crosses the screen and pointedly beats his chest before calmly leaving in the other direction. The *hyper-focalization* on the white players brings about a *hypo-focalization* on everything black on the screen, to the point that you do not notice something so obvious that it should stand out a mile. As William James pointed out in the quotation at the beginning of this chapter: 'Focalization, concentration, of consciousness are of its [attention's] essence. It implies withdrawal from some things in order to deal effectively with others.' So, every effort of focalization necessarily brings about forms of ATTENTIONAL BLINDNESS, which is to say, of *perceptive self-amputation caused by the need to concentrate your attentional resources on a narrowly determined centre of relevance, which leads to their withdrawal from other competing centres.*[22]

As is the case here, laboratory research into attention often only confirms what we suspected already: it is in fact the filtering operation performed by the old principle of pertinence that is so strikingly confirmed and illustrated by Simons' experiment. Once you have taken the time to re-situate the functioning of individual attention in the relational and media frameworks by which it is thoroughly over-determined – instead of making out that laboratory conditions and magnetic resonance devices give us access to *the* truth about human behaviour – the data gathered by experimental psychology and the neurosciences proves to be fascinating and essential to a better understanding of attention.

What an ecological approach can add to this can be summed up in two points. On the one hand, as James Gibson rightly highlighted in his essential work on visual perception,[23] laboratory psychology tends to reify into objects what would more pertinently be approached in terms of flux and process. By necessity, experiments usually measure the state of things or modes of operation defined at a time *t*. It is therefore difficult for them to evaluate correctly the PLASTICITY which everyone nonetheless recognizes as a characteristic of both attention and the human brain: inasmuch as they provide the interface with a constantly changing world, *our attention capacities are constantly opening up new modes of operation, which ceaselessly redistribute the complementary proportions of automated procedures and intentional effort.* Which is why we should speak of individuating attention rather than individual attention.

To learn a task is, we saw, to 'incorporate' inextricably mental and somatic knowledge, which enables us to operate automatically and free up the limited resources of our live attention – which prove to be potentially unlimited once the development of skills is historicized. 'As you become skilled in a task, its demand for energy diminishes.'[24]; 'generally, the expert can produce the same gesture with less attention, which leaves the prefrontal cortex free to take on board other factors that the novice, completely overwhelmed, must leave aside'.[25] The neuronal attentional nanoeconomy is being permanently restructured, according to a process which here too seems to reflect the 'productivity gains' produced by the automation of tasks at the social macroeconomic scale. The historicizing of the laws of attention discovered in the laboratory is, therefore, as important as the historicizing of economic laws, which have clearly varied a great deal from ancient slavery and medieval feudalism, to the first factories and digital finance.

The second point relates to a central presupposition of the vast majority of experiments carried out on attention in laboratories. We observe the subjects' ability to perform certain tasks (carry out a mental calculation, identify letters, count how many times a ball is passed). What about situations when our individual attention is not directly orientated towards a particular task? Listening to music, watching a film, walking in the country, chatting with a friend: of course, all of these activities imply sub-tasks that are necessary for them to go well, but it would be difficult to reduce them to the (successful or failed) accomplishment of a 'task'. It is to these kinds of practice that we will turn in the next chapter, in order that we may articulate more subtly the very problematic reference to *multi-task* activities – which may be defined not only as the (potentially schizophrenic) effort to carry out several separate and rival operations in parallel, but also as the superimposition of multiple confused and convergent aims within the same activity.

— 7 —

REFLEXIVE ATTENTION

Within the multi-layered attentional structure sketched out at the beginning of the last chapter, we should take note of the very thin stratum relating to REFLEXIVE ATTENTION, defined by the fact that *the individual may pay attention to the dynamics, constraints, apparatuses, and above all to the evaluations, conditioning their attention.* It is, of course, in this layer that this book, along with most of those cited in it, is situated. Asking questions as an individual about the objects or mechanisms that attract, stimulate, awaken, captivate or alienate our attention, necessarily amounts to asking questions about the *value* of these objects or mechanisms.

Indeed, as soon as we leave the laboratory, the 'millions of items of the outward order [. . .] present to my senses' take hold of me and inscribe me in the dense and conflictual fabric of human practices and their interwoven interests.[1] As we saw at the collective level of media dynamics, attention works like a filter which pre-selects what is supposedly of value to us. At the individual level too, I am defined as a 'subject' precisely by what I find myself paying more attention to (my wife, my parents, my cat, new philosophy books, free-jazz concerts), when compared with the millions of things that I may choose as worthy of interest in their place (the beggar on the corner, the pigeons at my window, Marseille's Olympic victory, the opera programme). In an AUTO-REFERENTIAL CIRCLE – which is only 'vicious' insofar as it must be selectively 'virtuous' – *I give my attention to what I value and I value what I give my attention to*, according to the self-reinforcing dynamic discussed in Chapter 3. It is because I am a jazz fan that I pay attention to a notice publicizing a Mary Halvorson concert, and it is because I attend concerts like those of Mary Halvorson that I am a jazz fan. While we easily understand, in light of the pertinence principle, why we pay attention to what we already value, it is to one of Flaubert's letters that we may look for the opposing principle, which closes the auto-referential circle: 'For something to be interesting, we need only look at it long enough.'[2]

While attention must be understood as an evaluating activity geared towards orientating us with respect to anything that may warrant attaching us to one aspect of our environment rather than another, the function of the laboratory is, as far as possible, precisely to cut us off from those bonds (of attention/evaluation) which attach us to one another and to the things that circulate among us. Laboratories try to produce results that are as weakly subjective and axiological as possible – 'objective' results. At the same time that they help us to measure and evaluate the parameters that condition the functioning of our attention, they are condemned to leave undisclosed, as though suspended in the void, everything that is truly incorporated by our individual attention in the relational web in which we live – that whole weave of attachments in which evaluation and valuation are intimately combined.

The Wailing Wall

So, if we leave the laboratory to listen to discourses concerned with accounting for the interplay of attachments forming or falling apart between us as individuals at the beginning of this third millennium, we hear an increasingly insistent build-up of voices proclaiming a 'crisis of attention'. In the 1970s, we sought to solve the problem of information overload by asking ourselves about the optimal allocation of resources and the organization of society. In tune with the great social protest movements experienced by Western countries at the end of the 1960s, and with the spectacular democratization of access to higher learning, it was a time for imagining new apparatuses (technical, societal, political) which would be up to the new challenges and the new hopes of a new (post-industrial) economy, a new (post-disciplinary) society, and a new (post-modern) world.

From Alvin Toffler's *Third Wave*[3] to Félix Guattari's *Three Ecologies*,[4] from the most consensual analyses to the most militant programmes, a new environmental sensitivity was learning to question the lifestyles produced by industrialization and mass consumerism, as it explicitly questioned the values governing our vital ecosystems. As a general rule, this questioning was based on the obvious fact that entirely new modes of subjectivation and valorization were starting to develop, called forth by the social transformations underway – at issue in the debates was knowing how to fulfil the hopes kindled by the general improvement in living standards (in Western countries), the reduction of time spent working, the democratization of knowledge and the erosion of oppressive forms of authority.

In contrast to this necessarily brief sketch, while we complain more than ever at the beginning of the third millennium of information overload, our wailing is now, generally speaking, devoid of hope – except the hope that the future may be wise enough to return us to ways and qualities of life associated with the past. The assessment is unremarkable: our collective inability to pay (serious and effective) attention to the ecological threats and social injustices that threaten our common future translates into an intellectual horizon that is so overcast that it appears completely closed off. Forty years of crisis discourse have revealed the futility of declarations that we are at the end of the tunnel and convinced many that we should turn back – towards the 'Les Trente Glorieuses' of a triumphant wage system (which were also the years of unprecedented environmental destruction), towards the Nation State as the sole defender of the politics of social solidarity (sending anything that smacks too much of the world's misery back to the borders) or towards the tribal values that supposedly guarantee the superiority of our civilization (Christianity, the heterosexual family, the Republic).

Reflections on the fate of our individual attention are particularly prone to the MELANCHOLIC NOSTALGIA that characterizes our intellectual atmosphere: *insight into the current dynamics that are casting a shadow over the future leads people to extol earlier lifestyles.* The most critical and clear-sited among us describe the sociotechnological transformations underway almost universally in terms of the danger of dumbing-down and enslavement. A quick overview of some (good) recent publications will enable us to pick out three broad analytical currents, which may of course come together in a particular author or book.[5]

A first current seeks to analyse the CAPITALIST PATHOLOGIES OF INDIVIDUAL ATTENTION: *the structural pressure to maximize financial profits brings about a steady exhaustion of the attentional and intellectual resources of the individual.* Under the heading of 'semiocapitalism', Franco Berardi has incisively demonstrated the imbalance produced by the disparity between the overabundance of semiotic goods made available to individuals and the paucity of attentional time necessary for their intelligent ingestion. He characterizes our predicament through the relationship between cyberspace and cybertime:

> Cyberspace is the infinite productivity of collective intelligence in a net-worked dimension. The potency of the General Intellect is enormously enhanced when a huge number of points enter into connections with each other thanks to the telematic network. Consequently, info-production is able to create an infinite supply of mental and intellectual goods. But while cyberspace is conceptually infinite, cybertime is not infinite at all. [. . .] Cybertime is the organic, physical, finite capacity to elaborate information. This ability is found in our mind, and our mind needs slowness in elaboration time, it needs to affectively singularize information. If elaboration time disappears the human mind is forced to follow the rhythm of the machinic network, and this brings about a pathology that manifests itself as panic and as depression on an individual level, and as generalized aggressiveness on a collective scale. [6]

While advocating political revolt and encouraging the emergence of anti-capitalist alternatives in support of the autonomist ideal, Franco Berardi notes above all the multiple symptoms of a 'pathological crash of the psycho-social organism', which is the fundamental truth of the countless crises coming one after the other at the surface level of our economies (recessions, market crashes, public debt) and deep down in our subjectivities (the consumption of Ritalin, Prozac or Viagra, burn-out and depression, suicide and attempted suicides).[7]

A second kind of discourse emphasizes the MACHINIC EROSION OF SOCIALIZING ATTENTION brought about by our intensely mediatized lives: *the proliferation of communication machines bombarding us with urgent messages inhibits our ability to be attentive towards others and attentive to our own desires.* When Winifred Gallagher characterizes our existence through the experience of *'focus interruptus'*, or Edward Hallowell emphasizes that the real question is not whether or not you are overoccupied, but whether you are overoccupied by things that you yourself value,[8] they join a long line of authors subscribing to the analysis developed in Maggie Jackson's book:

> The seduction of alternative virtual universes, the addictive allure of multi-tasking people and things, our near-religious allegiance to a constant state of motion: these are markers of a land of distraction, in which our old conceptions of space, time, and place have been shattered. This is why we are less able to see, hear, and comprehend what's relevant and permanent, why so many of us feel that we can barely keep our heads above water, and our days are marked by perpetual loose ends. What's more, the waning of our powers of attention is occurring

142

at such a rate and in so many areas of our life, that the erosion is reaching critical mass. We are on the verge of losing our capacity as a society for deep, sustained focus. In short, we are slipping towards a new dark age.[9]

This thesis of attentional erosion under the influence of new technologies finds its most developed form in a third kind of discourse, which specifies the threat of an imminent Dark Age as it proclaims the risks of a DISPLACEMENT OF THE MEDIOLOGICAL REGIME: *our modern and democratic civilizations are founded on the primacy of a book-based attention that encourages concentration, which is currently being replaced by a new regime of digital distraction dominated by the image and the hyperlink.* Behind the erosion of the presential attention that we are no longer able to give to one another, and more dangerous than it, we must locate a civilizational displacement (sometimes decried as irreversible), operative in the way in which our digital screens stimulate, activate and structure our attentional capacity (and our neuronal networks).

It is without doubt Nicholas Carr who has articulated the most seductive and well-known defence of this thesis, which he elaborates at the intersection of mediologically inspired macrohistorical schemas and the most recent discoveries in neuronal plasticity:

> We seem to have arrived, as McLuhan said we would, at an important juncture in our intellectual and cultural history, a moment of transition between two very different modes of thinking. What we're trading away in return for the riches of the Net – and only a curmudgeon would refuse to see the riches – is what Karp calls "our old linear thought process." Calm, focused, undistracted, the linear mind is being pushed aside by a new kind of mind that wants and needs to take in and dole out information in short, disjointed, often overlapping bursts – the faster, the better. [. . .] Just as neurons that fire together wire together, neurons that don't fire together don't wire together. As the time we spend scanning Web pages crowds out the time we spend reading books, as the time we spend exchanging bite-sized text messages crowds out the time we spend composing sentences and paragraphs, as the time we spend hopping across links crowds out the time we devote to quiet reflection and contemplation, the circuits that support those old intellectual functions and pursuits weaken and begin to break apart.[10]

In accordance with its original subtitle, the aim of the book is to understand 'how the internet is changing the way we think, read and remember'. His reasoning is particularly dramatic when, no longer content to reveal the 'stupidity' of our online behaviour, he describes a durable dumbing-down of our species as it is permanently

143

physiologically reprogrammed by its new digital practices. It is less our attention than our attention *capacity* that is threatened by a distraction machine that condemns us to an incurable superficiality. So, current reflections on the new digital-capitalist ecology of individual attention are certainly gloomy – situated between erosion, obscurantism and suicide.

A Literary Brain Heading Towards Extinction

It is perfectly possible to acknowledge the lucidity of the critiques discussed just now while nevertheless maintaining a certain scepticism with respect to their apocalyptic tone. Following Marshall McLuhan, thinkers like Vilém Flusser, Félix Guattari or Ivan Illich had, starting in the 1970s, already described a major mediological displacement taking place, at the end of which the book-object and the text-form, along with associated cultural practices and systems of authority, would in all likelihood be profoundly reconfigured as interactive apparatuses gained momentum – whose pitfalls they were able to anticipate at the same time as they espoused their benefits. In his last book, situated almost exactly at the point where the three currents distinguished above come together, Jonathan Crary is quite right to note that, in contrast to the promised emancipation of interactivity, the attentional machines that now surround the consumers of 'late capitalism' are even more alienating than the good old television on which our elders unleashed political critiques.

> What was celebrated as interactivity was more accurately the mobilization and habituation of the individual to an open-ended set of tasks and routines, far beyond what was asked of anyone in the 1950s and '60s. [. . .] So-called "smart" devices are labeled as such less for the advantages they might provide for an individual than for their capacity to integrate their user more fully into 24/7 routines. [. . .] As the opportunity for electronic transactions of all kinds becomes omnipresent, there is no vestige of what used to be everyday life beyond the reach of corporate intrusion. An attention economy dissolves the separation between the personal and professional, between entertainment and information, all overridden by a compulsory functionality of communication that is inherently and inescapably 24/7. [. . .] when [new] devices are introduced (and no doubt labeled as revolutionary), they will simply be facilitating the perpetuation of the same banal exercise of non-stop consumption, social isolation, and political powerlessness, rather than representing some historically significant turning point.[11]

The diagnosis is irrefutable. The reading given of the current historical moment in the evolution of attentional apparatuses is both lucid
and illuminating. We might, however, wonder about the 'form of
attention' that orientates these reflections on attention, in the etymological sense of the term (*ad-tendere*). *Towards what do they tend?* –
if not a nostalgia for the good old days that are now lost: 'what used
to be everyday life beyond the reach of corporate intrusion', 'our
old linear thought process', 'our old conceptions of space, time, and
place'. Where Illich, Flusser or Guattari situated the (radical) critique
of the present in the perspective of the new forms of emancipation
made possible (and already taken up) by the digital development of
our collective intelligence, the last decade seems to have condemned
itself to lamenting a past that is fading away.

It seems ill-advised to leave the privilege of hope to the visionaries
of post-humanism and other web 3.0 entrepreneurs who promise
to regulate our attentional overloading through the miracle of technological innovation – like Ray Kurzweil when he declares that our
email accounts will soon be able to communicate directly with each
other, without us having to waste time looking at our messages.[12]
How can we re-situate a reflexive reading of our attentional transformations in a collective movement of hope and new development,
without for all that losing the lucidity of the above critiques of
capitalism and machinic alienation? This is without doubt the major
challenge of the reflexive discourses that we might hold on attention
today – a challenge that is illustrated by the exemplary case of the
status of *the reader* in contemporary reflections.

So as to contrast the distraction inflicted on us by the digital media
with the concentration encouraged by the culture of the book, as it
was established when we began to read in silence, Nicholas Carr has
written a fine eulogy of the 'literary brain':

> Reading a book was a meditative act, but it didn't involve a clearing
> of the mind. It involved a filling, or replenishing, of the mind. Readers
> disengaged their attention from the outward flow of passing stimuli in
> order to engage it more deeply with an inward flow of words, ideas, and
> emotions. That was – and is – the essence of the unique mental process
> of deep reading. It was the technology of the book that made this
> "strange anomaly" in our psychological history possible. The brain of
> the book reader was more than a literate brain. It was a literary brain.[13]

The many knights of the literary cause, who battle valiantly today
against reductions in jobs, status and budgets in their discipline,
can only delight to see one of the new masters of the web change

allegiance and join in their fight. Indeed, we will see that it is essential that the kind of 'deep' or 'literary' reading described here by Nicholas Carr should be valued in the framework of an attention ecology.

In our reflections on the developments of our individual attention, the orientation of our analyses is as important as their object. In keeping with the works of George Steiner, the championing of books, literature and the humanities has usually taken a nostalgic tone, clinging to the remains of an experience of deep reading that is heading towards extinction to decry the superficiality and the illusions to which our new 'post-literary' spirit is victim. But this analytical orientation is not only debatable from the perspective of our historical knowledge; it above all risks becoming a self-fulfilling prophecy. The quotation given from Nicholas Carr's book will allow us to illustrate better what this is all about.

Historians of cultural practice tell us that this deep reading dating back to a distant time when our ancestors started to 'engage [their attention] more deeply with an inward flow of words, ideas, and emotions' represents just *one* of the different ways of relating to writing, and that our 'civilization of the book' was largely built on an overcoming of this meditative absorption. Ivan Illich's fine book on Hugues de Saint-Victor shows brilliantly how what we have thought of for centuries as a 'text' had to free itself from its original state of immersion in the flow of oration typical of religious writings until the twelfth century – a state of immersion which today is the model of attentive reading.[14] It was just as important to invent tools enabling the 'navigation' of texts and books (division into paragraphs, insertion of headings, table of contents, references) as it was to be 'immersed' in them. Even if these two movements are at right-angles and incompatible at any given moment, they are in fact complementary – and it would be absurd to suggest that I am not an attentive reader because I lose track of the argument when I consult an endnote.

And yet it is on this kind of exclusive and monomaniacal fundamentalism that many of our current complaints are based. Another whole series of recent publications – unfortunately much less frequently cited in French debate – tackles these same questions from a direction that is unencumbered by declinism. After having dedicated a chapter to deconstructing the presuppositions of the standardized intelligence tests on which most studies showing an alleged 'lowered level' for 'digital natives' are based, Cathy Davidson recounts how public debate around the internet and video games (played by 97 per cent of this generation) was dramatically upended in the United States following the school massacre at Columbine in 1999. She highlights that the most extensive study of video games (published by Pew Research Centre in 2008) suggests that 'absorption in games doesn't contradict social life, civic engagement, focus, attention, connection with other kids, or collaboration'.[15] Her conclusion goes against the grain of the dominant nostalgic discourse:

> By all statistical measures these digital natives happen to be the happiest, healthiest, most social, most civic-minded, best adjusted, and least violent and self-destructive teens since large demographic surveys began at the end of World War II. [. . .] If kids cannot pay attention in school, it may be less because they have ADHD and more because we have a mismatch between the needs and desires of students today and the national standards-based education based on the efficiencies of a classroom created before World War I. Are kids being dumbed down by digital culture or by our insistence on success and failure as measured by testing geared to lower-order and largely irrelevant item-response skills? Are video games the problem, or, as I suspect, is the problem our widespread abdication of the new three Rs (rigor, relevance, and relationship) in favour of antiquated testing based on rote memorization of random facts that has little to do with the way kids actually read, write, and do arithmetic online – or will need to do it in the workplace?[16]

While Cathy Davidson's optimism should certainly be tempered to the same degree as the declinism of the authors she is criticizing, her analysis provides two important reframings. On the one hand, we wonder if the new obscurantism noted in the development of our attentional attitudes might – like the drunk who looks for his keys under the streetlight because of its light, even though he lost them elsewhere – stem from the fact that we are incapable of turning our attention (and above all our measuring devices) to the new expertise peculiar to the digital age. On the other hand, as we saw above, many of our anxieties are based on the very debatable premise of an exclusive alternative and a natural incompatibility between digital hyper-attention, symbolized by videogames, and deep attention, identified with literary reading.

It is in order to overcome this deceptive alternative that Katherine Hayles has called for the humanities to pluralize their understanding of reading. Yes, the practice of close textual reading is a central exercise in literary studies but, no, literary studies have nothing to gain from closing up around this one exercise. Instead of cowering in yesterday's definition, they would do better to redeploy in a broader disciplinary field, yet to be established – comparative media studies:

> Learning to read complex texts (i.e. 'close reading') has long been seen as the special province of the humanities, and humanities scholars pride

themselves on knowing how to do it well and how to teach students to do it. With the advent of digital media, other modes of reading are claiming an increasing share of what counts as 'literacy', including hyper reading and analysis through machine algorithms ('machine reading'). [17] Hyper reading, often associated with reading on the web, has also been shown to bring about cognitive and morphological changes in the brain. Young people are at the leading edge of these changes, but pedagogical strategies have not to date generally been fashioned to take advantage of these changes. Students read and write print texts in the classroom and consume and create digital texts of their own on screens (with computers, iPhones, tablets, etc.), but there is little transfer from leisure activities to classroom instruction and vice versa. A Comparative Media Studies perspective can result in courses and curricula that recognize all three reading modalities – close, hyper, and machine – and prepare students to understand the limitations and affordances of each. [18]

So, COMPARATIVE MEDIA STUDIES may be defined as a reconfiguration of literary studies which seeks to *'teach literacies across a range of media forms, including print and digital, focusing on interpretation and analysis of patterns, meaning, and context through close, hyper, and machine reading practices'*. [19] It would be a question, therefore, of studying how, through which attributes, and with what effects on human attention and intelligence, our different media apparatuses structure our environments.

Literary studies and the humanities should certainly be defended, but this in no way exempts them from the need to transform themselves so they can better face the challenges and the hopes that have arisen (so rapidly) with digitalization. It is right to worry about their institutional status, but it is not by advocating a return to the past or grasping at what remains of it that we will further their cause. In its own provocative way, Pierre Bayard's book teaching us how to speak about books that we have not read belongs to the same pluralizing movement promoted here by Katherine Hayles, as it runs through the multiple ways we may look at a book – from far away and very superficially (we hear people talk about it, glance at its title and back cover), to the close, deep, meditative and almost religious study of a short story or poem. [20] The humanities should adopt a PLURALIST UNDERSTANDING OF READING, recognizing the *complementary (rather than rival) nature of close reading, distant hyper-reading and machine reading.*

In the development of an attention ecology we will be helped above all by an ability to modulate our focus – in such a way that we can, depending on the moment and our mood, alternate between very deep absorption in a book and looking at it from a great distance in the context of the landscape that it forms with other cultural objects. Valuing only the deep immersion cultivated by our good old books, as opposed to the superficial navigation brought on by the internet is like being made to choose between drinking and eating. No doubt you could live only on soup, or get all of your liquids from watermelons, but is this really how to get our contemporaries and our descendants back to the literary table?

Nicholas Carr's well informed and subtle book is better served by its English title (*The Shallows*) than by the sensational question (taken from a polemical article) that serves as a title to the French translation [*Is the Internet Making Us Stupid?*]. Far from advocating a return to the Middle Ages, the author reflects on a general tendency towards shallowness brought on by the different 'distraction machines' that we are surrounded by in our digital environment. The real – and excellent – question he asks is not about knowing whether the internet is making us stupid, but about whether we will be able to *adjust our environment so as to protect profound experiences*. His reflection brings us, therefore, to the heart of what must be thought of as an attention *ecology*. In this heart we will rediscover what he characterizes as 'a literary brain', but extended to a whole range – at once very broad and very specific – of experiences, that may be broadly qualified as 'aesthetic'.

Aesthetic Laboratories

Reflecting on attention poses an apparently unsolvable problem, whose knot paralyses our most essential socio-political debates. Our epoch often complains – and rightly so – that it is weighed down by evaluation procedures that have become simultaneously invasive, so time-consuming as to be paralysing, and disfiguring, since they are destined to ruin what they are trying to account for. A classic argument of the defenders of the humanities consists in highlighting the extent to which their disciplines are doomed from the start, from the moment we purport to subject them to a numerical logic when by 'essence' they are situated in the incalculable. Despite its hypocrisies – the same teachers serving as apologists for the incalculable hardly hesitate to give their students a numerical mark – the argument indicates a problem that is actually extremely important, the problem of VALORIZING EVALUATION, which attention ecology helps

149

us to identify (as we have been doing since chapter three): if *giving your attention to something helps you to recognize in it a value that will justify the attention you will give it later, then all of our evaluation procedures are affected by a fundamental flaw, since they actively contribute to* produce *the value they claim only to* measure *objectively.*

As we have already had the opportunity to see, this fundamental flaw that grounds an auto-referential circle is nevertheless only the flip side of a virtue. The force [*virtus*] of human attention consists precisely in its ability to discover new 'values': among the 'millions of external things that are present to our senses', it identifies certain objects or phenomena that deserve to be noticed for the contribution they might make to our wellbeing. We are often, therefore, right to reject existing evaluations, since their procedures conceal processes of valorization that they reproduce and impose occultly. But, most importantly, this rejection should lead us to question our modes of valorization – the most general, and clearly hegemonic even if it has not yet colonized every sphere of our social life, being CAPITALISTIC VALORIZATION, *which measures the value of a good or activity based only on its capacity for maximizing the profits of an investor.* Behind the rejection of the rating of universities in the Shanghai rankings, and behind the rejection of certain redundancies, or the occupation of public parks from Madrid to New York and Istanbul, we see the rise of one same awareness – still confused in certain milieux, but undergoing accelerated clarification – of the profoundly harmful character of this hegemony.

As a reflection on the processes of valorization, attention ecology comes, therefore, to play a central role in denouncing the illusions and deceptions which, through certain modes of evaluation, seriously and tragically distort the values that we bestow (or that we should bestow) on external things. But what the particular case of the literary attention valorized by Nicholas Carr brings home is the role played by our aesthetic experiences in general as VALORIZATION LABORATORIES: in line with Jacques Rancière's characterization of a 'reconfiguration of the distribution of the sensible',[21] *the immersion in an aesthetic experience leads to the valorization of previously unexpected sensations and feelings, and/or to the modification of associated valorizations.*

As he seeks to summarize the 'ecology of literary studies', taking the reading of poetry as a privileged example, Jean-Marie Schaeffer gives a very good analysis of the central role played by attention in our aesthetic experiences:

150

The aesthetic relation is a human conduct whose central stake is (linguistic, perceptive, etc.) attention itself, in its deployment: the success or failure of an aesthetic experience is not decided by the characteristics of the (real or represented) object, but by the satisfactory or unsatisfactory quality of the attentional process that we invest in that object. [. . .] The default dynamic of the act of verbal comprehension is founded on a principle of economy: it is a matter of understanding as quickly as possible while expending the least attentional energy. [. . .] In the framework of the aesthetic relation, on the other hand, it is attention itself, and so in this case reading as act, which is the aim of the conduct, and it no longer follows the principle of economy, but on the contrary maximizes the attentional investment.[22]

An 'ecological' approach emerges from our aesthetic laboratories because they constitute a place where the laws of the (cognitive) economy are suspended: to approach these situations in terms of an 'attention economy' is, therefore, to risk crushing their specific character. Jean-Marie Schaeffer shows more precisely that the attentional style called forth by poetry in particular, but by aesthetic experiences more generally too, is based on a 'delay in categorization':

The drawing out of the treatment of the linguistic signal due to the maximizing of attentional investment, does not produce only an attentional overloading, but also a delay in categorization, which is to say, a delay in the activity of hermeneutic synthesis (we accept that we will not understand 'straight away'). And this delayed categorization is always experienced as a dissonance, since it thwarts the principle of economy that seeks cognitive consonance. The capacity an individual has to give their sustained attention to the sonorous materiality of a text is, therefore, proportional to their capacity to tolerate situations of delayed categorization.[23]

The term 'laboratory' proves particularly apt here as it brings together three kinds of attitude which we tend to think of as incompatible with each other, but which are in fact typical of the artistic sphere – from the installations of avant-garde galleries to big-budget films, passing by rock concerts and hip-hop dances. Even if their methods are not 'scientific' in the usual meaning of the term, our aesthetic experiences relate to an attitude of (collective) *experimentation* which corresponds closely with how we imagine the laboratory: a space that is temporarily isolated from the daily world becomes a place of investigation, where we test certain limits of what can be done, perceived, felt, discovered, thought or justified. To be more precise, artistic modernity has taught us to make our encounter with the work the occasion for an 'experience' (of cognitive dissonance): even if there is

151

no attempt to quantitatively measure its effects, this encounter has the value of a 'test' through which we may appreciate what an artist can do and a spectator experience.

Our aesthetic experiences also relate to the laboratory in the etymological sense of the term, in that they are the place of a *labour*. On the side of the 'creator' – which, along with Étienne Souriau, we would do well to think of as an 'instigator'[24] – even the art of improvisation or the found object, which establish an important role for serendipity, are largely based on a sedimentation of the efforts necessary to bring about interesting encounters or discoveries. The participation of the reader, the listener or the spectator, are also a kind of 'labour' in that all our aesthetic experiences constitute, each in its own way, a certain challenge brought to our attention capabilities (a challenge to our tolerance for classification delay): we are invited to labour on ourselves to raise our sensitivity, our sentiments, and our understanding to the level of the programme that the work offers us. In their research and labour aspect, these aesthetic laboratories that might be books, theatres or cinemas, are certainly places for the verification and reprocessing of values: they set up a double experiment which is undergone in parallel by the work (will it 'hold up', bringing something that will sustain the attention we are to give it?) and the receiver (will they be able to enjoy and take advantage of the opportunity that is presented to them?). The experiment is only conclusive if the work and the attention it solicits are both successful in demonstrating their value – independently and yet jointly.

Finally, from the moment that our aesthetic experiences come to be situated beyond and before the principle of economy – in the suspense of a classification delay where the urgency of action briefly gives way to the unknown of contemplation – a third kind of attitude necessary to the constitution of the aesthetic laboratory reveals itself as intimately connected with that inactive activity that is *prayer* (if we are willing to read 'lab-oratory' as the place of a labour orientated towards oration). By highlighting the 'meditative' dimension of deep reading or literature, by having it emerge from the medieval religious tradition, by giving it the function of 'satisfying the spirit' and 'renewing its contents', Nicholas Carr already indicated how our aesthetic experiences are always related to 'oration' (from which they doubtless originate historically). Risking the trial of the work – which you instigate as an artist or expose yourself to as a spectator – always involves praying that the improbable and aleatory encounter will take place. We go to a show or open a book animated by the hope that we will momentarily connect with something that is bigger than us – on the occasion of a properly mystical communion, capable of initiating us into a higher form of existence.

The Gaze of the Third Bird

It is perhaps in tribute to this oratory dimension inherent in the experimentations of our aesthetic laboratories that an international collective – whose precise origins and real extent remain quite mysterious – gets together intermittently at various places around the world to develop attentional exercises under the auspices of the enigmatic Order of the Third Bird. Its members have assigned themselves the double and complementary mission of actively cultivating their attentional capabilities while nourishing through their active contemplation a work that they think suffers from a lack of attention. Their rituals consist in gathering in front of a painting that has been buried for decades in the deep recesses of a museum, or placing themselves in front of an architectural eccentricity that hurried passers-by neglect in the daily rush, or, again, assembling around a found object that bears witness to a lost practice or defies explanation. So, acting as 'attention attendants', they generously dedicate different forms of precisely assigned sustained attention to this human production, over time periods that may vary from thirty minutes to twenty-four hours. We may speak here of ATTENTIONAL PERFORMANCE in that, far from being considered a phenomenon coming after the fact that remains external to works that supposedly exist autonomously, here the reception of the work is rooted in *the production of a joint co-presential attention to the work, an attention which is itself raised to the level of artistic activity.*

Over the years, the members have developed a broad (and still incomplete) range of precise and ritualized rules which enable them to establish a certain JOINT ATTENTIONAL PROTOCOL for each individual performance: in this way, they play with the fact that *our aesthetic attention is structured by temporalities, phases, attitudes, focusing and distancing modes which can be the subject of shared exercises.* Five or six members may decide to stand in a line in front of a painting for two hours, dividing this period into four previously differentiated phases.

These exercises are of course rooted in joint attention, firstly because it is the progressive and synchronized convergence of their looking that makes up the substance of the attentional performance, and, secondly, because these practices do not fail to have an effect on people who were not part of the ritual to begin with. When they take place in the exhibition rooms of a museum, and not in its storage area, visitors cannot fail to be struck by the alignment of surprisingly still and perfectly silent Birds. The intensity and the ritualized nature of their sustained attention powerfully attracts the attention of passers-by who, in turn, look at the work with a curiosity that is quite exceptional in the contemporary museum context, where busloads of tourists are discharged only to bow before half a dozen seminal works (also in a very ritualized manner) while passing very quickly over the rest of the collection. Even if this is probably not their primary ambition, the members of The Order of the Third Bird illustrate the possibility of an ATTENTIONAL ACTIVISM in which one *makes a conspicuous demonstration of one's joint attention so as to draw collective attention to an unjustly ignored object.*

We still need to understand better, however, the way in which the laboratories of the Third Bird constitute a properly attentional 'practice' or 'labour'. Did not a whole swathe of twentieth-century aesthetico-political thought make the 'activity' of looking into the very opposite of activity, practice and (productive or revolutionary) labour? Mark Hansen's 'new philosophy for new media' might help

---

The Order of the Third Bird is currently engaged in a silent practice of Sustained Attention to Made Things. You are welcome to stand with members of the Order and join in giving your generous attention to the work.

ESTAR (SER)

The ORDER of the THIRD BIRD

For inquiries & information, the Order may be contacted through thirdbird.org or at orderofthethirdbird@gmail.com.

---

14. Notice outlining the Order of the Third Bird's practice of sustained attention

us to enlarge upon what was so well outlined by Jacques Rancière in his now famous essay on the *Emancipated Spectator*:

> Emancipation begins when we challenge the opposition between viewing and acting, [. . .] when we understand that viewing is also an action that confirms or transforms this distribution of positions. The spectator also acts, like the pupil or scholar. She observes, selects, compares, interprets. She links what she sees to a host of other things that she has seen on other stages, in other kinds of place.[25]

How can we explain this 'action' peculiar to the way of looking practised and trained by the Birds during their attentional performances? In the framework of a debate with the 'technological determinism' with which Friedrich Kittler's[26] thinking of the media is often charged, Mark Hansen highlights the role played by our bodies in the treatment of images, taking up the problematic of 'embodiment' we have already encountered with Richard Shusterman and Katherine Hayles. Where many digital theoreticians reason in terms of information, he emphasizes that this information only has meaning as a function of the labour carried out by an attentive body. Observing, selecting, comparing, interpreting – to pick up Jacques Rancière's terms – all relate inextricably to both *filtering* and *creation*. Images are never simply 'received', as though they had already been fixed in themselves for an eternity by a transmitter or a technology: they only make sense – a sense which is always a little different – in the reprocessing operations carried out by an (always differently) attentive receiver. It is the reflexive (slowed down and intensified) protocols developing these communal operations and lifting them to a higher power that constitute the Bird's ceremonies.

> [R]ather than selecting preexistent *images*, the body now operates by filtering *information* directly and, through this process, *creating* images. Correlated with the advent of digitization, then, the body undergoes a certain empowerment, since it deploys its own constitutive singularity (affection and memory) not to filter a universe of preconstituted images, but actually to *enframe* something (digital information) that is originally formless. Moreover, this "originary" act of enframing information must be seen as the source of all technical frames (even if these appear to be primary), to the extent that these are designed to make information perceivable by the body, that is, to transform it into the form of the image.[27]

As they line up several pairs of eyes in front of a neglected work, the *low tech* exercises practised by the Birds constitute a laboratory in which the processes that in reality 'shape' all of the images that affect us can be observed and experienced with great subtlety. As we have been repeating since the beginning of this book, attention functions as a selection operator. However, as Mark Hansen helps us to clarify, attention does not select between preformed images, but amongst information which is only constituted into images through this operation – an operation that transforms information into signification, thanks to a labour of the frame (enframing, deframing, reframing).

Ancestral practices of attentional exercises – coming from multiple traditions of 'spiritual exercises' – become central to a new set of concerns with digitalization. It is often repeated, and rightly so, that the digital image (made up of pixels on our screens) differs ontologically from the analogue image (exemplified by photographs produced through the gelatin-silver process) in that the second imposes on the receiver a block of characteristics that have been materially fixed, while the first allows anyone to independently adjust its different parameters (size, framing, colour intensity, even the internal composition with Photoshop).[28] Far from leading inexorably towards an extreme alienation of our way of looking, the DESTABILIZATION OF THE IMAGE permitted by our digital devices *only exteriorizes the active and creative labour of reframing which has always been constitutive of the peculiar function of human attention.* So, Mark Hansen suggests that the 'digital image' characteristic of our epoch should be defined as the process carried out by the attentive body through which information is transformed into signification: 'the image can no longer be restricted to the level of surface appearance, but must be extended to encompass the entire process by which information is made perceivable through embodied experience.'[29]

We can determine better now what is at stake in the attentional protocols developed by the Order of the Third Bird. By giving a neglected work several hours of sustained attention, structured in several phases with each operating a particular attentional reframing, the members work towards a RE-STABILIZATION OF THE IMAGE – something that has become indispensable in the context of our digital cultures: in an environment in which everything undergoes endless reframing according to heterogeneous, often contradictory and always rushed, demands, the look of the Third Bird is positioned such that it can *experiment in a reflective way with the processes by which information is stabilized into a meaningful image.* The members do not only work as attention attendants for the forgotten works to which their ceremonies are dedicated, but also as auxiliary nurses for our attention itself, which is chronically lacking in stability in our universe of digital images.

So, aesthetic laboratories come into focus as places for the exercise and testing of a labour, at once mysteriously initiatory and perfectly common, through which our attention puts pieces of information together to constitute them as perceptions, images and meanings. These laboratories are well suited for making our attention reflect on the objects to which it gives itself over, and on the valorizations in which it participates. It will therefore necessarily be of central interest for an attention ecology. 'The arts' are often presented as 'secondary' realities of our social life, 'luxury' 'diversions' that we sacrifice (regretfully, but in the front line) to the merciless gods of austerity – so that we can save the essential (read: 'the economy') as we wait for the crisis to pass and the end of the tunnel. The artistic practices and cultural apparatuses in place to disseminate their mystical pleasures to the population must on the contrary be thought of as being at the very heart of our social life: it is through their intercession that the processes of valorization – on which not only the totality of our economic activities but the very constitution of our lives depend – are renewed, altered, adapted and revolutionized.

Leaving the Laboratory

To those who would doubt – not without reason – that the fate of capitalism, of carbon-based industry or the production of microprocessors is at stake in the processes of valorization cobbled together in the ultra-minority laboratories that are art galleries, independent cinemas or free-jazz concerts, we should give two provisional responses, which only apparently contradict each other.

Firstly, we do not only observe the aesthetic experiences we are speaking of here in traditional places of 'high culture', in the elitist hangouts of the avant-garde and in cultural arenas where the public are invited into an 'ascetic' participation (which is demanding, difficult and therefore rare) – but also, in more or less diluted form, in the mainstream cultural offering which draws millions of spectators into its multiplex cinemas and in front of its small screens. Rare are the television series or Bollywood films that do not contain a fleeting moment of aesthetic adjournment – in the recess of an unforeseen twist in the plot, a suddenly inspired dialogue, a musical treasure or an unexpected edit. As standardized and mind-numbing as they may seem, the products of the cultural industries also distribute traces of past aesthetic experiences among the most extensive of audiences – whose forms may have a sense of *déjà-vu* for *aficionados*, but whose effects on less informed spectators are, for all that, no less real. So we must take into account processes of DIFFUSION BY DILUTION: *what dilutes the radicalism of aesthetic experiences allows them progressively to infiltrate the broadest strata of the population, and in this way generalize the reprocessing of values taking place in a concentrated and narrow way in ascetic experiences.*

Before we even get to the moments of aesthetic experimentation that exit the laboratory to infiltrate the products of commercial culture, Steven Johnson has sought to show that the development of American television series over the last fifty years has tended to provide viewers with ever more complex mental exercises. If he is to be believed, we should look beyond the explicit *content* of (violent, stereotypical, 'immoral') entertainment productions, to try to measure the kinds of *intellectual operations* that they ask of their receivers when they attempt to follow the narrative or character developments. The mass media should be analysed as providing 'a kind of cognitive workout, not a series of life lessons'. We then realize that 'the most debased forms of mass diversion – video games and violent television dramas and juvenile sitcoms – turn out to be nutritional after all'.[30] Following very popular series like *Seinfeld, ER* or *The West Wing* demands much more complex mental operations than was the case in the 1960s.

> For decades, we've worked under the assumption that mass culture follows a steadily declining path toward lowest-common-denominator standards, presumably because the "masses" want dumb, simple pleasures and big media companies want to give the masses what they want. But in fact, the exact opposite is happening: the culture is getting more intellectually demanding, not less.[31]

Despite some weaknesses in Steven Johnson's demonstration, his intuition should be taken seriously. Of course, the ostensible values on display in mainstream entertainment provide plenty of ammunition for the most acerbic critics of the cultural industries. But, in this sphere, what we see is probably less important than the way in which our attention is mobilized to make sense of what is to be seen. And, from this point of view, it is not unreasonable to hope that the slow but progressive infiltration of aesthetic experiences into mass cultural products will bring with it an increase in the complexity of the cognitive procedures induced in the spectators. Following a fiction requires a multi-dimensional attentional labour,[32] and we would certainly be wrong to exclude mass entertainment from the laboratories where our valorizations to come are continually being reprocessed.

Secondly, however, this dynamic by which values are constantly adjusted through their diffusion in mainstream cultural industries is based on the protection of privileged spaces of aesthetic experimentation. An attention ecology must, therefore, understand and actively defend the environmental conditions necessary for these artistic practices and aesthetic experiences to develop, sheltered from the pressure of profitability that tightly limits what can come through commercial channels. Aesthetic laboratories should be understood as VACUOLES which allow for *the temporary suspension of the demands of communicational attention, so as to be able to concentrate full attention on a privileged cultural object over an extended period.*

You can easily tell today that you are entering a vacuole of this kind when you are reminded to turn off your mobile phone. Reading rooms,[33] classrooms, cinemas,[34] concert halls, dance theatres and theatres[35] are without doubt, along with churches, the last sacred spaces where the attentional vampirism of communication still respects the superior values of a certain mystical communion – which would be sacrilegiously disturbed by a mobile phone ringing. Like the circle drawn on the ground in which the shaman can receive divine inspiration, like the laboratory we can only enter wearing a white coat and gloves, the white cube of the art gallery and the black box of cinematic projection or theatrical performance constitute paratopic spaces that establish attentional ecosystems ruled by their own laws, invested with magical properties and opening onto a perspective of elevation whose closest anthropomorphic equivalent is mystical initiation.

A strategy that is diametrically opposed to the constitution of aestheticizing vacuoles may nonetheless contribute to the sharpening and heightening of our reflexive attention. With a few accomplices gathered around the publisher *Questions Théoriques*, the poet and theoretician Christophe Hanna has for nearly two decades been developing a demonstration that he speaks of in terms of 'direct action poetry' and a thinking of 'apparatuses'. Instead of seeking to suspend communicational pressures and withdrawing into a vacuole that is protected in its temporary isolation, he advocates forms of APPARATUS-BASED INTERVENTION which aim to *take a position in communication flows in an attempt to short-circuit them from the inside.* Like advertising or political storytelling, direct action poetry seeks to insert spin, buzz, memes or viruses into the normal avenues by which information and art circulate. So, under the pseudonym La Rédaction, Christophe Hanna publishes 'poetic documents' on the decapitation of hostages by Abou Moussab al-Zarqaoui, on a short-lived reality TV star, or on the memory traces left by a hostage situation at a nursery school in Neuilly in 1993, which gave the then mayor, Nicolas Sarkozy, the opportunity to appear as a man of providence.[36] In every case, it is a question of making direct contact with our mediatized attention – the work dedicated to the Neuilly news item appeared right in the middle of the 2012 presidential campaign.

More than 'works' to be contemplated in mystical stasis, we are here dealing with 'apparatuses' that exit the laboratory in an attempt to occupy the most important field of our social conflicts: the mediasphere. Not, however, to discreetly infiltrate mainstream culture, as was suggested by the work of Steven Johnson, but to introduce elements productive of blockages, crashes and sudden bifurcations. Of course, this joins in a long tradition of modern art seeking to escape the ghettos of the museums and theatre stages to directly invade the social space as it reorders 'situations' there. Apparatus-based interventions are, however, explicitly rooted in a 'reflected' attention in the optical sense of the term, which involves grasping immediacy rather than a reflexive step back: our collective attention looks at itself in the mirror, without being able to separate itself from its own image, even if it knows that what it is contemplating is a distortion of the truth. We find the symmetrical twin of this in recent work by the Russian artist Arseniy Zhilyaev, who pretends to expound and venerate the works of Valdimir Putin, elevating him to the status of the greatest performance artist of our time, since the Russian President is able to 'produce an event', 'cause disruptions' and 'impact the real' thanks to the performerly and performative staging of his public persona.[37]

It is probably not La Rédaction's apparatus-based intervention that caused Nicolas Sarkozy's defeat in the 2012 presidential election. It is certainly, however, on the basis of his staged performances, and their prominence in the global and Russian mediasphere, that Valadimir Putin has been able to get himself re-elected to the Kremlin so often. Christophe Hanna's and Arseniy Zhilyaev's work share the same paradoxical gesture of attentional adhesion resulting in rejection through over-proximity: through both we are made aware of a staged fiction while at the same time immediately grasping a reality in the making. That towards which our reflexive attention tends (*ad-tendere*) belongs to what narratology calls a *metalepsis*, by which it refers to the collapse of two narrative levels that are imagined to be distinct and impermeable – like when the fictional character Don Quixote meets the real-life character of his author Cervantes.[38] In order to better understand this kind of metaleptic short-circuit, we will need to specify the structure on which the reflexive attention implemented in our aesthetic experiences is based.

Seeing (by) the Attention of the Other

At the level of individual attention, museums, cinemas, fictional narratives, classrooms and performance venues are characterized by the same structure of META-ATTENTIONAL ENGAGEMENT: *the spectator's attention is found to be plugged into the attentional experience of another more or less strongly subjectivized perception of the world, through which a certain reality is revisited.* This kind of apparatus is defined by four characteristics (Figure 15).

Firstly, there is a *difference in level* between two (or more) attentions, one of which (that of the spectator) enters into the other (that of the narrator, painter, filmmaker, producer, character) from above.

Secondly, this difference in level brings about the possibility of an *objectification* of our attentional experience. The terminology that Bernard Stiegler takes up from Husserlian phenomenology may help us to clarify the nature of this objectification: these engagement apparatuses enable our 'primary retentions' (our perceptions) and 'secondary retentions' (our memories) to externalize themselves, to materialize themselves, to stabilize themselves and to share themselves as 'tertiary retentions', namely as media objects like books, poems, films, videos, CDs and mp3 files.

Thirdly, the attention that my perception plugs into is always rooted in a certain *subjectivation*, even if each apparatus is characterized by a degree and a mode of subjectivation that are particular to it. Even an experimental film like Michael Snow's *The Central Region*, where the camera is placed on a horizontal and vertical rotating mechanism (360° x 360°) sweeping across a deserted landscape for three hours – even this kind of objectivist mechanism is rooted in a

DIFFERENCE IN LEVEL

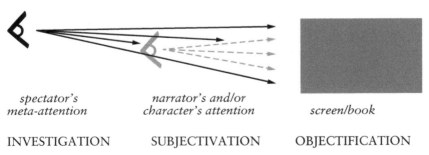

spectator's	*narrator's and/or*	
meta-attention	*character's attention*	*screen/book*
INVESTIGATION	SUBJECTIVATION	OBJECTIFICATION

15. Meta-attentional engagement

certain subjective project attempting to reduce as much as possible the filtering practised by a human subject on our perceptual data. The main virtue of meta-attentional engagement is precisely that it helps us to question the limits, the presuppositions, the blind spots and the other dead zones of our subjectivity: by repackaging the focusing, deframing and reframing effects through which we perceive reality, narrative and aesthetic apparatuses lead us to reconsider and readjust the parameters of our subjectivation.

And finally, fourthly, even though it is directly plugged into the attention of another subjectivity that is external to me, my attention retains a certain *investigative* margin within this kind of apparatus: within the work of production in words, sounds and images undertaken by creators, which is to say, within the attentional flow into which I plug my attention, I may focus on this actor rather than that actor, one theme, instrument, colour or form rather than another. Of course, the margin granted to our freedom of investigation by individual meta-attentional apparatuses varies greatly – and is doubtless one of the criteria that allows us to differentiate them, categorize them and recognize their different values. A typical Hollywood action film, jam-packed with car chases, yelling, explosions and constant gunshots, is like the old-style lecture where students had to copy word-for-word, in that it leaves practically no room for freedom of investigation by an attention destined to remain almost completely 'receptive'.

Our pedagogical and aesthetic experiences relate, therefore, to two very different forms of attentional joining. On the one hand, my attention is joined to that of the other spectators, other listeners, even the other readers, whereby we share our laughter, surprises, applause and now clicks ('like', 'dislike'). Other than the instance of reading a novel on a desert island, it is always a question of experiences inscribed in a collectivity – even with books and literature, as was aptly recalled in a recent article by François Cusset.[39]

At the same time, on the other hand, watching a film, listening to music or reading a text are always profoundly personal adventures – more *individuating* than individual. By virtue of the freedom of investigation from which our attention benefits in the attention flow with which we have engaged our senses, every reading, listening, or viewing maps out its singular exploration of the work, contributing to the parallel individuation of the work and the subjectivities that are developed through it. It is certainly another subjectivity that we are plugged into by meta-attentional engagement – be it minimal like that of *The Central Region*, or collective like that of a theatrical improvisation company – but it is a subjectivity that has been *objectivized* in the form of a tertiary retention. We are not joined to the author, the filmmaker, the actress or the painter, but to the work itself, in that its objectivized attention constitutes a vector of subjectivation.

We are here well and truly in the sphere of *reflexive* attention: every time that I open a book, listen to a lecture, or start a video, my attention takes someone else's attention as its object, which I enter into so as to re-imagine the world from a different point of view, while retaining the liberty to wander freely inside this objectivized attention. By putting our attention onto another attention, meta-attentional engagement opens a space whose reflexive structure helps us to reflect on what determines our attention.

The reflexive structure of meta-attentional apparatuses explains how readers, listeners and viewers are drawn into a constant back and forth between two mutually exclusive but complementary levels. Indeed, the meta-attentional adventure is based on an OSCILLATION BETWEEN IMMERSION AND CRITIQUE, where we are invited to *become absorbed in the represented attention (and in the universe in which it immerses us), while keeping one foot in the real situation from which we consider this attention* (Figure 16). I share the surprise and fear of the protagonist when a monstrous figure suddenly comes out of the dark, and yet I know that I am at the cinema and that I am not in danger. This double, two-levelled consciousness, through which I live in the territory and on the map by which it is represented at the same time has, until now, been the defining factor of aesthetic

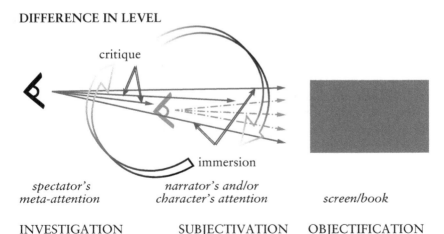

DIFFERENCE IN LEVEL

critique

immersion

spectator's   *narrator's and/or*
meta-attention   *character's attention*   *screen/book*

INVESTIGATION   SUBJECTIVATION   OBJECTIFICATION

16. The oscillation between immersion and critique

163

experiences taking place in the reassuring context of theatres or books. If these vacuoles need to be reevaluated and more carefully protected today, this is also because this simultaneously immerged and overarching double attention is in the process of being generalized to our very experience of reality – erasing the limits separating 'spectacles' from 'life'. It is no doubt on this dizzying merry-go-round that we encounter the metalepses mentioned above with respect to Christophe Hanna and Arseniy Zhilyaev.

The analyses of Guy Debord, Jean Baudrillard or Paul Virilio have shed light on the SIMULACRAL PERMEATION of human attention, which manifests itself unavoidably today in our social arrangements and technological gadgets. It has become commonplace to say that *all our perceptions of the world are informed by the representations circulating among us and through us*.[40] As our media apparatuses became more numerous, more efficient and more ubiquitous, we learned to look at territories according to the maps that we had stored up in our heads. When Google today offers us glasses which enable us to superimpose live – in real time and real space – all the information of the web onto the reality in front of us, this simulacral permeation of the map onto (or rather into) the territory is only the exteriorization in a technical apparatus of what already largely determined the internal functioning of our cultural apprehension of reality.

But, even if the effects of this technological externalization are likely to be considerable and difficult to anticipate, we may already observe how our attention accommodates itself to the intrinsically permeated nature of our attention. Risking oxymoron, we might qualify this accommodation as 'instinctively reflexive': it has become obvious to large sections of the younger generations that everything we look at today is always-already mediatized by simulacra that result from diverse interests. If these generations can seem disconcertingly naive in one study or another, you can be sure that it is often because the questions asked could not coax them to repeat something that is so overwhelmingly obvious that it goes without saying: no need to reflect (for very long) to know that I only see (through) simulacra. When I travel, I follow advertising images, and I do so to take pictures to post on Facebook. My reflexive consciousness of the import of images does not require a moment of self-critical epiphany: it is at the very centre of everything I experience.[41]

What Google's projecting glasses help us to see is that this instinctively reflexive double consciousness relates less to the collapsing of the map into the territory (and to mental confusion) than to a *detachment* between the two. Judging from their current form, which is still very crude,[42] glasses of this kind, by indicating that there is a service station or a pizzeria hidden round the corner of the road, enable us to alternate very quickly between mediatised information and immediately perceptible data, while giving us a sensory experience of their separation: my eye must focus on one *or* the other. As in narrative immersion, we simultaneously keep one foot outside and one inside – while advancing directly on the two levels at once.

Interpretative Attention

This two-levelled, out of sync, double-focused, unavoidably immersive and instinctively reflexive attention, in reality places us in a position which has nothing new about it, but which has characterized human attention since the start. It is the position of REFLEXIVE INTERPRETATION to which we may return here, thinking of it in terms of *an attentional regime founded on an oscillation between immersive adjustment and reflexive critique*. As soon as an awareness knows itself to be an 'interpretation', it incorporates a (self-critical) dimension that separates it from the simple certitude associated with sensible obviousness: whether I am looking at animal marks in the snow or the behaviour of a human in society, when I put my analysis forward as an 'interpretation', I recognize that it is in part subjective, fallible and relative, which forces us all (myself included) to maintain a certain critical distance with respect to it. But, as soon as an awareness claims to be an interpretation, it must also endeavour to adjust itself to a pre-existing given, in which it is constrained to immerse itself as deeply as possible: it always bears on something already-given (a trace, a gesture, a text, a score), with respect to which it claims a certain conformity, which allows it to legitimately lay claim to a certain objective reality.

Even if they seem to move in contrary directions, immersive adjustment and reflexive critique belong together: it is by patiently immersing myself in the details and nuances of the interpreted object that my attention seeks to respond in advance to the criticism addressed to its subjectivity. It is its (self)critical dynamic that provides the impetus for the dynamic by which it goes deeper into itself. We recognize here the reversed terms of the oft-repeated condemnation of the 'younger generations' for their supposedly absent-minded and a-critical use of the internet. The web provides us with a vast amount of information which we must learn to *interpret*. Behind denunciations of the internet considered as a distraction machine, behind the supposed dying-off of 'deep reading' and the 'literary brain', it is possible to discern two questions which should make us think about reforming our old institutions instead of pointing the finger at the young.

The declinist discourse likes to direct two contradictory criticisms at digital natives. On the one hand, 'the young' are completely devoid of critical spirit, naively swallowing all the nonsense posted on the internet; on the other hand, they are considered to be uncivilized wild things, rebelling against all forms of authority. We wonder instead whether they might not be demonstrating *another* form of critical spirit, which their elders find all the more offensive because of the way it exposes naivety and hypocrisy. What are we intellectuals and teachers complaining about when we lament the attentional deficits that characterize our different audiences? That they are not listening in large enough numbers or with enough devotion to the precious words coming from our mouths and pens? And what if, as was suggested above by Robert Caron and Cathy Davidson, it were also (a little) because what we are saying is (perhaps) ultimately not so brilliant or fascinating as we would like to imagine? Aside from the narcissism that quite naturally affects every author – and every speaker more generally – the complaints which, for the last two centuries, have been directed at the plethora of books published, rarely fail to expose power conflicts in which the traditional holders of authority find themselves threatened by newcomers.

And what if our efforts at democratization – as universally celebrated in principle as they are decried in their actual consequences – should bring into view a world in which anyone could say that they had *become an author*? Should we be whining that, because everyone is busy writing their articles, blogs, essays and books, no one has the time to read anyone else? Or should we celebrate our success in drastically reducing the inequalities of access to the 'scriptural economy' that Michel de Certeau considered one of the central sites of power in the system of modernity?[43] So, we should learn to think kindly of a Republic of Letters, which is all the more accomplished for its lack of readers[44]. . . More seriously, a good attention ecology above all invites us to rethink the publication institutions and the editorial protocols that determine the distribution of offices of authority.[45]

At the same time that we must keep in mind that digital natives may be making good use of their critical spirit when they give their attention to something other than our authority-lacking words, it is always worth repeating that this critical spirit does not emerge fully armed from simply looking at the internet. It needs to be fitted out, and the second question posed by the supposed inattention of digital natives is, therefore, that of knowing how best to develop our critical literacy and interpretative abilities.[46] And, to confront this task, while we should not rue the good old days, we should nevertheless recognize that they do contain lessons from which we may greatly benefit.

For at least two and a half thousand years our culture has been reflecting on the practices of textual interpretation that it has established over the course of its development, from commentaries on Homer, the legal rhetoric of the Romans, Christian exegesis of the Middle Ages, the Cabala, humanist learning, rationalist criticism of the classical age, to the more recent emergence of philology, literary history, structuralism or deconstruction – not to mention, of course, all the non-European traditions which, working with the text of the Koran or aphoristic Eastern wisdom, have developed hermeneutic practices that are easily as rich and subtle as our own. More than as reservoirs of knowledge in the process of being absorbed by the internet, world cultures should be considered above all as repositories and illustrations of interpretative practices, which, while often convergent with one another, are all equipped with their own nuances and tools.

But these cultures of interpretation *cannot* be digitalized and made accessible in one click through the magic of Google. We may try to describe them, understand them, explain them, and even formalize a number of their mechanisms – but, since they are rooted in practical abilities and not only in information, in knowing-*how* (to make sense) and not only knowing-where-to find-the-right-answer, it is up to each individual to incorporate them through habit, repetition, trial and error, through exercises, memorization and continual refinement. When, in the fourth chapter, the principle task of educational institutions was shown to be providing students and teachers with the opportunity to 'research together', we were in fact prescribing the apprenticeship of interpretative practices. And it is precisely the *reflexive practice of interpretation* that unites in one project what artists and spectators do in aesthetic laboratories, and what students and teachers do in the classroom: interpreting (together), while reflecting on the multiple way in which we can interpret – because it is on our ability to interpret our present and our past that the fate of future societies depends.

We might suggest, at the end of this chapter, situating the singular form of attention required by interpretative labour on the table of four attentional regimes described by Dominique Boullier. What, then, are we doing when we are 'analysing a text' at the (provisional) end of a tradition which brings together in time a handful of Greek scholiasts, a few hundred medieval scholastics, a few thousand humanist students and, now, millions of adolescents (in our countries where 80 per cent of the population complete secondary education) who are made to endure these kinds of school exercise? When things go the best they can, inspired by Hugues de Saint-Victor, Michel de Montaigne, Pierre Bayle and Jean Starobinski, we seek to combine the four attentional regimes discussed in the first chapter.

1. Everything begins with an advance of trust, an *investment of confidence* typical of the regime of 'loyalty': on the basis of a canonical author's name, a friend's recommendation, or a school exercise, we wager that a few hours spent studying a profane text as though it were a sacred writing (invested with a quality beyond the human) will indeed enable us to extract a higher meaning, capable of elevating us above ourselves.

2. The attention we grant it is, therefore, typical of the 'immersion' regime: we submerge ourselves in the text on the basis that it belongs to a radically foreign universe where every word must be questioned, where nothing is to be taken for granted *a priori*, where everything must be built anew, as though we have landed on a previously unknown planet.

3. The two other regimes now appear as threats, to which we are necessarily exposed, but which we do our best to repel as far away as we can and for as long as we can. We can never fully neutralize the 'alertness' regime: a fire alarm or someone close to us having an accident may always smash the vacuole in which we had taken shelter; we may endeavour to put ourselves in a state of automotive alertness, as it were, so that we can hone our sensitivity to discreet textual clues that may contain unimagined interpretive perspectives. But, in general, the less we are distracted by the tensions and appeals of the alertness regime, the better we interpret.

4. The same goes for 'projection': of course, everything we end up finding in a text follows from the questions that we project onto it; we cannot so easily escape from the hermeneutic circle: from its prejudices, its habitual findings, its self-involved interests; we never get away from ourselves – except, precisely, in the mystical experiences of possession and trance which constitute the perspective in which literary interpretation and aesthetic experience are situated here. The difficulty consists, precisely, in pushing back as far as possible the inevitable projection of our subjectivity onto the alterity of the text and, in this sense, the projection regime and the alertness regime represent antagonists to which we only concede what we are unable to refute.

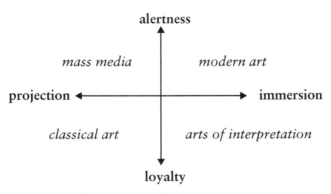

17. The attentional regimes compass

When we situate *the arts of interpretation* in the bottom right corner of the ATTENTIONAL REGIMES COMPASS suggested by Dominique Boullier, we immediately notice that three other combinatory possibilities appear, which will help us roughly to map out the aesthetic dimension of individuating attention (Figure 17). In the bottom left, the kind of attention called for by *classical art* seems to come out of the loyalty creation guaranteed by an institution of authority (an academy, a school, a style, a creator) and the projection of immutable rules that we expect to find comfortably established wherever we may go. In the top right, *modern art* strives, on the contrary, to keep us in a state of permanent alertness where all established conventions are threatened, and in a state of immersion, where we do not know which cause to take up or which criteria to cling to. Finally, in the top left – the polar opposite of the arts of interpretation – the kind of attention sustained by the *mass media* rests on the coming together of a state of permanent alertness where we are bombarded by emergencies, scandals and incessant distractions, on the one hand, and a projective standardization, on the other, through which we rediscover every night the same commentaries, the same muted ideology, the same refrains and the same weather forecast at the end of the news, whatever disasters have shaken us over the preceding half hour.

By making the arts of interpretation, exemplified by a certain practice of literary studies, into an antidote to the regime of alarmist distraction and standardized projection by which the mass media anaesthetize our sensitivities and our intelligence, we hope to contribute to a reevaluation of their status in light of an attention ecology concerned for our personal individuation and collective fate. Having warned against any attempt at a return to the past – literary studies and the arts of interpretation, far from being situated behind us remain more than ever to be invented – we should end by neutralizing in advance the 'interventionist' conclusions that might be drawn from what we have just said. As should be clear, it is not at all a matter of 'de-alienating the masses' by tearing them from their televisual stupor and forcing them to submit to a diet of interpretative amphetamines.

We should keep in mind the fine words of William James that opened the third part of this book: my experience is composed of 'what I *agree* to attend to'. We should take this as both an affirmation of liberty and an IMPERATIVE OF AGREEABLENESS: as we have seen, from the moment that 'attention cannot stay still', and that we can only get it from those who are happy to give it, *an attentional environment is only defendable if it is agreeable, and it is only agreeable if we know how to make it appealing.* This is the challenge of all pedagogy and all aesthetics: only what we are able to make enjoyable or exciting is truly useful. Simone Weil saw this clearly, 'intelligence can only be led by desire'.[47] There is no alternative to generating agreeableness – even if the highest pleasure often means an asceticism by which is it considerably deferred, as is illustrated by the strategies of modern art. Knowing how to make deferred pleasures, and the perspectives of elation to which they may lead us, shine out: this is what the proponents of aesthetic laboratories and the arts of interpretation must learn to do – rather than lamenting students' distraction or the superficiality of net users. Individuating attention is the first and last resource of what we call 'liberty'. At the same time that it seeks to understand the environmental factors conditioning the orientation of our individual attention, attention ecology can only contemplate subjects who *agree* to make themselves attentive to this rather than that. The stakes and the power of this liberty will be discussed in the conclusion to this work.

CONCLUSION

Towards an Attention Echology

Instead of asking *to what* we should *be attentive [faire attention]*, we might also try to understand *what* we can *do with [faire de]* our attention. Distinct from the economic metaphor found throughout the vocabulary of attention ('paying', 'lending', 'investing' one's attention), the French language has the peculiar feature of situating attention in the perspective of a particular kind of *doing [faire]* – which is fairly mysterious in principle and would seem to be untranslatable. The expression belongs to the order of intransitive activity and process (that of the German *tun* and the English *to do*), rather than that of production (*machen, to make*). But this 'doing' seems to give rise to a certain self-production, whose virtue was so well articulated by Simone Weil: 'never, on any occasion, is any true attentional effort lost; [. . .] whenever a human being carries out an attentional effort with the sole desire of becoming more apt at grasping the truth, they acquire this greater aptitude, even if their effort has not produced any visible fruit'.[1]

'Paying' attention to something or to someone is always understood in terms of a certain external purpose – gaining something, avoiding a danger, helping another. The attention that we 'pay' is a means that is dissolved in the end to which it is assigned – implying that you have wasted your time and effort if, despite the attention paid, the hoped-for return does not materialize. 'Being' attentive [*'faire' attention*], on the other hand, implies the practice of an activity that constitutes its own end (like doing sport or playing music [*faire du sport ou faire de la musique*]). The attentional effort carries its own benefit with it: in the increase in our ability to be attentive – which now appears as a good in itself.

So, what are we doing when we are being attentive? What kind of 'general economy'[2] are we talking about when the effort gains even

171

if it does not produce any visible fruit? How can we be attentive together without condemning ourselves to the paranoia of a common enemy or the univocity of aligned perspectives? And, above all, in what way should the alternative economy delineated by this kind of activity be thought of in the framework of a certain ecology? This is what we will be seeking to clarify in these concluding pages.

Individuations

Like sport, like music, attentional effort is first of all worthwhile for its individuation effects. The most important thing that it produces is not simply the *possibility* of pursuing the individuation of our being (helping us to avoid external threats of destruction), but, above all, the *concrete realization* of this individuation. To take up the vocabulary that Bernard Stiegler borrows from the Heideggerian tradition, attention does not only allow us to secure our 'subsistence' by avoiding death, and our 'existence' by bringing about the emergence of a unique and unprecedented life form through us; but, above all, it enables us to acquire a greater 'consistence' within the relationships that are woven in us. Far from helping us only to continue in being, it enables us to become ourselves.

These seemingly abstract, even abstruse, distinctions have very practical consequences. It is the reversal of priority between subsistence and consistence that characterizes the security craze of our dominant attentional regime. The shameful Guantanamo Bay or the Patriot Act in the United States, like the mantle of fear maintained in France by the Vigipirate Plans, by warnings against pickpockets, the Romany community and beggars, along with all the toxic rhetoric around 'terrorism' – all of this only (seemingly) protects our subsistence by preventing us from becoming anything but submissive and terrified zombies. The security attention regime is a tragic example of the terrible things that we can 'do to ourselves' when we are attentive to some things (mortal threats that have been exaggerated to the great benefit of a few political and commercial interests) rather than others (possibilities for a better life that we might all share in on a planetary scale).

We become together the individuals that we are depending on the paths along which our attention is stabilized. But the wayfaring which results in such paths takes time: it implies a waiting period and a waiting room, which are being squeezed with increasing impatience by the modes of communication that have been imposed on us by the intensification of modernity over the last two centuries. One of the major criticisms that should be addressed to our current socio-political regimes is precisely that they do not grant us *the time of waiting* [*le temps de l'attente*], the time of *anticipation* – which is the time in which our attention is formed. This has been quite rightly emphasized by Bernard Stiegler:

> Attention is something that forms, slowly, through a complex system of care, from the first gestures the mother dedicates to the infant to the most elaborate forms of sublimation, by way of everything constitutive of the superego. I can capture the attention of an animal and create conditioned reflexes which resemble anticipations, like Pavlov and his dog – but these are not anticipations [*attentes*]: they are instinctive and automated behaviours, which is to say, the opposite of anticipation, which, precisely, presupposes attention. [. . .] Anticipation is not a reflex, and attention is something that is formed: to produce attention in a psychological being is necessarily to participate in psychic *and* collective individuation, and so to produce *social* attention with *psychological* attention, to produce, that is, the social *bond*.[3]

From the flight from immediate danger to the considered care of valorizing interrelations, the time has come to go over the five broad levels of attentional individuation that we have had occasion to look at over the course of the preceding chapters. At the broadest, *collective*, scale, our attention takes shape according to the pre-individual fashion of the school of fish or swarm of bees: awareness of certain dangers or certain opportunities comes across us like groundswell or media waves, which are only visible from very far away since the criss-crossing of surface waves tends to conceal the deepest dynamics. We might think of our common languages (French, Spanish, Russian, English, Mandarin) as receptacles that have become filters for this sequence of awareness, which means that they bear an implicit transindividual knowledge which is infinitely richer than can be elucidated by our formalized understanding. These sedimentary collective flows which sweep through human history when considered from Saturn, serve as framework and canvas for our personal individuations.

At the smaller scale of *joint* attention, it is through the attention of other specific people who are present to our senses that we progressively (and endlessly) animate the consistency of our personality. At the same time that they bear on the different objects that we identify in the world, the valorizations inherent in attentional processes constitute the value that we acquire in our own eyes. We are here in the domain so well circumscribed by Georg Franck in what he called *Selbstwertgefühl* and *Selbstwertschätzung*: 'people's attention

173

income determines how much feeling of their own worth they can enjoy'.[4]

> Attentiveness as such is more than, and of ontologically higher order than, anything appearing to or in it. Dedicated attentiveness imparts dignity to the person receiving the attention. This alone makes receiving somebody's benevolent attention a most highly valued good for creatures who are attentive themselves. Receiving alert attentiveness means becoming part of another world. No attentive being has direct access to the world of another being's attention. By receiving another being's attention, however, the receiving one becomes represented in that other being's world. And it is one's representation in the other being's consciousness which makes the desire to be noticed so irresistible.[5]

As well as being taken up in the media flows that orientate my attention towards this rather than that, my individuation receives its structure and its substance from the attention given to me by people who are 'close to me' (parents, friends, teachers, neighbours, colleagues), since joint attention is a matter of presence and proximity (even if of a telesthetic nature thanks to the telephone or Skype). The strength available to my person comes, to a great extent, from its 'representation' in the attention of the other – which should be understood in the strong sense in which we speak of political representation: bringing into play questions of power and not just appearance.

At a third level, restricted this time to the *individual* relationship that unites a subject to the object receiving its attention, the processes of individuation are determined by the fact that these objects are the specific matter on which our bodies and spirits are nourished. If it is true that we are what we eat, then we are what we watch and listen to, since, from the hunting grounds of old to today's supermarkets, what enters our mouth has first of all entered our eyes, nostrils and ears. Attention is individuating to the extent that it chooses what I will be tomorrow by getting entangled in what I see, hear, smell and touch today. The relation of a subject to an object is rooted in mutual individuation: I give myself form (as subject) by distinguishing a figure (object) against the background of the sensory flow by which I am affected. It is the identification of such figures (*Gestalt*) that defines my identity. The distinction between figure and ground, performed by my attentional habits, divides the material universe between the *elect* (*e-ligere*) objects of a world that has become meaningful and the *neglected* (*neg-legere*) mass of present things that I am unaware of (but which do not cease to affect me).

We cannot, however, limit ourselves to just these three levels of collective, joint and individual attention, which seem to subject us to the impulse of media enthralments, alienation in the look of the other and the determinism of our material environment. The aleatory interplay of these factors would doubtless be enough to produce the infinite diversity of human subjectivities but, if we were to limit ourselves to this, we would miss the most powerful resource of our individuation capacity. Indeed, besides the automatic attention that makes us notice our name being spoken in the background noise of a cocktail party, we have the ability to focus our voluntary attention on one or another field in our sensory space.

Now, this voluntary attention is inextricably linked to a fourth level of individuation, whose wellspring is our *reflexive* attention. We are frequently brought to make our collective, joint and individual attention the object of a 'meta-attention' which makes us question the way in which we think about a particular fragment of reality, and the possibility that it may be considered differently. On such occasions, we are, therefore, 'led to lead' our own attention in an intentional and (more or less) reflexive way. As we saw in Chapter 7, our aesthetic and pedagogical experiences have precisely this vocation of opening up these kinds of spaces for meta-attentional reflection – and so catalysing our individuation. It is to the extent that it comes from an effort of reflection on our attentional habits, on their blind spots as well as their virtues, that our attention becomes properly 'individuating' – in the more demanding sense in which we are lifted from an individuation to which we are subjected to an individuation orientated towards what we value as our greatest good.

We should, however, take note of a fifth level, which accounts for the repositioning of the study of attention in *ecological* terms. Indeed, we risk getting caught up in pointless debates about 'liberty' or 'determinism' when we hope to define precisely the extent to which a reflection I carry out on my attention comes from my own free will or responds to an external stimulus. It is precisely the relationship between the two that constitutes my identity as it is destined to continue evolving as long as I am alive. As we have seen, attention should be thought of as an *interface*: it is what links a subject to the object it has selected in something external to it. So, it is irrelevant to wonder if it should be situated on one side rather than the other.

It is, on the other hand, a truth of practical obviousness that helps us to short-circuit this kind of abstract debate, and which suffices for grounding both ecological action and concern: *we have a certain control over our immediate environment*. I may move the paper on my desk a few centimetres; I may reduce or increase the size of the window in which I am typing this text; I may turn down or turn up the volume of the Big Satan CD I am listening to at the moment; I may also change the disk or turn off my stereo, reopen my email account which I had closed so I could work in peace, or put my telephone on silent.

Of course, this control that I have over my immediate environment is always extremely limited: I cannot stop the pneumatic drills which have been deafening me for three weeks as they renovate the gas mains in my neighbourhood, any more than I can escape the unpleasant smell of the person sitting next to me on the plane; I cannot choose to spend the day in front of my computer if I have to work as a cashier to earn a living; I cannot even close my email account or turn my phone to silent if I am waiting for a job offer which could be taken by a competitor if I do not respond immediately. There are even extreme conditions in which I may be led to lose all voluntary control of my attention (when a torturer or rapist subjects me to intolerable suffering, when learning of the death of someone close to me makes the ground open under my feet, when depression crushes all hope for the future). But, other than these exceptional cases, I may always direct my look, my listening or my hand towards this rather than that.

While it may be appropriate to speak of 'liberty', 'emancipation', or 'empowerment', it is less so at the level of the immediate control I have over my sensory organs than at the level at which I am able to (re)organize my environment. Not only looking at the open page or listening to the music, but moving the paper and lowering the volume. Not only 'acting', but *modifying the environment that will condition my future perceptions*. It is at the precise level of this knotting together of reflexive attention and environmental intervention that the alpha and omega of what we mean by 'liberty' is to be found. It is here that an ecosophy of attention must be developed.

Twelve Maxims of Attentional Ecosophy

The logics that today determine the interpretation and organization of our collective, joint and individual attention are at best unsatisfactory, and at worst self-destructive. It is therefore of the greatest importance that they be reworked so that we might reorient our attention towards commonly held and articulated priorities rather than see it diverted to the profit of particular financial interests. In this effort of reorganization and reorientation, we might turn to a number of ecosophical maxims that follow from the analyses developed in the different chapters of this study – at the point of convergence between ethics and politics, sociology and psychology, ecology and ethology.

Félix Guattari thought of 'the ecosophical object as articulated according to four dimensions: of flux, machine, value and existential territory'. The preceding chapters have demonstrated sufficiently that attention consists in filtering the flow of our sensations, within communicating and capturing machines, in always singular existential territories, 'based in coordinates of independent, extrinsic determinations', which gives attention 'an alienating, "embodying" dimension, along with a dimension of enrichment through process'.[6] But if, as Arne Naess wished, 'all 'sophical' insight should be directly *relevant for action*',[7] then this pragmatic wisdom works principally towards effecting a 'reorganization of values':

> This ecosophical object [. . .] is important for rethinking the problem of value, including capitalist value and exchange value in the Marxist sense, along with the other systems of valorization hidden away by autopoietic systems: social systems, groups, individuals, individual, artistic and religious sensitivities; for articulating them among themselves, without their being crushed by an overarching economic value.[8]

Rather than claiming to invent or promote 'new values' – according to a programme that may always fall back into pious commitments or moral positioning – the twelve maxims gathered below are all intended 'to be directly relevant for action', so that the processes of valorization already underway (but still in need of deeper study) might be better understood, better guided and better orientated.

1. *Distrust maxims of attentional standardization.* As much as some general maxims might help us to orientate ourselves in the labyrinth of attentional choices, any 'attention methodology' should be considered with the greatest of suspicion. All approaches of a scientific nature tend to generate this kind of methodology, which standardizes its object as it pushes it into already routine categories. A great deal of today's enormous mess results from the thoughtless full-scale application of analysis frameworks which are rigidified in economics departments and vulgarized in business schools (before being translated into the bureaucracy of *new public management*). Attentional hygiene demands on the contrary that every decision be subjected to a double and apparently contradictory, but indivisible, question: *in the name of what maxim of attentional ecology must I reorganize*

177

my environment AND in what way does this concrete situation require the qualification of the general maxim?

2. *Understand the consequences of the primacy of filters.* Attention being a matter of selection, the positions of power in an attention economy are defined according to their ability to filter the flows that pass through us. The teams of journalists selecting the day's news have as much power as the government teams regulating the circulation of our taxes. Wherever they are situated in these hierarchies and intertwined power networks, every individual and every group should be understood as a filtering operator in a circulation that now takes place on a planetary scale. From which comes a question in which our political demands converge, along with our ethical responsibilities: *what will we (or will we not) allow to pass through us* (discourses, words, types of goods and modes of production)?

3. *Get behind mediatized questions.* Because of the self-reinforcing loops that structure the mass-media space, the questions that circulate among us often tend to concentrate our attention on (at best) secondary issues or (more often) problems that are deceptive because they have been badly articulated. Rather than worrying about answering these questions with a yes or a no, as the polls require, or about knowing whether what we are being told is true or false, we would do better to get behind the implicit presuppositions of the questions that pass through us: *is it truly important that our attention should be focused on this issue?*

4. *Be strategic about your attentional valorization.* Our individual and collective attention is the most precious thing that we possess, since it affects the wellspring of all our valorizations. We transform ourselves into 'representatives' of the other the moment we give him our attention – often against our will. Even when we denounce, attack, or criticize ideas or people, we contribute to drawing our joint and collective attention to them, and so valorizing them ('there is no such thing as bad publicity'). Faced with the positivity of adverse attention, two questions follow from one another: *what will we chose to speak about? Should we do our enemies the favour of criticizing them?*

5. *Instead of hoping to free yourself, learn to choose your alienations.* Attention means 'alienating yourself': apart from the case of meditation, being attentive to something brings about an exit from the self and an absorption in the thing in question. So, from the perspective of an attention ecosophy, alienation cannot in itself be a bad thing: it expresses the relational condition of the

178

attentive being, called by what he tends to (*ad-tendere*) to become other than what he is. What the denouncers of our contemporary distraction lament is precisely that we no longer can, or no longer know how to, alienate ourselves profoundly in the contemplation of an experience or a work. The aim of individuating attention is not, therefore, to escape alienation, but to judiciously choose our alienations: *what forms of alienation enrich us?*

6. *Struggle against apparatuses of attentional enslavement.* The reason we must choose our alienations is because certain kinds of alienation can be exhausting or overwhelming – like those denounced by Simone Weil in her analysis of the worker's conditions on the assembly line. We impose on the soldier responsible for standing guard, and the Taylorian worker, 'the paradox of an attention that is appealed to and kept alert without being invigorated': there is suffering and enslavement because the agent 'cannot make do with carrying out their gestures in an automatic and unconscious way, but must, on the contrary, give them all their attention'.[9] Far from decreasing with the progressive replacement of humans by machines in industrial production, this enslavement tends to become more generalized with the increasing hold of neoliberal bureaucracy: the combined pressures of an intensified competition, a generalized surveillance and ubiquitous evaluation have brought this enslavement out of the factory to overrun offices, hospitals and schools. From which emerges a question that is inextricably economic, ethical and political: *how do we organize* all *our work places so that we make them places of invigorating rather than enslaving attention?*

7. *Beware of the risks of inhibition inherent in opportunity cost calculations.* Faced with any choice, the 'opportunity cost' represents the loss of potential gains brought by alternative possibilities that we are made to forego by the choice taken. This is the cancer eating away at globalized capitalism, as it requires of all our businesses that they align themselves with the highest profit level of the moment. You 'lose' even as you win when you do not gain as much as you could have with another investment. This is also the perspective that stresses all of our decisions: faced with the overabundance of information, cultural goods and virtual possibilities, have I considered with enough attention all of the alternatives before I get involved with something? Instead of helping our decision making, opportunity cost calculation leads to (financial) lurching or (psychological) paralysis. It tends to inhibit any enjoyment by taking up our attention with (the

179

potentially infinite) work to be done before taking a decision or making us lament the alternatives which we are 'denied' by any decision. From which comes a double question: *is the maximization of hope not paid for by the sacrifice of reality? Doesn't the time spent choosing expropriate the time of enjoyment?*

8. *Extract yourself from the hold of the alertness media regime.* Like opportunity cost, vigilance is a double-edged sword. On the one hand, helping us to avoid the ills that threaten us is an essential function of attention. On the other, a state of permanent alertness stifles reflection as surely as the infinite calculation of possible alternatives stifles enjoyment. But it is just such a state of permanent alertness that is made to hover over us by our current media enthralments, through 'crisis' discourses, images of catastrophes, political scandals and violent news items. From which we may pose a question (even to the informed catastrophism that wakens us to the ecological threats obscured by the growth race): rather than on the anxieties of alertness, *on what already existing regimes of loyalty can we count to counteract the predicted dangers?*

9. *Set up vacuoles protected from the assaults of communication.* Even if, as Jean-Philippe Lachaux says, it is a peculiar property of attention that it 'does not stay still', and even if our perceptive and mental apparatus experiences constant twitches and movements, the intensification of our technologies and communication practices is leading to the gradual disappearance of moments and places where our attention is not being solicited by a chaotic multiplicity of external stimuli. Beyond calls for individual choice, which exposes the most helpless to the requirements of being permanently available, it is becoming necessary to foster the material conditions of possibility for attentional concentration, by, for example, demanding a right to unplug. Before disapproving of a distracted person for their inattention, we should start by asking: *what attentional vacuoles are available for successful completion of the task (and for self-development)?*

10. *Learn to devote yourself, at different times, to hyper-focusing, open vigilance and free-floating attention.* Even more than the ability to concentrate, good attentional health is characterized by an aptitude for modulating your level of attention to the situation at hand. It is just as essential to be able to immerse yourself in methods of sustained hyper-focusing, which make us impervious to any external stimulus, as it is to sweep broadly across the field of possibilities to note something entirely new, or to allow your free-floating attention to transgress the barriers of habit.

The question, then, is not simply of knowing how to concentrate, but rather: *how can we vary the sampling rate so as to discover the new in (or at the borders of) what is already known?*

11. *Distrust idols, have confidence in icons.* In Jean-Yves Leloup's fine book, *Un art de l'attention [An Art of Attention]*, we find an illuminating distinction between the idol and the icon: 'The idol arrests my look on what it sees: my look is replete, blocked, arrested. The icon does not arrest my look on what is there to be seen; here, there is a presence that opens me further. From the visible, I go towards the invisible; the look becomes broader. . .'[10] Things as different as a Hollywood action film, a photograph of a bearded 'terrorist' or a rise in GDP have an idol effect on most of our attentions, 'arresting our look on what is there to be seen'. On the other hand, a page of Edouard Glissant, a Gaston Chaissac painting, a Kiripi Katembo Siku photograph or a Pedro Costa film offer us icons, which broaden our look to make us attentive to an invisible presence inhabiting the visible. From which come two complementary questions to bear in mind: *how can we look at all images as icons? How can we increase the proportion of icons in the images that circulate among us?*

12. *Learn to value background properties.* The work of attentive focusing consists in noticing significant figures in what seemed to be an insignificant background. But, as every attentional effort is necessarily limited, we might suspect that any background contains figures that are only waiting to be identified as such. Beyond this progressive discovery of the neglected wealth of the background, it is above all urgent that *we become attentive to the properties of the background as background* – to what in its very indistinctiveness enables it to make figures appear. What we today call the 'common(s)' provides a good illustration of this productivity peculiar to the background: water, air, climate, seeds, languages, know-how and accumulated manners – all of these are usually situated below the level of private property, protected from individual appropriation by their status as a common background to all human activities. It is by blinding itself to the imperceptible (because ubiquitous) role played by the commons in the continuation of our societies that individualist ideology has been able to undermine the very foundations of our existence. Hence these now vital questions: *what kinds of common backgrounds support the prominence of the individualized figures that we see so clearly? How can we valorize and foster the environmental power whose abundance is concealed in the background?*

Five Echo Dynamics

From economy to ecosophy by way of attention ecology: the echoes of *eco-* have multiplied over the preceding page and chapters. Behind the *oikos* of our homes, our towns and our shared planet, the problematic of attention has also made us aware of the importance of *echo* phenomena in the constitution of our subjectivities and communities. The 'mediasphere' very quickly came into view as an 'echosystem': against our habitual way of thinking, in which the media are thought of as *channels* through which information circulates, it seemed sounder to see them as *vaults* in which resonance phenomena are organized, resulting in the synchronization of our movements, affects and imaginations. Joint attention is also based on the play of echoes: when my interlocutor turns to look in a particular direction, my look tends to follow his with a very slight delay, in the same way that the nymph Echo repeated what was said to her after a short interval. Finally, like every Echo has its Narcissus, we saw that at the level of individuating attention, the confidence that enables me to take part in human interactions comes from the positive resonances that my behaviour produces in the attention of the other, nurturing the sense that my narcissism has of its own value.

Not only has everything in the preceding chapters encouraged us to think that attention is a matter of echoes, but the very material of these chapters is made from echoes: what have I done since the beginning if not collect quotations from the most disparate authors, only to myself bring them into a harmonising echo? So, the time has come to see how what appeared to be only a metaphor or a composition method in fact belongs to the fundamental structure of attentional dynamics. More perhaps than an ecology or an ecosophy, it is an *attention echology* that we should be seeking to ground.

At the most fundamental level, attention is an echo because, like the nymph in Ovid's myth, it does not know either how to speak for itself or listen in silence. 'Attention does not stay still', says Jean-Philippe Lachaux,[11] himself echoing a refrain already intoned by Théodule Ribot in his 1888 treatise:

> If we take a healthy adult male of average intelligence, the ordinary mechanism of his mental life consists in a perpetual coming and going of internal events, in a procession of sensations, sentiments, ideas and images which come together or repel one another according to certain laws. [. . .] [Attention] is an exceptional, anomalous, state, which

cannot last long because it contradicts the fundamental condition of psychic life: change.[12]

If attention does not stay still, this is not only because it feels the urge to move, but because it has no proper place: attention is essentially 'alienated' in that it is always attention *to something* other than itself. Always? Not quite . . .

Among the many blind spots of the discourse on attention held over the preceding chapters, there is doubtless one which will not have failed to strike the (attentive) reader by its absence. It is certainly revealing of the historic moment, the cultural context and the social origin of this work (and its author) that it has been possible to fill seven chapters without ever really analysing the attentional practices of meditation and prayer, which are nonetheless extremely important and widespread throughout world history and world cultures. In such practices, all effort is aimed towards performing a folding back of attention on itself. The – enormous, superhuman – difficulty is in arresting the spontaneous movement of attention which (almost) always carries it outside itself, to that creaking floorboard, that bird crossing your visual field, that call you have again forgotten to make, to that pain that you are trying to ignore. Meditational discipline does not so much aim at 'emptying' attention of any content than at stabilizing it (exceptionally) on an unmoving and fundamental content (the regularity of breathing, God's infinity, identification with the All).

Our Western modernity seems to have renounced this asceticism. We accept that attention has nothing to tell us: no need to silence everything, outside and inside us, to listen to what it has to say. Besides, clear-thinking or defeatist, we know moreover that it cannot shut itself up: it is impossible to stop the incessant echoes of the noise of the world that it makes resonate in us. From birth to death, our attention never stops going from one echo to another, and we are its resonance.

Paul North is right to highlight that 'attention and distraction are not opposites at all, but rather contraries, the one, distraction, consists in the other, attention, to the lowest degree. The age of distraction, it turns out, was always but the age of attention.'[13] If, at any moment of the day, one hundred and seventy thousand American drivers are sending or receiving text messages at the wheel of their car, and if a quarter of the thirty-five thousand car crash deaths result from the use of mobile telephones – as do a fifth of the two hundred and thirty thousand Indian road deaths[14] – then it is just as correct to speak of fatal distraction (with respect to driving) as of lethal attention (with respect to the conversation). As Paul North also notes, the true opposite of attention is not distraction, but thinking of nothing, or not thinking at all. The incessant echo of attention only ever changes object, and as indicated by its etymology, 'distraction' like 'diversion' are only displacements – very natural for something which, in any case, cannot stay still.

If being distracted is in no way equivalent to *not* being attentive, but simply being attentive to *something else*, then we can better understand why attentional problems are often described simultaneously in terms of deficit and hyperactivity. It seems paradoxical: either there is a lack or an excess. We might think we can resolve the problem by situating the paradox in a temporal succession: at one moment the child is inattentive, and, the next, over-attentive. But the truth is more complex, and more interesting: the child is *both* not attentive enough to the echoes that we would like him to repeat *and* excessively attentive to other echoes from which we would like to distract him.

From a very exacting reading of Husserl's phenomenology, Natalie Depraz helps us to get beyond simplistic oppositions (distracted *vs.* concentrated, passive *vs.* active, automatic *vs.* voluntary) by developing a processual approach to attention as an *integrative dynamic*. This dynamism explains why attention 'cannot stay still': its function is precisely to 'modulate' together different scales and different perceptual sources, different processing regimes and different categories of action – different modes of resonance.[15]

This model of a selective and integrative echo chamber can extend to a variety of attentional dynamics, which we will look at by way of conclusion – the first of them valorizes of the attunement of echoes. Christopher Mole developed a highly formalized understanding of this when he defined attention as the constitution of 'cognitive unison':

> Let α be an agent, let τ be some task that the agent is performing, and call the set of cognitive resources that α can, with understanding, bring to bear in the service of τ, τ's 'background set'.
> α's performance of τ displays cognitive unison if and only if the resources in τ's background set are not occupied with activity that does not serve τ.[16]

So, ATTENTION AS UNISON asserts in conformity with current instincts that '*an agent performs a task attentively if and only if its performance of this task displays cognitive unison*'.[17] This definition has the virtue of not requiring that attention be conceived as a particular faculty belonging to a specific organ – a problem that has haunted all

184

its psychological and philosophical theorizations. Attention here has no proper substance: it is only defined as a dynamic that puts different functions in unison, whatever they may be. It is even wrong to use the substantive, which makes you think that it refers to something that is isolatable as such. In fact, it would be more correct to designate this particular reality by an adverb: attention is nothing in itself, it is only a collection of tasks performed *attentively*.

Christopher Mole explains, however, that carrying out a task attentively is not necessarily desirable: 'In general, the capacity for inattentive engagement with a task is a sophisticated achievement.'[18] When we first drove a car, changing gear doubtless mobilized all of our background resources, and we are very lucky to be able to multi-task, carrying on a conversation with our passenger as we drive. Attentional unison is only, therefore, a particular and passing moment of our mental dynamic – a moment of concentration. To start with, there is the multiple: many things solicit us at the same time, generating scattered and contradictory echoes in us. Then comes the phase of attentional attunement, when our resources are concentrated on a single task, which may nevertheless call for multiple forms of simultaneous action – to change gear: press the left foot, lift the right foot, push the right hand, watch the pedestrian who is stepping into the road, listen to the firemen's siren coming from the next crossroads. After this punctual unification, we return to our normal state of multiple competing and parallel tasks, among which our divided and often 'distracted' attentional resources oscillate.

Because it begins in the multiple, this model can be transferred without much difficulty from the individual to the collective scale. Christopher Mole mentions the example of a sports team who, when they execute a task with good judgement and by mobilizing all of the necessary resources, can be considered to be demonstrating cognitive unison.[19] We may of course also mention the example of an orchestra or a theatre group – and, by extension, we may now specify the way in which our epoch is dramatically 'inattentive' to the threats of climate imbalance brought about by the continuation of our unsustainable lifestyles. It is not a question of 'being conscious' of a problem, of thinking about it or even worrying about it, but of dedicating the necessary background resources for solving it. The attunement of echoes here implies both an agreement on certain priorities and a certain behavioural alignment.

It is this alignment that a second conception of the echo-play constitutive of attention seeks to denounce and surpass. Of course, the echoes generated by our incessant interactions with the world must

185

be organized to avoid the chaos of a haphazard floundering, and the construction of a certain internal consistence is the object of all our 'educational' efforts. There is nothing to say, however, that this internal consistence should be based in unison, which is to say, the alignment of several voices on one single melody. Cathy Davidson's book *Now You See It* condemns the reduction of attention to the model of unison as the central problem of our epoch – and as the cause of most of our (false) debates and our (exaggerated) anxieties about the supposed attentional collapse among the youth.

She sets out in her reasoning from Daniel Simons' famous gorilla experiment (mentioned in Chapter 6 above). As they concentrate on the number of passes made by the players in white shirts, the participants suffer an attentional blindness that makes them miss the obvious presence of a gorilla crossing through the game. This experiment seems to her to provide the key to a major development in our modes of being attentive, which are having to transform themselves as they confront an increasingly complex world. She takes up the notion of CONTINUAL PARTIAL ATTENTION from Linda Stone to describe 'the way we surf, looking in multiple directions at once, rather than being fully absorbed in only one task'.[20] From this she develops an analytical framework that overturns a good number of our habitual judgments:

> Rather than think of continuous partial attention as a problem or a lack, we may need to consider it as a digital survival skill. In most of life, our attention is continuous and partial until we're so forcefully grabbed by something that we shut out everything else. Those blissful episodes of concentrated, undistracted, continuous absorption are delicious – and dangerous. That's when we miss the gorilla – and everything else. The lesson of attention blindness is that sole, concentrated, direct, centralized attention to one task – the ideal of twentieth-century productivity – is sufficient for the task on which you are concentrating but it shuts out other important things we also need to be seeing.
>
> In our global, diverse, interactive world, where everything seems to have another side, continuous partial attention may not only be a condition of life, but a useful tool for navigating a complex world. Especially if we can compensate for our own partial attention by teaming with others who see what we miss, we have a chance to succeed and the possibility of seeing the other side – and then the other side of that other side.[21]

Starting with the example of her own journey from dyslexic child to education advisor to President Obama, Cathy Davidson notes the extent to which people suffering from 'academic handicaps' (dyslexia, attention deficit, etc.) tend to be overrepresented among successful scientists, artists and entrepreneurs. She attributes this to the fact that, since they are unable to attune their attention to that of others, these people have had to invent workaround procedures which have enabled them to perceive better certain hidden faces of things. If you hate counting or you have not understood the test instructions, you will be in a much better position to see the gorilla. It is because all our perspectives are aligned on the returns of GDP growth that we have missed the gorilla of climate imbalance.

As a consequence, Cathy Davidson points to an attentional dynamic that is very different to the dynamic of unison. Far from having to align with a single melody repeated on everyone's lips, echoes are to be valued more highly when they diverge from the melodic line that we already have in our heads. This ATTENTION AS COUNTERPOINT *makes the illumination of our blind spots through the decentring of perspective the essential aim of attentional effort.* When we are not clones reacting in the same way to the same stimuli, teamwork will increase our strengths. For Cathy Davidson, the almost exclusive privilege enjoyed by the dynamic of unison and the valorization of concentration in current discourses on the collapse of attention bears witness to an obsolete fixation on an industrial model inherited from Taylorism, where every worker on the production line did indeed have to stay concentrated on a single task, repeated in identical fashion day after day, and executed in parallel by many workers who did not really interact with their neighbours. The parallel evolution of our modes of production and our modes of sociality requires, on the contrary, that we learn to get away from this unique and centralized absorption that was imposed on the population during the twentieth century, so that we may cultivate a continual partial attention through which everyone tries at every instant to revaluate the opportunities and dangers present in their environment, to reorient their behaviour according to previously unsuspected factors, to collaborate ceaselessly with others so as to notice the hidden faces that inevitably escape their always situated point of view.

Even if we need unison when we concentrate our efforts on a task that requires us to mobilize all of our resources, attention as counterpoint tempers these alignment effects with a taste for difference and contradiction. It is where you do not agree with me that I should pay attention to what you are saying: not so as to prove to you that I am right, so as to reduce our disagreement to a unison (even if this exercise in argumentation is healthy in its own right), but above all to benefit from the enriching complementarity of counterpoint composition. As we saw in Chapter 5 when we discussed 'inter-attentional added value' and promoted a 'politics of convivial dissensus', the progress of thinking is honed by the effects of opposing viewpoints, in the same way that melody is further enriched by the introduction of a counterpoint than by the addition of another voice to the unison.

Where the counterpoint model remains a little constrained by a binary logic (conceived in terms of contradiction), it is salutary to lead it towards the more open and pluralist dynamic of a POLYPHONIC ATTENTION: *the challenge of continual partial attention is in adjusting our behaviour as subtly as possible to the heterogeneous multiplicity of constraints, voices and projects that are superimposed on one another in the great collective improvisations that are our social formations.* When she highlights the importance of 'compensating for our own partial attention by teaming with others who see what we miss', Cathy Davidson rediscovers what Bernard Aspe (rereading Gilbert Simondon) valued in the virtues of 'transindividual communities'. The principles of reciprocity, affective agreement and improvisation are central to the dynamics of polyphonic attention. Everyone is called on to make themselves the contrapuntal echo of multiple heterogeneous voices, according to modes of interaction that Vilém Flusser admirably described when he suggested a parallel between the coming 'telematic society' and the musical improvisations of the past – not without giving a central role to repetition and echo phenomena:

> Chamber music can serve as a model of the telematic social structure. In itself, it precedes telematics, the apparatus, and automation. It is a preindustrial form of communication. And yet it is now possible to see in it (and perhaps in jazz, so strongly reminiscent of chamber music) many aspects of postindustrial communication. [. . .] The basis for such music making is an original score, a program, a set of rules. But using recordings of recordings of recordings, this score will soon disappear behind the horizon of musicians who are improvising with continually reprogrammed memories. In chamber music, there is no director, no government. The one who sets the tempo is only temporarily directing things. And yet chamber music demands an exceptionally close adherence to rules. It is cybernetic. Chamber music is pure play, by and for the players, for whom listeners are superfluous and intrusive. It employs participation (strategy) rather than observation (theory). Precisely to play as though it were playing solo, each instrument plays as though it were an accompaniment. To play for himself, each player plays for all the others. Each improvises together with all the others, which is to say, each adheres to precise rules (consensus) to jointly change them in the course of the playing.[22]

188

While the digitalization of our attention of course opens unprecedented perspectives – for the better and for the worse[23] – often, it only leads to the reinvention of modes of interaction that have already been experimented with in earlier contexts. The description of musical improvisation put forward here by Vilém Flusser describes a relationship to the rule, programme and prescription, as well as to concentration, focusing and collaboration, that is very different to the one we inherited from the industrial era. It becomes much more difficult to fully absorb yourself in the assimilation of a predefined object when the rules of interaction are continually evolving around you – calling for that continual partial attention that we hastily condemn in digital natives as a form of distraction.

Most importantly, the analogy with improvised music gives us a good feeling of the potential of the *echological* model for an understanding of our attentional dynamics. When guitarist Otomo Yoshihide takes up a standard theme, like Ornette Coleman's *Lonely Woman*, he echoes it as he reprogrammes it. The evolution of this theme 'from recording to recording to recording' is nothing but a sequence of echoes incessantly affected by variation. From unisons to counterpoints, the incessant collective 'reprises' which make up the musicians' interactions weave a fabric of communal resonances where – in the best scenario – it becomes impossible to distinguish the soloist from the accompanist. 'To play for himself, each player plays for all the others': Narcissus and Echo finally combined. . .

The most important echosystem for our attention echology is nevertheless the one whose dynamic is described by Katherine Hayles in terms of *technogenesis*. Like Cathy Davidson, her colleague at Duke University, she highlights the equal importance and the complementarity uniting deep attention and hyper-attention.[24] Like Nicholas Carr and all those who gravitate towards these questions, she recognizes the dynamic interaction that links the evolution of our technical devices with neuronal plasticity: through the process of *synaptogenesis*, 'synapses are pruned in response to external stimuli, with those that are used strengthening, and the neural clusters with which they are associated spreading, while the synapses that are not used wither and die'.[25] While recognizing the determining role played by our technical devices in the stimulation, and so the structuring, of our brains' attentional operations, she nevertheless highlights the importance of the feedback effect that constitutes this recursive loop: from the vast range of functions that our machines are able to carry out, our attention selects only a very small number – and it is this selection that orients the pursuit of certain technical developments, at the expense of other possible developments.

Across the attention interface, it is as true to say that technogenesis conditions synaptogenesis (as is rightly maintained by Nicholas Carr and the declinists) as it is to say that synaptogenesis, itself guided by our social practices and our ethico-political biases, conditions technogenesis (something that is noted much less often). So, the dynamics of unison, counterpoint and polyphony determining the play of echoes between our different activities take place within a more general TECHNOGENETIC ATTENTION whose dynamic comes to determine any attention echology: *the materiality of the devices that will condition our attention tomorrow depends on the way in which our attention today selects certain properties offered by the devices produced yesterday.*

> [A]ttention is an essential component of technical change (although undertheorized in Simondon's account), for it creates from a background of technical ensembles some aspect of their physical characteristics upon which to focus, thus bringing into existence a new materiality that then becomes the context for technological innovation. Attention is not, however, removed or apart from the technological change it brings about. Rather, it is engaged in a feedback loop with the technological environment within which it operates through the unconscious and nonconscious processes that affect not only the background from which attention selects but also the mechanisms of selection themselves. Thus technical beings and living beings are involved in continuous reciprocal causation in which both groups change together in coordinated and indeed synergistic ways.[26]

The technogenetic dynamic analysed here by Katherine Hayles enables us to recognize the complementarity that joins the 'technological determinism', so often decried by Friedrich Kittler, with the 'new philosophy for new media' developed by Mark B. N. Hansen to highlight the creative dimension inherent in the attentive body. Technogenesis is based just as much on the conditioning of my attention by the technological equipment which permeates me with information as on my ability to reframe this information so as to extract its meaning. The wellspring for this reframing is to be found in the 'responsive' dimension elucidated by Bernhard Waldenfels in his *Phenomenology of Attention*. Whether I am looking at an animal, reading a book or watching a screen, my perceptions as an attentive subject never represent a simple echo of the object I am confronted with: my reaction always implies a portion

190

of creative response, which is indispensable for *making sense of the sensation*:

> Attention is a double event: *something strikes me – I pay attention* [*etwas fällt mir auf – ich merke auf*]. [...] 1. The first part of attention is constituted by the fact of something happening to me, striking me, moving me, affecting me. [...] 2. The second part of the double event should be understood as a response that I give or withhold, beyond its propositional content. When something is said or done, the event of the response does not coincide with what is said or done. [...] The gap between sensation and response, being crossed over by attention without being abolished, is accompanied by a division of the so-called subject. The subject divides into two figures: on the one hand, the *patient* (in the broad sense of the word), and on the other the *respondent*. We become what we are by being affected and responding to it. So we will never be fully what we are.[27]

So, at the heart of technogenesis, we should note a fifth echo dynamic peculiar to the responsive dimension of ATTENTION AS FRAMING: of course, our individuation is only fed by the echoes generated in us by the information circuits passing through and constituting us, but *our proper activity, as individuals, consists in projecting interpretive frameworks onto this information, which alone are able to give it meaning.* It is these frameworks, as they condition certain singular effects of resonance among the information, which make some characteristics and not others emerge within the technological systems available to us: they are what make each of our reactions a singular and meaningful response to what comes to us as a flow of data.

This is what allows Mark Hansen to appropriate the Bergsonian conception of the human individual as a 'centre of indetermination': each of us is the place of an unpredictable potential reaction to the stimuli that affect us ('equipotentiality'). Although echoes and images of each other, we are all creators of new meanings through the singular way in which we en-frame and en-capture what passes through us:

> [A]ny technical circuit or image is necessarily the product of an embodied framing of information [...]. Insofar as it serves to actualize the equipotentiality of the living in empirical informational circuits, framing furnishes the mechanism through which meaning inheres in information, and for this reason, can properly be said to create information.[28]

It is in this way that an attention echology articulated in terms of technogenesis and responsive framings comprehends the echosophical principle evoked in the first pages of this conclusion: our 'freedom of action' is proportional to *our ability to alter today the environment that will condition our future perceptions* – our technological environment, but also our social, institutional and political environments.

By making the devices currently available to us the 'backgrounds' from which our attention extracts a few properties destined to become prominent in future devices, Katherine Hayles and Mark Hansen also invite us to *be attentive to the properties of the ground as ground*: what potentials for action are *already* available to us – in what we have in common and which constitutes our current environment – which we do not know how to assess, because we are not looking at the ground but at the figure which imposes itself on it? This work will conclude with a reflection on our attention to the 'ground', bringing us back from (the apparently 'superficial') questions of echoes to (the more 'fundamental') problems of our physical ecology.

From Echo to Eco: Regrounding Politics?

In a youthful text inspired by Sartre, Paul Ricoeur describes the attentional dynamic in terms of excess: 'the object *exceeds* perception because attentive perception *extracts* the perceived from the total field. Extraction by attention, excedence by the object are one and the same thing.'[29] The extraction carried out by attention must be excessive in the perceptual object for the good reason that, as we have seen, attention does not stay still. There is always something to be seen or heard next to what we are looking at or listening to. The laments of discourses on information overload could turn easily into astonishment when confronted by the *excedence of curiosity* that occupies the human mind. So, the distraction for which the young are berated would bear witness to the deepest wellspring of attention:

> There is a fundamental opposition between two attitudes, the one consists in *inflecting* perception in the direction of some anticipation, the other in seeking an innocence in the eye and the senses, in an opening of spirit, a welcoming of the other as other. Through this respect for the object, we give ourselves over to the object, much more than we subordinate the object to our past. The true name of attention is not anticipation but *astonishment*.[30]

An attention echology will have to learn to valorize this excedence of curiosity eager to be astonished by everything that, in our objects of knowledge or perception, exceeds the categories and anticipations through which we set about grasping them. If we believe Lacanian psychoanalysis, every desired object 'flees', following a metonymic movement that displaces itself at every step: I thought that I desired this object, but as soon as it comes into my possession, I realize that I wanted another one, its brother, its sister, its neighbour, its double – its echo. It is this movement of 'dis-traction' that we decry in online reading: if net users spend an average of twenty seconds on the pages that they visit on the Web,[31] it is because as soon as it is loaded, they are attracted by what in it exceeds itself – the hyperlinks promising unimagined opportunities excite their curiosity. In Chapter 3 we were concerned by the capturing apparatuses set up thanks to digital technologies to drive this always fleeing curiosity towards the sterilized highways of capitalist profit. The problem is not, however, with the excedence of curiosity but with the inadequacy of the switchboards that inflect our capacity for astonishment to enslave it to market-orientated anticipations.

As a good phenomenologist, Paul Ricoeur reformulates the excedence and astonishment belonging to attention in terms of relationships between foreground and background, between figure and ground:

> Of course, attention is always more or less in the service of a desire, an intention (in the current sense of anticipating project), of a task – in short, of a need or a volition. But neither need nor volition *constitute* attention. What is attentive in research is not anticipation, it is the fact of turning towards the background to *interrogate* it. [. . .] The passage from the background to the foreground, from the obscure to the clear, implies the apprehension of a new aspect that had not been perceived as an aspect.[32]

This may be the greatest challenge for our attention echology: how can we adapt our way of looking at backgrounds so as to see new aspects in them that had not yet been perceived as aspects. The whole of the work that is concluding here has been directed towards this end: how can we hear the echo chamber that nurtures the voice of the soloist? How can we perceive the resonating vault behind the media buzz? How can I do justice to the joint attention that gives me the confidence I need to speak? In other words, when all of our sensory and academic education has taught us to notice prominent figures, how can we see and hear the – inextricably communal and environmental – ground that supports our existence? How can we communicate with the commons?[33]

In terms of environmental wisdom (*ecosophy*) and awareness of the polyphonic properties of our attentional dynamics (*echology*), these questions call forth a double task. On the one hand, establishing (physical, social, legal) environments that will allow the greatest number of us to modulate our attention according to our own desires and our communal needs – rather than in accordance with the interests of a minority and a growth agenda that is dragging us all towards the abyss. And, on the other hand, learning to adapt our attention in new ways so as to make other figures and other values appear in the common ground by which we are constituted.

So, by way of these two goals, attention echology calls for a 'regrounding of politics'. Not in the sense of rediscovering a stable and unmovable foundation on which a new ideologico-political apparatus could be rebuilt – as the 'refoundationalist' Communist parties had hoped to do at the end of the Cold War. But in the sense sketched out in the preceding pages, in which politics is in need of a new relationship with the ground, understood as an environment and an echo chamber. 'Re-grounding politics' on the basis of an attention echology encourages us, therefore, to work along at least three major axes.

Firstly, conforming to a problem that is as old as politics, there is the question of finding (old and new) ways of *making numbers*. The forces of resistance to capitalist self-destruction suffer from the dispersal brought about by that same capitalism. Far from being made obsolete by new modes of communication on the internet, the efforts of organization within transindividual communities are more necessary, and must be more imaginative, than ever. In Chapter 5 we saw what the attention echology can contribute to these efforts in the area of group micro-politics. The real challenge is in moving from the 'micro' scale of collective presence to the 'macro' scale of media aggregations. How – through what mediations and through what media arrangements – can the digital class, formed by the millions of hackers whose libertarian and collaborative practices rejuvenate our commons on a daily basis, be constituted as a 'political class'? The basis of what weaves together the collective intelligence of the Web is already there: the problem is making it come as such into its own power, turning all of our attention towards it, so as to situate it on the horizon of our political practices.

The second axis of the grounding of politics seeks to evaluate the new potentials of *wikipolitics* – based on the distributed contributions of thousands or millions of collaborators who are unknown to one another (*crowdsourcing, crowdfunding*). Before they even dream of organization, these multitudes bear a potential that is inherent in their internal diversity and their swarm dynamics. It is less a question here of the old 'class consciousness' than of a (no less ancient) *collective sensibility*, constituted simultaneously by perceptive pluralism and communal intelligence. The strength of *wikis* comes from the fact that their ingenious apparatuses have found a way of benefiting from the stores of knowledge, attention and sensitivity that are always present among us in a latent state. To the inevitable verticality of organizational work (and the establishment of the *wikis* themselves), they bring the antidote of an essentially horizontal and anti-hierarchical dynamic.

As the title of a book by David Weinberger neatly encapsulates, we must rethink the very notion of knowledge – and be suspicious of traditional relationships between the figure of relevant information and the ground of implicit knowledge – 'now that the facts aren't facts, experts are everywhere, and the smartest person in the room is the room'.[34] The issue is not so much that that those who are sitting at the back next to the radiator, consulting Wikipedia on their smartphone, may 'know' more than the speaker who is professing from his lectern. Even if they may now and then correct a mistaken date or name, the professor still has a head start on them thanks to the syntheses and the schemas of understanding that he has had the opportunity to accumulate over the course of the years, his readings and his experiences. It is not a question of knowing who knows the most, but of realizing that we are more intelligent together than any one of us can be individually – as long as vacuoles have enabled each of us to enjoy moments of separation, necessary for the deepening of our singularization. Those sitting at the back may or may not know more than the person holding forth on the dais, but it is in the communal ground woven from our interactions – 'the room' inasmuch as it includes all its occupants – that we must learn to recognize the most important site of our individual and collective intelligence.[35]

But this fund of collective intelligence is only 'given' to any one of us provisionally and precariously. It is only regenerated to the extent that we know how to take care of its echosystem. It is at this level that current debates on attention may influence our future. Suppressing the excedence of curiosity in the name of good old disciplines dating from the industrial era may prove to be as harmful as abandoning it unprotected to the hegemony of financial logics. In the same way that it is important at the individual level to help everyone to supplely modulate periods of hyper-focusing with periods of partial attention and multi-tasking, we must, at the collective level, develop attention echologies that enable us to subtly harmonize dynamics of unison, counterpoint and improvising polyphony.

David Weinberger's choice of words nevertheless leads us to glimpse a third axis of the politics of the ground, which is perhaps

18. Rajarshi Mitra, *Rain in Calcutta*

more important. It is in fact essential that we extend what we mean by 'the room' beyond the human figures who are in it to include the assemblage of furniture and buildings that enable these people to demonstrate their intelligence together. The people sitting by the radiator will lose a great deal of (the use of) their knowledge if the internet connection stops working or the heating breaks down in the middle of winter. Our collective (human) intelligence would be nothing without the relational ground that allows it to continually (re)constitute itself, through countless forms of exchange with its material environment. The room is more than the sum of its bipedal inhabitants: its collective intelligence is also based on the tables, chairs, floors, cables and pipes – in short, on a whole material infra-structure saturated with human understanding and practices, which have been accumulated over the centuries but which are dependent on continual communication with our non-human environment.

It is the presence of *a double ground* conditioning our existence on planet Earth that was (re)discovered by ecological consciousness over the course of the twentieth century.[36] As important as the play of *echoes* may be in the organization of human society, they always depend in the last resort on the constraints of the *eco-*, which is to say, on the physico-chemical *oikos* on which our existence is based. When we encounter a painting like Rajarshi Mitra's *Rain in Calcutta* (Figure 18), we are spontaneously brought to recognize human figures carrying umbrellas, which instantaneously detach from the back-ground. In conformity with what was pointed out by Paul Ricoeur, an *attentive* look will quickly bring us to 'interrogate the background' (since attention does not stay still), from which 'a new aspect that had not been perceived as an aspect' will emerge – the upper window of the building on the right, for example, whose curved shape and slight inclination I note. This work of acclimatization allows me to see a primary ground, internal to the representation, which often goes unnoticed in our hurry to identify the salient (generally human) figures and their (usually narrative) developments, but which consti-tutes *the setting* from which these figures detach. This first attentional displacement clearly relates to ecology in that it bears on the environ-ment in which the represented characters live.

The true challenge of an attention ecology is, however, to be found elsewhere, in a second displacement that gives us access to the most important stratum of this double ground. The 'abstract' painting of the twentieth century taught us to pay attention to the concrete mate-riality of the canvas itself: in addition to the human figures sheltering under umbrellas, in addition to the background setting representing

197

buildings and a tree, I may also focus my attention on the diagonal scratches that scuff the surface of the painting. It is a *second material ground* that appears here: not located in a Calcutta street on a rainy day through a representation phenomenon, but situated here and now in front of me, in the concrete material presence of the painting. When I look at the original, this second ground is comprised of a watercolour on a thick weave coated in coloured pigments. If I look at this same image on a screen, like at the moment as I write this conclusion, it is pixels activated by an electric circuit. For you who are holding this book in your hands, it is black ink printed on a white page.

In general, we do not see this second ground: we read 'texts', we look at 'images' – not pigments, pixels, or ink. And yet, all of our representations and simulacra – now ubiquitous in our lives and decision making – are woven into the material realities of this second ground. The water that the Bengalese painter used for his watercolour may have been polluted by uncontrolled industrialization; the production of my liquid-crystal screen emitted sulphur hexafluoride, which is the most powerful greenhouse gas; the French version of this book has been produced by a printer who has been approved as Imprim'Vert . . .[37] In certain cases, the extremely complicated reality that constitutes this second ground is made accessible through an immediate demonstration (the French reader could look for the Imprim'Vert label on the last page of his book!). Usually, however, it has to be reconstituted through enquiry, research and calculation before we can become properly aware of it.

It is because of our indifference and negligence towards this second ground that Bengal is at immediate risk of seeing alternating floods and droughts destroy its multi-millennial civilization. As we watch the rain fall on the Calcutta pedestrians in Rajarshi Mitra's watercolour, we must learn to see how the circulation of images and texts, along with the circulation of barrels of oil and rare metals, contributes to the climate imbalance that threatens to engulf this city, one of the most exposed in Asia. It is only by adapting our way of seeing and our intelligence to this second material ground that the politics to come will be able to unite the ecology of attention with a real attention to the ecology.

In concluding this book, we must, therefore, insist on the need to take 'attention ecology' literally, in its most material sense – in the context of an ontology where, as in Spinoza's, 'bodies' and 'minds' are just two ways of envisaging one same reality. Being attentive to the second material ground (of the paper and liquid crystals), behind the visual ground of the images that we are presented with, requires that we be actively attentive to the concrete relational fabric which assures the consistency of the figures and functions that we project onto the different parts of our environment. The book or the screen, as the material grounds of our intellectual experiences, are part of a system that is simultaneously productive and destructive, whose fabrication cannot be separated from the weaving of the concrete demands of our lives. From the African migrant who sifts our recycled paper to the Chinese worker who assembles our smartphones, this system produces the pleasure and the leisure of some at the expense of the work and exploitation of others. In the context of the second material ground of our collective attention ecology, it is unfortunately at the expense of the over-occupation and attentional exhaustion of many of our contemporaries that you and I have been able to enjoy the privilege of wresting enough free time to read and write the book that is coming to an end here.

From the assembly line to the recycling conveyer belt, by way of the scrolling letters passing under the saccades of our eyes, our attention is like the needle that constantly weaves this ground of concrete links that hold us together, at the price of the greatest global inequalities. Attention ecology remains at the level of vague generalities so long as it does not involve itself with the singularity of our multiple inter-linked ecosystems. At every level, its challenge is to help us identify what we are able to change in our different environments, so that we can pay better attention to what deserves it. If the media flows observed from Saturn and the neuronal activation revealed by MRI remain largely outside our field of action, *your* generous effort to read *this* book to the end – even if it was by jumping from key term to key term – concretely illustrates, on a very small scale, both the hopes and the limits of what our attention might be able to do. Like all cultural objects, this work only exists through the attention of its readers: thank you for having nurtured its existence with yours.

NOTES

Introduction: From Attention Economy to Attention Ecology

1 For more on the critique of the ideology of the immaterial see, for example, Matteo Pasquinelli, *Animal Spirits: A Bestiary of the Commons* (Rotterdam: NAI, 2008) and Éric Méchoulan, *La Crise du discours économique. Travail immatériel et emancipation* [*The Crisis of Economic Discourse: Immaterial Labour and Emancipation*] (Quebec: Éditions Nota Bene, 2011).

2 On the question of the ecological impact of digital cultures, see Richard Maxwell and Toby Miller, *Greening the Media* (Oxford: Oxford University Press, 2012); on the new forms of exploitation on the internet, see the special collection 'Luttes de classes sur le Web' ['Class Struggles on the Web'] published in no. 54 of *Multitudes* in November 2013.

3 Gabriel Tarde, *Psychologie économique* [*Economic Psychology*], vol. 1 (Paris: Alcan, 1902) pp. 92 and 162.

4 Ibid., pp. 186 and 189.

5 Ibid., pp. 71 and 231. On Tarde, see the fine works by Maurizio Lazzarato, *Puissances de l'invention. La psychologie économique de Gabriel Tarde contre l'économie politique* [*Powers of Invention: Gabriel Tarde's Economic Psychology against Political Economy*] (Paris: Les Empêcheurs de penser en rond, 2001), and Bruno Latour and Vincent Lépinay, *L'Économie, science des intérêts passionnés. Introduction à l'anthropologie économique de Gabriel Tarde* [*Economics, Science of Passionate Interests: Introduction to Gabriel Tarde's Economic Anthropology*] (Paris: La Découverte, 2008).

6 Herbert Simon, 'Designing organisations for an information-rich world' in *Computers, Communication, and the Public Interest*, ed. Martin Greenberg, p. 40. [NB. YC cites the manuscript version of the paper given at the Brooking's Institute on 1 September 1969 (available online). In this translation, I have cited the corresponding passages from the version in *Computers, Communication and the Public Interest*, which do not differ from the MS version. Trans.].

7 Alvin Toffler, *Future Shock* (New York: Bantam Books, [1970]1984).

8 Daniel Kahneman, *Attention and Effort* (Englewood Cliff (NJ): Prentice Hall (1973).

9 Georg Franck, *Ökonomie der Aufmerksamkeit: Ein Entwurf* (Munich: Carl Hanser (1989, 1993, 1998, 2005, 2013). The articles were as follows: 'Die Neue Währung: Aufmerksamkeit. Zum Einfluß der Hochtechnik auf Zeit und Geld', *Merkur*, vol. 486, August 1989, pp. 688–701, and 'Ökonomie der Aufmerksamkeit', *Merkur*, vol. 534–535, September–October 1993, pp. 748–761 (in English translation by Silvia Plaza: "The economy of attention", *Telepolis*, http://www.heise.de/tp/artikel/2/2003/1.html).There was a ferment of multi-dimensional analyses around questions of attention in the German-speaking world, whose trace we pick up, for example, in the multi-contributor volume *Aufmerksamkeiten*, edited by Aleida and Jan Assmann (Munich: Fink, 2011).

10 Michael H. Goldhaber, 'Principles of the New Economy', available at www. well.com; see also 'Some Attention Apothegms', 1996, available on the same site, and 'The Attention Economy and the Net', *First Monday*, vol. 2, no. 4, 1997, available at www.firstmonday.org.

11 John Beck and Thomas Davenport, *The Attention Economy: Understanding the New Currency of Business*, (Cambridge (MA): Harvard Business School, 2001), p. 213

12 Richard Lanham, *The Economics of Attention: Style and Substance in the Age of Information*, (Chicago (IL): University of Chicago Press, 2006), p. xi.

13 Josef Falkinger, 'Attention Economies', *Journal of Economic Theory*, vol. 133, 2007, pp. 266–7.

14 Emmanuel Kessous, Kevin Mellet and Moustafa Zouinar, 'L'économie de l'attention. Entre protection des ressources cognitives et extraction de la valeur' ['The Attention Economy: Between protecting resources and extracting value'], *Sociologie du travail*, vol. 52, no. 3, 2010, p. 366.

15 See, for example, Maggie Jackson, *Distracted: The Erosion of Attention and the Coming Dark Age* (New York (NY): Prometheus, 2009), or Nicholas Carr, *The Shallows: How the Internet is Changing the Way we Think, Read, and Remember* (New York (NY): W. W. Norton and Co., 2010).

16 N. Katherine Hayles, 'Hyper and deep attention: the generational divide in cognitive modes' *Profession*, 2007, p. 187.

17 On Google Ngram Viewer, see Erez Aiden and Jean-Baptiste Michel's *Uncharted: Big Data as a Lens on Human Culture* (New York, Riverhead: 2013).

18 See, for example, Philippe Aigrain 'Attention, Media, Value and Economics' *First Monday*, vol. 2, no. 9-1, September 1997.

19 Ann M. Blair, *Too Much to Know: Managing Scholarly Information before the Modern Age*, (Yale University Press: Connecticut, 2001). Ivan Illich's splendid book, *Du lisible au visible. Sur L'Art de lire de Hugues de Saint-Victor* [*From the Readable to the Visible: On Hugues de Saint-Victor's* The Art of Reading] (Le Cerf: Paris, 1991), suggests that the need to make information directly available as a 'text', rather than dependent on the temporal development of speech transcribed in the book, stems from a mental revolution which should be traced back to the twelfth century.

20 Charles Tiphaigne de La Roche, *Giphantie*, v.1 (Paris, 1760), p. 52.

21 Charles Bonnet, *Analyse abrégée de l'Essai analytique* [*Abridged Analysis of the Analytical Essay*] § XXI, in *Œuvres d'histoire naturelle et de philosophie* [*Works of Natural History and Philosophy*], vol. 7, 1783, p. 35. We await to see a research programme for such a history of attention taken up in the

university, better yet, by a collective of researchers brought together for a project comparable to the *Histories of Women*, or *private life* or *publishing*.

22 In the rest of this book, the term 'media' will be used to refer not only to mass media (newspapers, radio, television), as is generally the case in France, but sometimes also – in a broader 'mediological' understanding as it is used in the English *Media Studies* or the German *Medienstudien* – to designate the very different mediations that humans have been able to make use of to record, disseminate and process information, from the sonic vibrations transmitted through the air between mouth and ear to the global network that is today's internet.

23 Jonathan Crary, *Suspensions of Perception: Attention, Spectacle and Modern Culture* (Cambridge (MA): MIT Press, 1999), pp. 13–14.

24 On this point, see Yann Moulier Boutang, *Cognitive Capitalism.* (2007), Cambridge, Polity, 2012.

25 Jean-Philippe Lachaux, *Le Cerveau attentif. Contrôle, maîtrise et lâcher-prise* [*The Attentive Brain: Control, Mastery, Letting Go*] (Odile Jacob, Paris: 2011).

26 Jacques Thomas, Célia Vaz-Cerniglia and Guy Willems, *Troubles de l'attention chez l'enfant* [*Attention Disorders in Children*] (Masson, Issy-les Moulineaux : 2007), pp. v–vi and pp. 38–40.

27 Colette Sauvé, *Apprivoiser l'hyperactivité et le déficit de l'attention* [*Mastering Hyperactivity and Attention Deficit*] (Éditions de l'hôpital Sainte-Justine, Montréal: 2007), pp. 16–17.

28 On this subject, see Bruno Falissard, 'Les médicaments de l'attention: les doutes d'un praticien' ['Attention Medication: A Practictioner's Doubts'], *Esprit*, no. 401, January 2014, pp. 34–43.

29 Georg Franck, "Mental capitalism", in *What People Want. Populism in Architecture and Design*, ed. by Michael Shamiyeh and DOM Research Laboratory (Basel, Boston & Berlin: Birkhäuser, 2005), pp. 98–115.

30 Bernard Stiegler, *Économie de l'hypermatériel et psychopouvoir* [*Economy of Hypermaterial and Psychopower*] (Paris: Mille et une nuits, 2008), pp. 117 and 122.

31 See Aurélien Gamboni 'L'*Escamoteur*: économie de l'illusion et écologie de l'attention' in *Technologies de l'enchantement. Pour une histoire multidisciplinaire de l'illusion*, ed. Angela Braito & Yves Citton (ELLUG, Grenoble, 2014), ch. 2.

32 Jean-Marie Schaeffer speaks in this way of an 'attentional ecology' in a characterization of aesthetic experiences; Matthew Crawford, who is writing a book on the subject, highlights the extent to which 'our attention ecology is weakened' (interview in *Le Monde*, Saturday 27 July 2013); Daniel Goleman dedicated two chapters (XIII and XIV) of his book *Focus: The Hidden Driver of Excellence* (HarperCollins, New York: 2013) to our systemic inability to focus our collective attention on ecological issues over the long-term.

33 Arne Naess, *Ecology, Community and Lifestyle,* trans. David Rothenberg (Cambridge: Cambridge University Press, 1989), p. 37.

34 Félix Guattari, *Qu'est-ce que l'écosophie?*, texts assembled by Stéphane Nadaud (Lignes/IMEC, Paris : 2013), pp. 33 and 66.

35 Arne Naess, *Ecology, Community and Lifestyle*, pp. 56.

36 I tried to develop this in *Renverser l'insoutenable* (Seuil, Paris: 2012).

1 Media Enthralments and Attention Regimes

1 Jonathan Beller *The Cinematic Mode of Production: Attention Economy and The Society of the Spectacle* (Hanover: Dartmouth College Press, 2006), pp. 112, 115, 181.

2 On this point see 'Envoûtements médiatiques' published in *Multitudes*, 51, Winter 2012, in collaboration with Frédéric Neyrat and Dominique Quessada. For a broader perspective on media spells, see also the essential book by Jeffrey Sconce, *Haunted Media. Electronic Presence from Telegraphy to Television* (Durham: Duke University Press, 2000). [The French word translated here as 'enthralment' is 'envoûtement', which resonates with the word 'voûte', meaning vault. The rest of the chapter plays on this phonic proximity to describe the mass media as communication architectures consisting of vaults (*voûtes*) which generate effects of resonance putting certain spells (*envoûtements*) on our collective attention. The reader should be aware of this in the discussion of the media 'echosystem' below. [Trans.]].

3 Niklas Luhmann *The Reality of Mass Media*, (Stanford: Stanford University Press, 2000).

4 See, for example, Aristotle *Physics*, book II, ch. 3, §2–5, or *Metaphysics*, book V, ch.2, §1–7.

5 Marshall McLuhan: 'Since formal causes are hidden and environmental, they exert their structural pressure by interval and interface with whatever is in their environmental territory.' Lance Strate: 'The formal cause is the cause of emergent properties, it is the cause that media ecologists often have in mind when they consider the impact of technical change on individuals and societies, on communication, consciousness and culture.' (Marshall and Eric McLuhan, *Media and Formal Cause* (Houston: NeoPoiesis Press, 2011), pp. x and 129–30, cited by Thierry Bardini 'Entre archéologie et écologie: Une perspective sur la théorie médiatique', *Multitudes*, 62, Spring 2016).

6 On this point, see the two classic works by Neil Postman (*Amusing Ourselves to Death* (New York: Methuen, 1985)) and Pierre Bourdieu (*Sur la television* (Paris: Seuil, 1996)).

7 A reference is implicit here in French to the extremely popular series of flashy photographs made from air balloons by Yann Artus-Bertrand under the title *The Earth from Above* (*La Terre vue du ciel*).

8 In *Everything Bad is Good for You: How Today's Popular Culture is actually Making Us Smarter* (New York: Penguin, 2005) Steven Johnson develops a whole line of argument suggesting how the popular culture despised by elites could actually be contributing to the development of our communal intelligence. In 'Le divertissement: un défi pour l'esthétique', in *Le Style à l'état vif* (Paris: Questions théoriques, 2004), Richard Shusterman lays some solid foundations for a positive reevaluation of what we too quickly condemn as alienation or dumbing-down.

9 Here, I am taking up the stratification suggested by Bernard Stiegler between (a) a level of *subsistence* reduced to bio-psychological survival (corresponding to Giorgio Agamben's 'bare life', *zoe*), (b) a level of *existence* that is characterized by the desire to affirm a singularity indispensable to the process of human individuation and (c) a level of *consistence* which gives to this singularization the means by which it can find a lasting place within a collective

whose timeframe extends beyond the limits of individual survival, as exemplified by a work of art valued long after the death of its author. See, for example, Bernard Stiegler 'Faire la révolution' in *Constituer l'Europe*, vol. 1 (Paris: Galilée, 2005).

10 This is the thesis developed by Tim Ingold in 'From the transmission of representations to the education of attention' in *The Debated Mind: Evolutionary Psychology versus Ethnology*, ed. Henry Whitehouse (Oxford: Berg, 2001), pp. 113–53.

11 This is the definition that Richard Shusterman gives to the work of interpretation in *Sous l'interprétation* [*Beneath Interpretation*] (Combas: L'éclat, 1994). See also my book *L'Avenir des humanités. Économie de la connaissance ou cultures de l'interprétation* [*The Future of the Humanities: Knowledge Economy or Interpretation Cultures*] (Paris: La Découverte, 2010).

12 Paul Valéry, *Cahiers*, vol. 2, edited by Judith Robinson (Paris: Gallimard, 'La Pléiade', 1974), pp. 269 and 273.

13 On these dichotomies see, for example, John Beck and Thomas Davenport, *The Attention Economy*, pp. 22–6.

14 Dominique Boullier, 'Composition médiatique d'un monde commun à partir du pluralisme des régimes d'attention' ['The media composition of the common world from the point of view of the pluralism of attention regimes'] in *Conflit des interprétations dans la société d'information* [*The Conflict of Interpretations in the Information Society*], ed. Pierre-André Chardel (Paris: Hermès, 2012), p. 43.

15 Dominique Boullier, 'Les industries de l'attention: fidélisation, alerte ou immersion' ['The attention industries: loyalty-creation, alertness or immersion'], *Réseaux*, no.154, 2009, p. 244.

16 Dominique Boullier, 'Composition médiatique d'un monde commun...', p. 44.

17 Ibid., p. 46.

18 On this subject we may indicate Anthony Down's pioneering article which touches directly on the complex and literally burning interactions between attention and ecology, 'Up and down with ecology – the 'issue-attention' cycle', *Public Interest*, vol. 28, Summer 1972, pp. 38–50.

2 Attentional Capitalism

1 Herbert Simon, 'Designing organisations for an information-rich world', in *Computers, Communication and the Public Interest*, p. 41.

2 Michael H. Goldhaber, 'Principles of the new economy', §6.

3 Michael H. Goldhaber, 'The attention economy and the Net'.

4 Thomas Mandel and Gerard Van der Leun, *Rules of the Net* (New York (NY): Hyperion, 1996).

5 Michael H. Goldhaber, 'Attention Shoppers!', *Wired Magazine*, vol. 12, no. 5, 1997 (available on Wired.com).

6 Barbara Carnevali, *Le Apparenze sociale. Una filosofia del prestigio* (Bologna: Il Mulino, 2012), p. 102. Georg Franck also comments on the principle *esse est percipi* in *Ökonomie der Aufmerksamkeit*, p. 178. In *A Short History of Celebrity*, Fred Inglis sets out a history of the notion of celebrity rooted in

eighteenth century London and in Romantic Paris in *A Short History of Celebrity* (Princeton (NJ): Princeton University Press, 2010). The main reference on this topic is Nathalie Heinich, *De la visibilité* [*On Visibility*] (Paris, Gallimard, 2012).

7 Georg Franck, 'The Economy of Attention'.
8 Georg Franck, *Ökonomie der Aufmerksamkeit*, p. 118. On this *Bekanntheitsgrad* (*Ruhm, Reputation, Prestige, Promienz*), see pp. 115–20.
9 Georg Franck, 'Capitalisme mental', p. 213.
10 Pierre Zaoui, *La Discrétion. Ou l'art de disparaître* [*Discretion. Or the Art of Disappearing*]. (Paris: Autrement, 2013), p. 27.
11 Jonathan Beller, *The Cinematic Mode of Production*, pp. 78, 115, 231.
12 Gabriel Tarde, *Psychologie économique*, vol. 1, p. 144.
13 Georg Franck, 'Économie de l'attention', pp. 57–8.
14 Jean-Michel Espitallier, *De la célébrité. Théorie et pratique* (Paris: 10/18, 2011), p. 86.
15 Georg Franck, 'Mental Capitalism', p. 8.
16 Ibid., p. 9. The German allows for the distinction between *Beachtung* (attention as *renown* and esteem) and *Aufmerksamkeit* (attention as the effort of *noticing* distinctive features) and *Zuwendung* (attention as the *orientation* of my perceptive or reflexive capacities *in the direction of* a particular object).
17 Michael H. Goldhaber, 'Some attention apothegms', §12.
18 Michael H. Goldhaber, 'Principles of the new economy' § 7.
19 Michael H. Goldhaber, 'The attention economy and the Net'.
20 Georg Franck, 'Mental Capitalism', in Michael Shamiyeh and DOM Research Laboratory (dirs.), *What People Want. Populism in Architecture and Design*, Birkhäuser, Bâle, Boston, Berlin, 2005, pp. 98–115; available online at http://www.iemar.tuwien.ac.at/publications/Franck_2005c.pdf (page numbers will refer to this version), p. 3.
21 Ibid., p. 204. For an interesting literary work on the multiple implications for subjectivities which find themselves caught, not necessarily against their will, in this inextricably attentional and financial game of media pulling power, see the work produced by Christophe Hanna in the guise of La Rédaction, *Valérie par Valérie* (Al Dante, 2008).
22 Georg Franck, 'Mental Capitalism', pp. 9–10.
23 Ibid., p. 3.
24 See on this point Philip M. Napoli, *Audience Economics: Media Institutions and the Audience Marketplace* (New York: Columbia University Press, 2003), which analyses the question by carefully distinguishing between *predicted* audience, *measured* audience and *effective* audience, which alone corresponds to what we generally mean by attention.
25 Georg Franck, 'Mental Capitalism', p. 2.
26 Josef Falkinger, 'Attention Ecomomies', p. 267.
27 Josef Falkinger, 'Limited attention as the scarce resource in an information-rich economy'. *Economic Journal*, vol. 118, 2008, p. 1612.
28 The translation loses the reference to a specific body. The French text mentions: 'les associations de maintien de l'agriculture paysanne (AMAP)' [Trans.].
29 Ibid., pp. 1613, 1615. The idea of a tax on advertising is not in itself new; we find it in an interesting form with the TA-SR (*Tax-Advertising/Subsidise-Readers*) suggested by C. Edwin Baker in 1994, which followed measures already proposed in the United Kingdom by Nicholas Kaldor in 1961 that

would 'reduce the influence of advertising on the editorial content' of papers. It would have meant the imposition of a 10 per cent tax on the papers' advertising revenue, and the redistribution of the money collected in this way as a subsidy based on the revenue that each paper received from its reader base. (See C. Edwin Baker, *Advertising and a Democratic Press* (Princeton: Princeton University Press, 1994), p. 83–117).

30 Matteo Pasquinelli, *Animal Spirits*, pp. 66–7.
31 John Beck and Thomas Davenport, *The Attention Economy*, pp. 15 and 68.
32 Michael H. Goldhaber 'The attention economy and the Net'.
33 Michael H. Goldhaber 'Principles of the new economy', § 4.
34 Georg Franck, 'Mental Capitalism', p. 18 (English translation altered to stay closer to the original German).
35 Ibid., p. 6.
36 Ibid., p. 18.
37 Georg Franck, 'The Economy of Attention', (non-paginated).
38 See Vilém Flusser, *La Civilisation des médias* (Belval: Circé, 2006).

3 The Digitalization of Attention

1 Félix Guattari, 'Vers une ère postmédia' ['Towards a Post-Media Age'], *Terminal*, No. 51, October 1990, Republished in the journal *Chimères*, No. 28, Spring/Summer 1996, and available online at Multitudes.samizdat. net.
2 Tiziana Terranova, 'Free Labour' in *Digital Labour: The Internet as Playground and Factory* (New York: Routledge, 2013), ed. Trebor Scholz, pp. 34, 50. See also, *Network Cultures: Politics for the Information Age* (London: Pluto Press, 2004) by the same author.
3 See 'Harnessing Human Computation', *The Economist*, 1 June 2013. See also Ayhan Aytes, 'Return of the Crowds: Mechanical Turk and the Neoliberal States of Exception', in *Digital Labour*, ed. Trebor Scholz, pp. 79–97.
4 Tiziana Terranova, 'Free labor', p. 50.
5 Kenneth McKenzie Wark, *A Hacker Manifesto* (Cambridge (MA): Harvard University Press, 2004).
6 Kenneth McKenzie Wark, *Telesthesia: Communication, Culture and Class* (Cambridge: Polity, 2012), p. 143.
7 Ibid., p. 164.
8 Ibid., p. 165.
9 Vilém Flusser, *La Civilisation des médias* [Media Civilisation], p. 62. We note that Flusser characterized *every* photographic image (both film and digital) as a techno-image structured by the (abstract) programming logic of the apparatus used to produce it. See his most important work, *Into the Universe of Technical Images* (1985) (Minneapolis: University of Minnesota Press, 2012).
10 On this point, see Alexander Galloway's wonderful books, *Protocol: How Control Exists after Decentralisation* (Cambridge (MA): MIT Press, 2004), and Alexander Galloway and Eugene Thacker, *The Exploit: A Theory of Networks* (Minneapolis: University of Minnesota Press, 2007).
11 Herbert Simon, 'Designing organisations for an information-rich world',

p. 42. Detailed analyses of the interfaces presently devised to optimize our use of these attention condensers can be found in *Human Attention in Digital Environments*, ed. Claudia Roda (Cambridge: Cambridge University Press, 2010).

12 Dominique Cardon, 'Regarder les données' ['Looking at Data'], *Multitudes*, 49, Summer 2012, p. 142. On these questions, see Viktor Mayer-Schönberger and Kenneth Cukier's overview of the subject, *Big Data: A Revolution That Will Transform How We Live, Work and Think* (London: Eamon Dolan/ Mariner, 2014).

13 On these questions, see Sergey Brin and Lawrence Page, 'The Anatomy of a Large-scale Hypertextual Search Engine', 1998, available on Infolab.stanford. edu; Amy N. Langville and Carl D. Meyer, *Google's PageRank and Beyond: The Science of Search Engine Rankings* (Princeton (N.J.): Princeton University Press, 206); Nicholas Carr, *The Big Switch: Rewiring the World, from Edison to Google* (New York (NY): W. W. Norton, 2008); and the collection 'Impact boom!' published by Éric Méchoulan in the review *SubStance*, no.130, vol. 42–1, 2013, pp. 3–81. Georg Franck analyses the counting of citations in scientific papers as an ideal model of the attention economy in *Ökonomie der Aufmersamkeit*, pp. 181–211, and in *Mentaler Kapitalismus*, pp. 105–32.

14 The ORTF (Office de radio-télévision française) [Trans.].

15 See Thomas Mathiesen, 'The viewer society: Michel Foucault's panopticon revisited', *Theoretical Criminology*, vol. 1. No. 2, 1997, and Vilém Flusser, *La Civilisation des medias*.

16 We speak of *serendipity* to designate a discovery coming out of an improbable mix of chance and intuitive insight. On the history of the epistemological stakes of this concept, see Sylvie Catellin, *Sérendipité. Du conte au concept* (Paris: Seuil, 2014).

17 To my knowledge, the differences between languages means (for how much longer?) that searches made on Google remain confined to different linguistic communities. Global standardization will have passed a particularly significant threshold when the results of my searches in French include – thanks to the mechanisms of automatic translation – the hyperlinks, visits and other participation collected on all sites judged to be equivalent, whatever the language serving as an interface with net users. Then, the Earth from Saturn could truly end up resembling a vast school of fish. This kind of 'semantic web' project situated above ethnic languages does however hold out some interesting perspectives when sketched out by Pierre Lévy in terms of an 'Information Economy Meta Language' (IEML) – see, for example, Pierre Lévy 'Au-delà de Google. Les voies de l'intelligence collective', *Multitudes*, 36, Summer 2009, special issue 'Google et au-delà'.

18 Matteo Pasquinelli, 'Google's PageRank Algorithm: A Diagram of the Cognitive Capitalism and the Rentier of the Common Intellect', in Konrad Becker, Felix Stalder (eds), *Deep Search*, London: Transaction Publishers: 2009, available on http://matteopasquinelli.com/google-pagerank-algorithm/, p. 5, Google PageRank: une machine de valorization et d'exploitation de l'attention', in *L'Économie de l'attention*, ed. Yves Citton, pp. 171–2. For good non-reactionary critical overviews of Google, see Ippolita, *La Face cachée de Google*, (Paris: Payot, 2008) and Ariel Kyrou, *Google God: Big Brother n'existe pas, il est partout* (Paris: Inculte, 2010).

19 Matteo Pasquinelli, 'The Number of the Collective Beast: Value in the Age of

the New Algorithmic Institutions of Ranking and Rating' (2014) available online at http://matteopasquinelli.com/number-of-the-collective-beast/(non-paginated).

20 Ibid.

21 Paul Valéry, *Cahiers*, vol. 2. pp. 254, 268, 271.

22 Michael Hardt and Antonio Negri put forward the notion of *excedence* to counter the discourses of crisis and lack that uselessly disfigure our political horizon. They designate by this a production of positive externalities, coming out of the commons but not taken into account by dominant economic calculations. See Michael Hardt and Antonio Negri, *Commonwealth* (Cambridge, MA, Harvard University Press, 2009).

23 In French, *faire attention* (paying attention) translates literally as "making attention".

4 Presential Attention

1 On joint attention, which is a recent area of study, see *Joint Attention: Its Origin and Role in Development*, ed. Chris Moore and Phil Dunham (Hillsdale (Mich.): Lawrence Erlbaum Associates, 1995); Naomi Eilan *et al.*, *Joint Attention and Other Minds* (Oxford: Oxford University Press, 2005); *Joint Attention: New Development in Psychology, Philosophy of Mind and Social Neuroscience*, ed. Axel Seeman (Cambridge (MA): MIT Press, 2012).

2 Vilém Flusser, *La Civilisation des médias*, p. 103.

3 In French, attentive (*attentif*) and considerate (*attentionné*) both clearly refer to attention.

4 Daniel Bougnoux, *Introduction aux sciences de la communication* [*Introduction to the Communication Sciences*] (Paris: La Découverte, 2001), pp. 71–2.

5 Robert Caron, 'Les enfants savent déjà résister' *Les Actes de lecture*, no.125, March 2014, p. 55. As well as Katherine Hayles' article 'Hyper and deep attention . . .', on these questions see also Philippe Meirieu, 'À l'école, offrir du temps pour la pensée', *Esprit*, no. 401, January 2014, pp. 20–33.

6 Cathy N. Davidson, *Now You See It: How Technology and Brain Science Will Transform Schools and Business for the 21st Century* (New York (NY): Penguin, 2011), p. 76.

7 I am here taking up Vilém Flusser's terms, which have already been quoted above, *La Civilisation des médias*, p. 103.

8 John Beck and Thomas Davenport, *The Attention Economy*, p. 68.

9 Michael H. Goldhaber, 'The attention economy and the Net'.

10 John Beck and Thomas Davenport, *The Attention Economy*, p. 68.

11 *L'Individuation à la lumière des notions de forme et d'information* [*Individuation in the Light of the Notions of Form and Information*] (Grenoble: Million, 2005).

12 Edmund Husserl, *Phénoménologie de l'attention*, edited by Natalie Depraz (Paris: Vrin, 2009) p. 126.

13 Jacques Rancière, *Le Maître ignorant. Cinq leçons d'émancipation intellectuelle* [*The Ignorant Schoolmaster: Five Lessons in Intellectual Emancipation*] (Paris: Fayard, 1987), pp. 85–92.

14 Paul Valéry, *Cahiers* vol. 2, pp. 254, 268, 271.
15 Bernard Aspe, 'Simondon et l'invention du transindividuel' ['Simondon and the Invention of the Transindividual'], *La Revue des Livres*, no. 12, July-August 2013, p. 78. The citation in quotation marks is taken from Gilbert Simondon, *L'Individuation psychique et collective* [*Psychic and Collective Individuation*] (Paris: Aubier, 1989), p. 211.
16 Steve Kolowich, 'The minds behind the MOOCs', *The Chronicle of Higher Educaton*, March 2013 (available on Chronicle.com).
17 On these experimentations and their fate in the nineteenth century, see Anne Querrien, *L'école mutuelle. Une pédegogie trop efficace?* [*The Mutual School: An Overly Effective Pedagogy?*] (Paris: Les empêcheurs de penser en rond, 2005).
18 Michael Meranze and Christopher Newfield, 'Remaking the University', Utotherescue.blogspot.fr.
19 We sense, however, the natural symbiosis maintained between MOOCs and the procedures of automated evaluation that have been developed since the beginning of the twentieth century in the form of multiple choice questionnaires (IQ tests, SATs, GREs and other standardized exams) – industrialized procedures which are the subject of a critique and a brief history in Cathy Davidson's *Now You See It*, pp. 111–25. 'Digitalization' is as much rooted in the overeconomies of scale particular to industrial Taylorization as it is in the technical development of microprocessors.
20 Nicholas Carr, *Internet rend-il bête?*, pp. 249–73.
21 On the notion of *gesture* – on its complexity and importance – I refer to my book *Gestes d'humanités: Anthropologie sauvage de nos expériences esthétiques*, (Paris: Armand Colin, 2012). On the gesture of searching, see the magnificent chapter dedicated to it by Vilém Flusser in *Les Gestes* (Cergy: Éditions Hors Commerce, 1999). In particular, we read there that 'the gesture of searching is the model of all our gestures' (p. 79).
22 Isabelle Barbéris and Martial Poirson, *L'Économie du spectacle vivant* [*The Live Show Economy*] (Paris: PUF, coll. 'Que sais-je?', 2013), p. 116.
23 See Edgar Morin, *Le Cinéma ou l'homme imaginaire* [*Cinema or the Imaginary Man*](Paris: Minuit, 1956) and *Les Stars* (Paris, Seuil, 1957).
24 Olivier Bosson, *L'Échelle 1:1. Pour les performances, conférences et d'autres live* [*1:1 Scale: For Performances, Conferences and Other Live Events*], (Paris: Van Dieren, 2011), p. 7–8. On these questions see also Guy Spielmann's book on *Le Spectacle vivant* [*The Living Spectacle*] forthcoming.
25 See n. X in Chapter 1 [Trans.].

5 The Micro-Politics of Attention

1 For a critique of this managerial ecology, see, for example, Geneviève Azam and Christophe Bonneuil's book published for Attac, *La nature n'a pas de prix. Les méprises de l'économie verte* [*Nature Has No Price: The Mistakes of the Green Economy*] (Paris: Les liens qui libèrent, 2012), as well as the edited volume *Non au capitalisme vert* [*No to Green Capitalism*] (Lyon: Parangon, 2009).
2 The expression comes from Franco Berardi, 'La fabrique de l'infélicité',

digital supplement to *Multitudes*, 8 March-April 2002, available at multitudes.net.

3 Citation taken from the agency website, ANMA.fr.

4 *Le Génie du Lieu. Journal d'expression libre du quartier des Lentillères* [*The Spirit of the Place: Journal of Free Expression of the Lentillères*], no.1, p. 1, available at Dijon-ecolo.fr. Ruth Stégassy produced two broadcasts of fascinating interviews in this concrete example of an alternative experience for her show *Terre à terre* on France Culture on 8 and 15 June 2013, available on FranceCulture.fr.

5 See Jérôme Thorel, *Attentifs ensemble! L'injonction au bonheur sécuritaire* (Paris: La Découverte, 2013).

6 Jean-Baptiste Fressoz, *L'Apocalypse joyeuse. Une histoire du risque technologique* (Paris: Seuil, 2012).

7 For a good presentation of the notion of *care*, see Pascale Molinier, Sandra Laugier and Patricia Paperman *Qu'est-ce que le* care? *Souci des autres, sensibilité, responsabilité* [*What is Care? Concern for others, Sensitivity, Responsibility*] (Paris: Payot, 2009). For good ways of thinking the articulation of the attention economy and *care*, see Dominque Boullier, 'Pour une conception cosmopolitique du *care*' ['For a cosmopolitan understanding of care'], *Cosmopolitiques. Laboratoire des pratiques de l'écologie politique* [*Cosmopolitics: Laboratory for the Practices of Political Ecology*], July 2010, available on www.cosmopolitiques.com.

8 See Arne Naess, *Ecology, Community and Lifestyle*, and Arne Naess and David Rothenberg *Vers l'écologie profonde* [*Towards the Deep Ecology*] (Marseille: Wildproject, 2009). See also the many articles (often in French) dedicated to deep ecology by the review *Wildproject: Journal of Environmental Studies*, available at www.wildproject.org.

9 On this point, see David Vercauteren's book *Micropolitques des groupes. Pour une écologie des pratiques collectives* [*Group Micropolitics: For an Ecology of Collective Practices*] (Paris: Les prairies ordinaires, 2011).

10 Sigmund Freud, 'Recommendations to Physicians Practicing Psychoanalysis' (1912).

11 Didier Houzel, 'Attention consciente, attention inconsciente' ['Conscious Attention, Unconscious Attention'], *Spirale*, no. 9, *L'Attention*, edited by Bernard Golse, November 1998, p. 34. See also, in the same edition, Christine Anzieu-Premmereur's study, 'L'attention flottante du psychanalyste' ['The Psychoanalyst's Free-Floating Attention'], pp. 67–78. The main reference is Wilfred R. Bion's *L'Attention et l'Interprétation. Une approche scientifique de la compréhension intuitive en psychanalyse et dans les groupes* [*Attention and Interpretation: A Scientific Approach to Intuitive Understanding in Psychoanalysis and in Groups*] (Paris: Payot, 1990).

12 Peter Szendy, *Écoute. Une histoire de nos oreilles*, (Paris: Minuit, 2001), p. 153.

13 André Carpentier, 'Être auprès des choses. L'écrivain flâneur tel qu'engagé dans la quotidienneté', 2009, available on the site of l'observatoire de l'imaginaire contemporain, OIC.uqam.ca.

14 For a justification of the definition of literary interpretation sketched here, I refer to my book *Lire, interpreter, actualiser. Pourquoi les études littéraire?* [*Read, Interpret, Actualise: Why Literary Studies?*] (Paris: Éditions Amsterdam, 2007). On the structure of the epistemological stakes of

interpretative debate, see *Pour l'interprétation littéraire des controversies scientifiques* (Versailles: Quae, 2013). For a rich consideration of the role played by attention in the formation of the literary canon, see Frank Kermode's book *Forms of Attention* (Chicago (IL):University of Chicago Press, 2010).

15 See Denis Hollier, *Politique de la prose. Jean-Paul Sartre et l'an quarante* [*Politics of Prose: Sartre and 1940*] (Paris: Gallimard, 1982).

16 The weekly broadcast *Terre à terre* presented by Ruth Stégassy on France Culture – which has informed many comments in this chapter – might represent a model of this humble but indispensable task of political echology. Periodicals such as *Vacarme*, *Eco'Rev*, *Z*, *Écologie et politique* and *Multitudes* are also trying to contribute to this labour.

6 Attention in Laboratories

1 William James, *The Principles of Psychology*, vol. 1. (New York (NY): Henry Holt, 1890), ch. XI pp. 402–4.

2 Jean-François Marmontel, 'Attention' in *Éléments de la littérature* [*Elements of Literature*] (1787), edited by Sophie Le Ménahèze (Paris: Desjonquères, 2005), p. 183, and Denis Diderot and Jean le Rond d'Alembert, 'Attention', *Encyclopédie*, vol. 1. 1751, p. 840.

3 See Lorraine Daston, 'Attention and the values of nature in the Enlightenment', in *The Moral Authority of Nature*, ed. Lorraine Daston and Fernando Vidal (Chicago (IL):University of Chicago Press, 2004), pp. 100–27. As far as we are aware, there is not yet an overview of the history of attention for the seventeenth and eighteenth centuries. The work of Jonathan Crary are crucial, but hardly go back before 1800 (*Techniques of the Observer: On Vision and Modernity in the Nineteenth Century* (Cambridge (MA): MIT Press, 1990) and *Suspensions of Perception*). Michael Hagner considers the end of the eighteenth century in 'Towards a history of attention in culture and science', *Modern Language Notes*, vol. 118, no. 3, April 2003, pp. 670–87, and in 'Aufmerksamkeit als Ausnahmezustand', in *Aufmerksamkeiten*, ed. Aleida and Jan Assman, pp. 273–9. A rich work by Margaret Koehler provides an excellent overview of the question in English poetry and philosophy, *Poetry of Attention in the Eighteenth Century* (New York (NY): Palgrave Macmillan, 2009). She notes that at the beginning of the eighteenth century, with Leibnitz correcting Locke, attention tended to be characterized as 'increasingly active and voluntary rather than as passive and automatic', and as 'a flexible set of resources rather than as a uniform phenomenon', p. 16.

4 Étienne Bonnot de Condillac, *Traité des sensations* (1754), (Paris : Fayard, 1984) Part 1, ch. 2, p. 21.

5 Jean-Paul Mialet gives a remarkably clear overview of this in *L'Attention* (Paris: PUF, coll. 'Que sais-je?', 1999), pp. 51–84.

6 On the (multiple) fantasies and the (still rather vague) realities of the action of 'subliminal' images, see Charles R. Acland's book *Swift Viewing: The Popular Life of Subliminal Influence* (Durham (NC): Duke University Press, 2012).

7 This chapter follows closely the excellent book in which Jean-Philippe Lachaux clearly presents what the neurosciences can teach us about

attention, *Le Cerveau attentif* [*The Attentive Brain*], p. 229. In English, see Michael Posner, *Attention in a Social World* (Oxford: Oxford University Press, 2012) ch. 6, pp. 127–55.

8 Frédéric Kaplan, 'Le cercle vertueux de l'annotation' in *Le Lecteur à l'œuvre*, ed. Michel Jeanneret and Frédéric Kaplan, (Geneva: Infolio, 2013), p. 62.

9 For all these examples, see Daniel Kahneman, *Thinking, Fast and Slow* (New York: Farrar, Strauss and Giroux, 2011), chapter 4. As Daniel Kahneman has himself recognized, we know that the experiments on which the theorizations of *priming* are based should be subject to caution because of the difficulty of reproducing them (and obtaining similar results) – see 'How science goes wrong', *The Economist*, 19 October 2013.

10 The expression comes from an 1896 treatise by the psychologist Edward Tichener, cited by Jean-Philippe Lachaux in *Le Cerveau attentif*, p. 139.

11 Ibid., pp. 169–85.

12 '[S]omaesthetics is concerned with the critical study and meliorative cultivation of how we experience and use the living body (or soma) as a site of sensory appreciation (aesthesis) and creative self-fashioning.' As the centre of a movement insisting on the importance of *embodiment* in the age of digital virtual worlds, Richard Shusterman emphasizes that the actual body 'must be recognized as our most primordial tool of tools, our most basic medium for interacting with our various environments, a necessity for all our perception, action, and even thought'. *Body Consciousness: A Philosophy of Mindfulness and Somaesthetics* (Cambridge: Cambridge University Press, 2008). Any consideration of attention must, therefore, include a somaesthetic which bases its analyses in an appreciation of the limits and potentials of our 'living and feeling bodies'. For an excellent case for an approach to new digital media in terms of embodiment, see N. Katherine Hayles, *How We Became Posthuman: Virtual Bodies in Cybrnetics, Literature and Informatics* (Chicago (IL): University of Chicago Press, 1999).

13 Étienne Bonnot de Condillac, *Traité des sensations*, p. 20.

14 Jean-Paul Mialet, *L'Attention*, p. 84.

15 Jean-Philippe Lachaux, *Le Cerveau attentif*, pp. 263, 264 and 272.

16 Daniel Kahneman, *Attention and Effort*, p. 9.

17 'Human beings, like contemporary computers, are essentially serial devices. They can attend to only one thing at a time.' Herbert Simon, 'Designing organisations for an information-rich world', p. 41.

18 Daniel Kahneman, *Attention and Effort*, p. 201.

19 Jean-Philippe Lachaux, *Le Cerveau attentif*, pp. 342–4.

20 Ibid., pp. 346–7. My emphasis.

21 See 'Gorilla experiment', TheInvisibleGorilla.com.

22 I am here taking up the term *self-amputation* from Marshall McLuhan's classic text *Understanding Media* (1964), (London: Routledge, 1964), ch. 4, where it is articulated in a sociological consideration of our collective attention.

23 James J. Gibson, *An Ecological Approach to Visual Perception* (London: Routledge, 1986)

24 Daniel Kahneman, *Thinking, Fast and Slow*, ch. 2.

25 Jean-Philippe Lachaux, *Le Cerveau attentif*, p. 327

7 Reflexive Attention

1 In his *Enquête sur les modes d'existence. Une anthropologie des modernes* [*Enquiry into Modes of Existence: An Anthropology of the Moderns*] (Paris: La Découverte, 2012) Bruno Latour has provided the most ambitious and stimulating description of this interlacing of practices and interests, as well as sentiments, beliefs, fictions, worries and spells that attach us, humans and non-humans, inexorably to one another.

2 Gustave Flaubert, Letter to Alfred Poitevin of 16 September 1845, in *Correspondance*, vol. 1 (Paris: Gallimard, Pléiade, 1973), p. 252.

3 Alvin Toffler, *The Third Wave* (New York: Bantam Books, 1980).

4 Félix Guattari, *Les trois écologies* [*The Three Ecologies*] (Paris: Galilée, 1989).

5 It is of course impossible to take into account the tens of book and the thousands of web pages dealing with the 'scourges of the internet', the 'secrets of multi-tasking', with 'how I unplugged' or the 'thousand and one ways to reconnect yourself'. I will make do with mentioning a few books that are symptomatic of the debates that have taken place over the last decade around the question of individual attention. The emphasis placed on the book-form in these reflections, and throughout the rest of this study, itself already implies, of course, a positon on the questions discussed in this section.

6 Franco Berardi, *Precarious Rhapsody: Semiocapitalism and the Pathologies of the Post-Alpha Generation* (London: Minor Composition, 2010), pp. 44 and 71.

7 Ibid., p. 82. On the intrinsically suicidal tendencies of contemporary 'hyper-capitalism', in direct connection with its 'hyperexploitation' of attentional time, see Jean-Paul Galibert's short work *Suicide et sacrifice. Le mode de destruction hypercapitaliste* (Paris: Lignes, 2012).

8 Winifred Gallagher, *Rapt: Attention and the Focused Life* (New York (NY): Penguin, 2009), pp. 145–62; Edward M. Hallowell, *CrazyBusy: Overstretched, Overbooked and About to Snap! Strategies for Handling your Fast-Paced Life*, (New York (NY): Ballantine Books, 2006).

9 Maggie Jackson, *Distracted*, p. 14.

10 Nicholas Carr, *The Shallows: What the Internet is doing to our Brains*.

11 Jonathan Crary, *24/7: Late Capitalism and the Ends of Sleep* (New York (NY): Verso, 2013), pp. 40, 75–6, 80, 81.

12 Ray Kurzweil, *The Singularity is Near: When Humans Transcend Biology* (New York (NY): Penguin, 2005), p. 31

13 Nicholas Carr *The Shallows: What the Internet is doing to our Brains*. The author takes up a distinction between deep attention and hyper-attention made by Katherine Hayles in 'Hyper and deep attention . . .'.

14 See Ivan Illich, *Du lisible au visible* [*From the Readable to the Visible*], Jack Goody, *La Raison graphique. La domestication de la pensée sauvage* [*Graphic Reason: The Domestication of Savage Thought*] (Paris: Minuit, 1978) and Ann M. Blair, *Too Much to Know*.

15 Cathy N. Davidson, *Now You See It*, p. 154.

16 Ibid., pp. 153–4.

17 The Organization for Economic Co-operation and Development defines *literacy* as 'the ability to understand and use written information in daily life, at home, at work and in the community with a view to achieving personal

goals and extending one's knowledge and capabilities' (OECD, *La Littératie à l'ère de l'information*, 2000, p. x, available at OECD.org). Katherine Hayles illustrates *hyper-reading* with studies showing that we glance over webpages in an F motion: the net user tends to 'read the first two or three lines across the page, but as the eye travels down the screen, the scanned length gets smaller, and by the time the bottom of the page is reached, the eye is travelling in a vertical line aligned with the left margin'. (N. Katherine Hayles, *How We Think: Digital Media and Contemporary Technogenesis* (Chicago (IL): University of Chicago Press, 2012, p. 61).

18 Ibid., p. 11. The term *affordance* was formulated by James Gibson to indicate what an object or an environment offers as a catch for human action.

19 N. Katherine Hayles, *How We Think*, p. 79.

20 Pierre Bayard, *Comment parler des livres qu'on n'a pas lus?*

21 Jacques Rancière, *Le Partage du sensible* [*The Sharing of the Sensible*] (Paris: La Fabrique, 2000).

22 Jean-Marie Schaeffer, *Petite écologie des études littéraires: pourquoi et comment étudier la littérature* [*Little Ecology of Literary Studies: Why and How to Study Literature*] (Vincennes: Thierry Marchaisse, 2011), pp. 112–13.

23 Ibid., p. 114. Jean-Marie Schaeffer and Agnès Levitte have moreover launched a very promising programme of research into 'The aesthetic experience: objects and contexts, attentional styles and attractiveness?', a description of which can be found at HISCA.univ-paris1.fr.

24 Étienne Souriau, *Les différents modes d'existence* [*The Different Modes of Existence*] (1943) (Paris: PUF, 2009).

25 Jacques Rancière *The Emancipated Spectator*, translated by Gregory Elliot (London: Verso, 2011).

26 See, for example, Friedrich Kittler's *Optische Medien* (Berlin: Merve, 2002).

27 Mark B. N. Hansen, *New Philosophy for New Media* (Cambridge (MA): MIT Press, 2004), p. 11.

28 On this subject see William J. Mitchell, *The Reconfigured Eye: Visual Truth in the Post-Photographic Era* (Cambridge (MA): MIT Press, 1992).

29 Mark B. N. Hansen, *New Philosophy for New Media*, p. 10 – see also pp. 70–85.

30 Steven Johnson, *Everything Bad is Good for You*, pp. 9 and 14.

31 Ibid., p. 9.

32 For an accurate overview of the cognitive operations involved for the consumer of fiction, see Thomas Mondémé's thesis *Fictions et usages cognitifs de la fictionalité: Kepler, Cyrano, Fontenelle*, [*Fictions and Cognitive Uses of Fictionality: Kepler, Cyrano, Fontenelle*] supervised by Jean-Charles Darmon and defended in February 2014 at Versailles University – book forthcoming.

33 On the aesthetic laboratory established by the experience of literary reading, see Marielle Macé, *Façons de lire, manières d'être* [*Ways of Reading, Modes of Being*] (Paris: Gallimard, 2011).

34 In the particular case of cinema, Gabriele Pedullà has clearly demonstrated how the progressive establishment of a completely dark space, the respect for silence, the individual isolation and the cutting off from the rest of the communicating world, during the first half of the twentieth century, was a condition of possibility for a certain kind of (ascetic) cinephilic experience developed during the era of the New Wave, explored in the framework of the 'art and essay' initiative ['*Art et Essai*' refers to a particular class of cinemas

in France which enjoy certain special protections in French law – Trans.] and threatened by the attentional regimes that dominate our contemporary world. See Gabriele Pedullà *In piena luce. I nuovi spettatori e il sistema delle arti*, (Milan: Bompiani, 2008).

35 On the live spectacle, see Jacques Rancière *The Emancipated Spectator*, and Olivier Neveux, *Politiques du spectateur. Les enjeux du théâtre politique aujourd'hui* [*Politics of the Spectator: The Stakes of Political Theatre Today*] (Paris: La Découverte, 2013), and for an historical perspective, Martial Poirson "Multitude en rumeur': des suffrages du public aux assises du spectateur' ['Multitude Rumbling: Public Sufferage in the Court of the Spectator'], *Dix-huitième siècle*, no. 41, 2009, pp. 223–48, and *Spectacle et économie à l'age classique (XVII-XVIIIe siècle)* [*Spectacle and Economy in the Classical Age (17th-18th Century)*] (Paris: Classique Garnier, 2011).

36 See, respectively, La Rédaction, *Nos visages-flash ultime* (Marseille: Al Dante, 2007); *Valérie par Valérie*; *Les Berthier. Portraits statistiques* (Paris: Questions théoriques, 2012). For the theoretical works, see Christophe Hanna, *Poésie action directe* (Marseille: Al Dante, 2007); *Nos dispositifs poétiques* (Paris: Questions théoriques, 2010); and Olivier Quintyn, *Dispositifs/Dislocations* (Marseille: Al Dante, 2007); Franck Leibovici, *Des documents poétiques* (Marseille: Al Dante, 2007); Dominiq Jenvrey, *Théorie du fictionnaire* (Paris: Questions théoriques, 2011).

37 Arseniy Zhilyaev, *M. I. R.: New Paths to the Objects* (Paris: Kadist Art Foundation, 2014).

38 On metalepsis, see *Métalepses. Entorses au pacte de la représentation* (Paris: Éditions de l'EHESS, 2005) edited by John Pier and Jean-Marie Schaeffer.

39 François Cusset, 'Ce que lire veut dire' ['What Reading Means'], *La Revue des Livres*, March-April, 2013, pp. 11–16.

40 Following on Walter Benjamin's insights, this is the thesis from which several Italian theoreticians have drawn fine and insightful conclusions – for example Antonio Scurati, *La letteratura dell'inesperienza. Scrivere romanzi al tempo della televisione* (Milan: Bompiani, 2006); Arturo Mazzarella, *Politiche dell'irrealità. Scritture e visioni tra Gomorra e Abu Ghraib* (Turin: Bollati Boringhieri, 2011); and Daniele Giglioli, *Senza trauma. Scrittura dell'estremo e narrativa del nuovo millennio* (Macerata: Quodlibet, 2011).

41 On this point, see Daniele Giglioli's fine article 'Trois cercles: critique et théorie entre crise et espoir ['Three Circles: Criticism and Theory Between Crisis and Hope'], *La Revue des Livres*, no. 6, July 2012.

42 For an excellent and surprising history of the glasses (preceding the latest developments), see Arnaud Maillet, *Prothèses lunatiques. Les lunettes, de la science aux fantasmes* [*Tempramental Prostheses: Glasses, from Science to Fantasy*] (Paris: Éditions Amsterdam, 2007). For a reflection on Google Glass, see Franco Berardi, 'Attention et expérience à l'âge du neurototalitarisme' ['Attention and Experience in the age of neurototalitarianism'] in *L'Économie de l'attention*, ed. Yves Citton, pp. 147–60.

43 Michel de Certeau, 'L'Économie scripturaire' ['Scriptural Economy'] in *L'Invention du quotidien*, v.1, *Les Arts de faire* [*The Invention of the Everyday, v.1., The Arts of Doing*] (1980) (Paris: Gallimard, 1990), pp. 195–224.

44 This is the situation I tried to envisage in 'Rethinking "impact": between the

attention economy and the readerless Republic of Letters', *SubStance*, no.130, vol. 42–1, 2013, pp. 69–81.

45 On this point, see the edited volume *Protocoles éditoriaux. Qu'est-ce que publier?*, [*Editorial Protocols: What is Publishing?*] ed. Olivier Bomsel (Paris: Armand Colin, 2013).

46 For a few proposals that are still far too general, I refer the reader to my book *L'Avenir des humanités* [*The Future of the Humanities*].

47 Simone Weil, 'Réflexions sur le bon usage des études scolaires en vue de l'amour de Dieu' (1942) in *Œuvres complètes*, vol. 4, *Écrits de Marseille*, vol. 1., 1940-2, edited by André A. Devaux and Florence de Lussy (Paris: Gallimard, 2008), p. 259.

Conclusion: Towards an Attention Echology

1 Simone Weil, 'Réflexions sur le bon usage des études scolaire. . .', p. 257.

2 Georges Bataille, *The Accursed Share. An Essay on General Economy* (1949), Zone Books, 1998.

3 Bernard Stiegler, *Économie de l'hypermatérial et psychopouvoir* [*The Hypermaterial Economy and Psychopower*], pp. 117 and 121.

4 Georg Franck, 'Mental Capitalism', p. 18.

5 Georg Franck, 'The Economy of Attention', (non-paginated).

6 Félix Guattari, *Qu'est-ce que l'écosophie?* pp. 72–73.

7 Arne Naess, *Ecology, Community and Lifestyle*, p. 37.

8 Félix Guattari, *Qu'est-ce que l'écosophie?* pp. 40 and 73.

9 Fréderic Moinat, 'Phénoménologie de l'attention aliénée: Edmund Husserl, Bernhard Waldenfels, Simone Weil', *Alter*, no. 18, *L'Attention*, edited by Natalie Depraz and Laurent Perreau, November 2010, p. 55. See also Simone Weil, *La Conditon ouvrière* (1937) (Paris: Gallimard, 2002); and Joël Janiaud, *Simone Weil. L'attention et l'action* (Paris: PUF, 2002).

10 Jean-Yves Leloup, *Un art de l'attention* (Paris: Albin Michel, 2002), p. 76.

11 Jean-Philippe Lachaux, *Le Cerveau attentif*, p. 229

12 Théodule Ribot, *Psychologie de l'attention* (1888), (Paris: Alcan, 1894), pp. 4–5.

13 Paul North, *The Problem of Distraction* (Palo Alto (CA): Stanford University Press, 2012), p. 5.

14 'Fatal distraction', *The Economist*, 3 November 2013.

15 Natalie Depraz, 'Attentionalité et intentionnalité. L'attention comme modulation', in *Husserl*, ed. Jocelyn Benoist (Paris: Le Cerf, 2008), pp. 223–48 and 'Attention et conscience: à la croisée de la phénoménologie et des sciences cognitives', *Alter*, no. 18, *L'attention,* edited by Natalie Depraz and Laurent Perreau, November 2010, pp. 203–26.

16 Christopher Mole, *Attention is Cognitive Unison: An Essay in Philosophical Psychology* (Oxford: Oxford University Press, 2011), p. 51.

17 Idem. Here again, we hear the distant echo of Ribot: 'Attention consists, therefore, in the substitution of a relative unity of consciousness for the plurality of states, for the change that is its norm.' (Théodule Ribot, *Psychologie de l'attention*, p. 7)

18 Christopher Mole, *Attention is Cognitive Unison*, p. 71.

19 Ibid., pp. 166–7.
20 Cathy Davidson, *Now You See It*, p. 287.
21 Idem.
22 Vilém Flusser, *Into the Universe of Technical Images*, translated by Nancy Ann Roth (Minneapolis: University of Minnesota Press, 2011), p. 163.
23 For a radical indictment of some of these dangers, see *La liberté dans le coma. Essai sur l'identification électronique et les motifs de s'y opposer* by the Groupe Marcuse (Paris: La lenteur, 2013).
24 N. Katherine Hayles, *How We Think*, p. 69.
25 Ibid., pp. 99–100.
26 Ibid., pp. 103–4.
27 Bernhard Waldenfels, 'Attention suscitée et dirigée', *Alter*, no. 18, *L'Attention*, edited by Natalie Depraz and Laurent Perreau, November 2010, pp. 35–6. See also Bernhard Waldenfels, *Phänomenologie der Aufmerksamkeit* (Frankfurt am Main: Suhrkamp, 2004).
28 Mark B. N. Hansen, *New Philosophy for New Media*, p. 84.
29 Paul Ricoeur, 'L'attention. Étude phénoménologique de l'attention et de ses connexions philosophiques' (1939), in *Anthropologie philosophique. Écrits et conférences 3* (Paris : Seuil, 2013), p. 64.
30 Ibid., pp. 69–70.
31 Nicholas Carr, *The Shallows*, ch.7.
32 Paul Ricoeur, 'Attention. . .', pp. 63 and 69.
33 Many recent publications have tackled this question head on, among which: Karen Barad, *Meeting the Universe Halfway: Quantum Physics and the Entanglement of Matter and Meaning* (Durham (N. C.): Duke University Press, 2007); Michael Hardt and Antonio Negri, *Commonwealth*; Bruno Latour, *Enquête sur les modes d'existence*; Georges Didi-Huberman, *Peuples exposés, peuples figurants* (Paris: Minuit, 2012); Dominique Quessada, *L'Inséparé. Essai sur un monde sans Autre* (Paris: PUF, 2013); Henri Torgue, *Le Sonore, l'Imaginaire et la Ville. De la fabrique artistique aux ambiances urbaines* (Paris: L'Harmattan, 2013); Robert Bonamy, *Le Fonds cinématographique* (Paris: L'Harmattan, 2013); Pierre Dardot and Christian Laval, *Commun. Essai sur la révolution du XXIe siècle* (Paris: La Découverte, 2014).
34 David Weinberger, *Too Big to Know: Rethinking Knowledge Now that the Facts Aren't the Facts, Experts Are Everywhere, and the Smartest Person in the Room is the Room* (New York (N Y): Basic Books, 2011).
35 On these questions see the research that Pierre Lévy has been conducting for a long time, in, for example, *L'Intelligence collective. Pour une anthropologie du cyberespace* [*Collective Intelligence: For an Anthropology of Cyberspace*] (Paris: La Découverte, 1997) or in *World Philosophy. Le Marché, le cyberespace, la conscience* [*The Market, Cyberspace, Consciousness*] (Paris: Odile Jacob, 2000).
36 *Re*-discovered because a whole series of safeguards forestalled the destruction of the communal environment in what we call 'traditional' societies. This has clearly been shown by, for example, Elinor Ostrom, *La Gouvernance des biens communs. Pour une nouvelle approche des ressources naturelles* (1990) [*The Governance of Common Goods: For a New Approach to Natural Resources*], (Liège: Commission Université Palais, 2010); Jean-Baptiste Fressoz *L'Apocalypse joyeuse* [*The Joyful Apocalypse*]; Eduardo

Gudynas, 'La Pacha Mama des Andes: plus qu'une conception de la nature', *La Revue des Livres*, no. 4, March–April 2012, pp. 683.

37 Imprim'Vert is a trademark established in 1998 that printing companies in France may incorporate into their branding, provided they comply with a number of regulations aimed at the reduction of their environmental impact [Trans.].

NAME INDEX

SUBJECT INDEX

223